The New Literacy

Moving Beyond the 3Rs

Paul J. Morris II

Stephen Tchudi

Jossey-Bass Publishers • San Francisco

Substantial discounts on bulk quantities of Jossey-Bass books are available to corporations, professional associations, and other organizations. For details and discount information, contact the special sales department at Jossey-Bass Inc., Publishers.
(415) 433–1740; Fax (800) 605–2665.

For sales outside the United States, please contact your local Simon & Schuster International Office.

Manufactured in the United States of America on Lyons Falls Pathfinder Tradebook. This paper is acid-free and 100 percent totally chlorine-free.

Library of Congress Cataloging-in-Publication Data

Morris, Paul J., date.
    The new literacy : moving beyond the 3rs / Paul J. Morris II,
Stephen Tchudi   —   1st ed.
        p.   cm.
    Includes bibliographical references and index.
    ISBN 0-7879-0292-6 (cloth : acid-free paper)
    1. Literacy—United States.   2. Literacy—Social aspects—United
States.   I. Tchudi, Stephen, date.   II. Title.
LC151.M67   1996
302.2'244—dc20
                                                                      96-25189
                                                                      CIP

FIRST EDITION
HB Printing   10 9 8 7 6 5 4 3 2 1

Contents

Preface

Since the Greeks first explored theories of rhetoric and criticism, Western society has perceived literacy as a key component of both education and citizenship. *Literacy*—usually defined in vague but heartfelt ways—is perceived as a vital skill that leads to improved participation in government. Literate citizenship is often linked, directly or indirectly, to economic success. Literacy is even promoted as a means to national growth in an international economy and as a tool for less-literate societies and economies to become more like our own. Finally, literacy has long been seen as providing access to the thoughtful life, to the aesthetic life, and to the ethical or moral life: we learn to read and write not only to do the business of the world but also to appreciate beauty and to develop strong value systems.

In our time, however, the meaning of literacy has changed. Since World War II, our society has become an electronic global village. The tools people use to send and receive language have been transformed—think merely of the evolution from scribbled memo to faxed lunch order—thus altering the very nature of communication itself. Using modern communication tools such as long-distance telephoning, faxing, E-mail, television news, MTV, and *USA Today* does not require the same literacies as using *The McGuffey Reader,* the Harvard Five-Foot Shelf of Books, the *New York Times,* or Samuel Johnson's *Rambler*; nor does society seem to place as much value on the knowledge that these previous literacies garnered. Thus, our concept of literacy has broadened: what once described the skill of encoding and decoding print now also refers to the skills necessary for operating in the automated office or for playing video games. The rhetorics of literacy, which once focused on political or forensic oratory, have expanded to encompass myriad social, political, and intellectual skills. In fact, the word *literacy* has nearly become synonymous with the concept of *competence*. It is possible, for example, to discuss *scientific literacy* as skill in experimentation, without any reference to writing; to refer to *mathematical literacy* as ability to manipulate numbers, without any reference to reading; to describe *technological literacy* as capacity for using the new communications media, without any consideration of their verbal contents; and even (thanks to Dr. Ruth) to debate a *sexual literacy* that has nothing to do with the reading of sex books. Thus, the word literacy—derived from the Greek *litera,* which means instructed in letters—has moved far from its root meaning.

Contemporary rhetoricians, educators, and critics have choices to make. They can lament the changing nature of literacy and long for the good old days of print dominance, or they can attempt to understand the new literacies, including new manifestations of print, and try to figure out what literate thinkers do with language. This book puts us in the latter category: we want to focus on what people—community members, business leaders, members of the media, and professional educators in both college and the K–12 system—can and should be doing with and about the language of today. To accomplish this, we took our research directly to the source, literate citizens. In a series of interviews, we asked individuals, young and old and from diverse backgrounds, how they learned to use language and how they use it now. The answers we received lead us to a broader view of literacy schooling, one that reaches beyond the traditional view of literacy as only "the three Rs"—reading, writing, and arithmetic—to embrace what we call a *renaissance of Rs.*

We hasten to add that this is not a school-bashing book. We respect the efforts of K–college educators to improve the teaching of language, and we reject the simplistic analyses of "why Johnny can't read and write." Further, we take sharp objection to cynical critiques of schooling that emphasize the alleged "dumbing down" of education or that make simplistic and uninformed critical comparisons between the American school system and the systems of other countries such as Japan and Germany.

Our driving observation (and our main reason for writing this book), however, is that an extraordinary number of people in this country are both consciously and subconsciously searching for and developing literacies *not* found or fostered in schools. It is not uncommon for people in all walks of life—blue-collar, white-collar, minority, and majority—to say: I didn't learn anything about reading and writing in school; I had to figure it out when I got into the real world. If that is the case, one solution would be to shut down the schools altogether and simply let nature take its course, assuming that, in the real world, folks would become literate through osmosis. However, an approach that is both more realistic and more idealistic is to explore the gap between what occurs in obtaining *real-life literacy* and what takes place with learning in the schools.

Further, there is a growing body of programs and methodologies that point in precisely that direction: they encourage bridging the gap between schoolhouse literacy and the literate knowledge required for functioning in a democratic society. The purpose of our book is to document some existing possibilities and some new directions, to project current research implications into visions of future education, and to acknowledge the productive directions we see presently taking place in school and college education.

With all this in mind, we have not written a manifesto for "revolution" in education. We see improved literacy education, like the development of language itself, coming about gradually and thoughtfully, through e-volution rather than re-volution, in classrooms across America. Nevertheless, we propose nothing less than to shake down the world of education and to shake up conceptions of schooling for a literate society.

In Chapter One, we redefine literacy in contemporary terms, examining its diverse meanings in a diverse society. We look at the connections between literacy and mass culture, the role of education in fostering these new literacies, the real ways citizens actually use language, and what it really means to be a literate citizen. Through case studies, Chapter Two examines the effects of encouragement and discouragement—parental, academic, and social—on literacy development. Chapter Three details the dynamic and critical literacies of people we call entrepreneurs and rhetorical inventors, individuals who are redefining what it means to be literate in the world of business. In Chapter Four, we highlight the lively, varied, and imaginative rhetoric of a new breed of political and community activists. Chapter Five examines the artists, writers, and musicians, those literate in the classic sense. Many people believe this kind of literacy is dying and unappreciated. The people we interviewed for this chapter prove that artistic literacy is, fortunately, alive and well. In Chapter Six, we look at the media literate, those mass communicators who are literate not only in written and spoken discourse but also in the new communications techniques and technologies. Chapter Seven goes to the source—kids. They explain what they like, what they want, what they do. From them, we learn what things engage them to become literate and what things do just the opposite. In Chapter Eight, we try to pull together all that we have learned from the literate citizens we interviewed. Through a dialogue, we examine opposing, conflicting, and contradictory points, to reach a synthesis on which we form a model of literacy learning. Chapter Nine assesses responsibilities for schooling for a literate society. We offer ideas to teachers, schools, colleges, districts, communities, businesses, political leaders, and the media—all of whom must take part in building the future of a literate society. Finally, in the Appendix, we discuss three pilot programs that actualize many of the ideas we recommend for schooling for a literate society.

We believe the new, broadened definitions of literacy discussed in this book are relevant not only for educators but also for businesses, parents, and policy makers. Understanding the new literacies, how they are being implemented today, and how they will grow and change in the future, is key to meeting the ever-increasing and often thorny challenges inherent in the global village. Becoming competent and comfortable with these new and varied literacies is also a requirement for achieving a happy and satisfying life for us and for our children.

Paul Morris   *Reno, Nevada*
Stephen Tchudi   *July 1996*

The Authors

Paul J. Morris II returned to college in 1973 after four years in the Navy. He received his A.A. degree from Hartnell Community College in 1975 and his B.A. in creative writing from the University of California at Davis in 1980. While attending school, he worked in television broadcasting as a broadcast engineer. From 1980 to 1990 he worked for ABC television in San Francisco and wrote fiction in his spare time. In 1990, he moved to Nevada to pursue his education, receiving an M.S. degree in English in 1992 from the University of Nevada. He will receive a Ph.D. degree in rhetoric and composition in 1997, also from the University of Nevada. Morris is a Vietnam veteran who has published articles and short stories about the Vietnam War in such literary magazines as *Brushfire*, *Halcyon*, and the *Redneck Review of Literature*. He is currently a freelance writer, a computer consultant, and a student and teacher of literacy in America. His initial interest in literacy began with the written word, but it has since grown into a passion for teaching and for research into the creative use of language in the classroom and society.

Stephen Tchudi received a B.A. degree in chemistry from Hamilton College in 1963, an M.A. degree in teaching English from Northwestern University in 1964, and a Ph.D. degree in English education in 1967, also from Northwestern. Tchudi first explored his literacy interests while teaching high school in Chicago, and he has held faculty positions at Northwestern University, Michigan State University, and the University of Nevada, and visiting faculty appointments at the University of British Columbia, Northeastern University, and the University of Virginia. He has published some forty books, including professional texts for teachers, books on education for the general public, and fiction and nonfiction for young adults. He presently coordinates the graduate program in composition and rhetoric at the University of Nevada and directs the interdisciplinary university seminar program for entering students. He is also editor of *Halcyon,* an interdisciplinary humanities series published by the Nevada Humanities Committee and the University of Nevada Press.

The New Literacy

Part One

The Literate Citizen

Chapter One

Redefining Literacy

> *Republics, one after another . . . have perished from a*
> *want of intelligence and virtue in the masses of the*
> *people. . . . If we do not prepare children to become good*
> *citizens; if we do not develop their capacities, if we do not*
> *enrich their minds with knowledge, imbue their hearts*
> *with love of truth and duty, and a reverence for all things*
> *sacred and holy, then our republic must go down to*
> *destruction, as others have gone before it; and mankind*
> *must sweep through another vast cycle of sin and*
> *suffering, before the dawn of a better era can arise upon*
> *the world.*
> —HORACE MANN, *LECTURES AND ANNUAL REPORTS*
> *ON EDUCATION*

A friend of ours was recently scolded for not appreciating the seriousness of the "illiteracy problem" in America. Our friend—we will call him Jim—was at a party, standing with a group of adults who were bemoaning a media factoid that "one-third of our population can neither read nor write." Suddenly, a man in the group pointed a finger at Jim and said, "You're a teacher, aren't you? How do you expect to teach the great books if nobody can read?" Jim told the man that his students actually could read fairly well and that he was more than willing to let them decide for themselves which books were great. At this point, the man began to lecture Jim on the need for a "return to the basics" and "more discipline" in education. A short while later, just after his wife arrived to rescue him, Jim heard the finger-pointer say to the others, "It seems to me a lot of the problems in this country could be traced to illiteracy."

The party goer's last remark suggests that if every American learned to read and write, many of the problems we face as a society would somehow disappear and our country would be great again. Like many people in America, this man probably thinks that the ability to read and write and cipher defines a literate citizen. Americans have traditionally equated education, especially in the 3Rs, with success, happiness, well-being, and even morality. They also seem to believe that there was a more educationally enlightened period in the near or distant past, when literacy supposedly thrived, education was in much better shape, and America was great. For whatever reason, many Americans are unwilling to believe that their present society is as literate, say, as it was in 1940 or 1950. No doubt, the people who lived during the forties and fifties were sure their society was less literate than the society their fathers and mothers grew up in at the turn of the century.

In this chapter, we address the inconsistencies in this view of literacy (and illiteracy) and offer our own definition of literacy, one as multifarious as the society we live in. First, we will examine the relationship between literacy and mass culture in order to reveal our culture's real and perceived effects on literacy. Second, we will examine literacy education, its traditional aims as well as those suited to our own broader definition of literacy. Third, we will discuss language as the literate citizen actually gives voice to it. Finally, we will portray the literate citizen as much more than someone who can read, write, and cipher.

TV, the Daily Rag, Cyberpunks, and Literacy

The mass culture of just about every era has been condemned as harmful to the nature and condition of literacy. To the concern of pious educators in the eighteenth and nineteenth centuries, the printing press was capable of running off as much sentimental pulp as it did newspapers, Bibles, and works of Shakespeare. Educators have long wondered and worried about the harm that hack writing might be doing to the moral fiber of America through dime novels and comic books. The electronic media have been and continue to be attacked on similar grounds, quite possibly with justification.

Television, for example, has been seen alternately to threaten and to enhance literacy in modern society. Social critics, educators, and even politicians have denounced it for hypnotizing people and for turning generations of children and adults into violent imbeciles, even as others of their kind have observed that television has opened up the world in astonishing ways. The computer, with its global Internet connections and virtual realities, with its hackers and cyberpunks, has taken over where television left off as a repository for both praise and criticism. Critics complain that nobody reads because of TV; nobody writes letters because of the telephone; nobody looks things up because of the Internet; and nobody can spell because of the spell checkers in computer word processors. All of this suggests (unreasonably, we believe) that American society has grown lazy as well as stupid because of technological advances in communication.

Presumably, magazines like *Time* and *Newsweek* perpetuate this indolence by running television ads that cater to society's preference for uncomplicated news. The well-dressed and obviously busy man on the TV is holding a copy of *Newsweek*. He looks into the living rooms of America and says something like this: "I like *Newsweek* because it gives me my news in easily digestible, bite-sized chunks." No time to read complex in-depth coverage of national and world events? Read *Time* or *Newsweek*. Better yet, why read at all? *CNN Headline News* broadcasts twenty-four hours a day.

Newspapers, which for obvious commercial reasons were once on the forefront of most literacy movements, have adopted many of the tricks used by TV to attract a wider audience. Papers like *USA Today* are figuratively television in newsprint. Their headlines and even their articles are similar to the sound bites and teasers used on local and national news shows. Despite *USA Today*'s attempt to copy television's format, most newspaper, magazine, and book publishers find it increasingly difficult to compete with the immediacy of television. In fact, taking their cues from Marshall ("the medium is the message") McLuhan (1967), people like Neil Postman (1985) see television as supplanting the written word. Whether or not people agree that television is actually replacing print, they cannot help but see how television has influenced culture. Most libraries now stock huge selections of videotapes as well as CDs and audiocassettes. Any bookstore that hopes to make a decent profit must do the same. The number of newspapers is in decline, while TV newsmagazine shows are on the rise. To attract more viewers, television moguls have even created specialized networks for viewer interests like shopping, sports, weather, video games, and music.

In the 1990s, the diversity of entertainment on television has become increasingly more sophisticated due to specialized programming for adults and children and to a less-charitable image of America. In its infancy in the fifties and early sixties, television projected a clean, trouble-free image of America. Beaver Cleaver's family lived in an upper-middle-class neighborhood in a mythical American town. Beaver spoke respectfully to his parents, went to school regularly, and did his homework every night. Bart Simpson, Beaver's cartoon counterpart in the nineties, constantly makes fun of his father, cuts school often, gets horrible grades, always gets into trouble, and has attained popular culture status as an anti-idol. The worst thing Beaver Cleaver ever did was to fib to his parents about trapping himself on top of a billboard in a huge coffee cup. Matt Groening, the creator of *The Simpsons,* satirizes topics as diverse as nuclear power (Bart's father, Homer, works in a nuclear power plant), political corruption (the mayor of the town sounds and looks suspiciously like Senator Ted Kennedy), and artistic freedom (Maggie, to her music teacher's consternation, would rather play the blues than classical music on her saxophone).

Some people worry that the latest threat to reading and writing can be found in computers. Whole subcultures have grown up around the use and abuse of computers. Cyberpunks, hackers, and travelers on the Internet have created microcultures with their own languages. In these languages, the traditional mechanics of English are often ignored. In E-mail, abbreviations abound and spelling errors are frequent because of the speed-typing encouraged by E-mail chats.

Still, educators and language purists are bothered less by the use of computers and E-mail than they are by the absence of traditional writing skills in those who use the computers for writing and ciphering. The PC is capable of solving programmed mathematical formulas very quickly, without the user's needing to know the underlying algorithms. Most word processors contain not only a spell checker but also a thesaurus and a grammar checker: touch a few buttons and the computer edits your spelling, gives you a larger vocabulary, and warns you about passive voice. Many programs now contain several style sheets formatted for a wide range of documents—for example, if you want to write a business letter, the program might have several different business-letter styles for you to choose from, including plug-in and revise-to-fit phrasings. Dictation-to-print systems will soon be operational, so your computer will literally spell and punctuate for you. Meanwhile, today's sophisticated word processors contain grammar checkers that examine your documents for subject-verb agreement and syntactical correctness. Each of these word processing features, the purist could argue, moves the writer further and further away from editing tasks, thereby slowly eroding sentence-level writing skills. Carrying this argument to its logical conclusion, the same purist might claim that at some point, the computer will end up doing not only people's editing but their thinking as well.

Doublespeak in Government and the Marketplace

Each of the technological advances mentioned so far has been seen by critics as contributing in some way to the decline in literacy in our society. Some critics also blame the way the English language is used in our culture. In the past two decades, people like former television news commentator Edwin Newman (1974) and columnist William Safire (1980) have been the watchdogs of the language. For Newman, the less grammatically and mechanically correct the "American word," the less pure the language itself. People like Newman and Safire take a somewhat narrow and formal approach in their analysis of the state of the word. Rather than examining the mechanical abuses of language, perhaps they should be scrutinizing the ways in which people abuse the language to further their own unethical purposes.

Politicians, known since the time of the Greeks for their evasive locutions, have become ever more adept at hiding or shading the truth. In the 1992 presidential election, candidates Bush and Clinton skillfully manipulated figures with regard to their tax plans and the national debt. Later, after President Clinton took office, he admitted that his staff may have hedged on its calculations concerning the national debt and his own tax plan.

The business community has taken doublespeak to new heights of rhetorical excess. In the 1980s, Lee Iacocca, the unflappable former head of Chrysler, used patriotic slogans and team spirit jargon to maneuver his autoworkers into taking a substantial pay cut. Later, the public learned that Iacocca had given himself an enormous pay raise. It is obvious that Iacocca, whom Americans viewed nightly on their television sets in front of a huge American flag, used patriotic symbols to sell not only Chrysler automobiles but also his own image as a decent and honest American businessman.

In 1994, Americans watched several top executives in the tobacco industry answering questions from a Senate committee investigating whether or not the tobacco industry was using dishonest advertising to target certain groups, like young people or minorities. Near the end of the hearings, each executive was asked, "Do you believe nicotine is addictive?" One by one, they replied, "No," in spite of the fact that most doctors, including former Surgeon General C. Everett Koop, now are convinced by research showing nicotine to be as addictive as heroin. Given the executives' answers, the public can guess rather easily how accurate the rest of their testimony was.

Incidents and situations like these indicate that our business and government leaders are often more concerned with manipulating the language than with using it to enlighten the public. Stephen Lafer, a teacher and researcher in education, worries that this trend is so widespread that the public has difficulty analyzing public rhetoric:

> Good people often are confused by public rhetoric into doing things that are anti-community, anti-self even. The other frightening thing for me is to hear the spin doctors discussing publicly how they doctored the message, and how well it sold and continues to sell despite their admission that the message was doctored! I am all for education, as my credentials show. . . . Yet, and this may be the lament of a frustrated educator, I find what I have called "the distorted message" undermining constantly my attempts to give students the kind of education we speak of here [Stephen Lafer, interview with authors, June 1994].

Lafer's concerns about truth and public rhetoric are as legitimate now as they were when people like Plato addressed them in his dialogues *Gorgias* and *Phaedrus*. Can schools educate people to see beyond "the distorted message," as Lafer calls it, to the truth?

Education: Critics and Consequences

Education critics like Rudolf Flesch (1955), E. D. Hirsch (1987), Allan Bloom (1987), and Harold Bloom (1994) are also worried about the kind of education students are getting. Their biggest concern is with what students are learning and how they are learning it. Flesch wrote *Why Johnny Can't Read and What You Can Do About It* in response to low test scores on standardized reading tests. He believed the reading problems in American schools could be remedied simply by teaching phonics. In his call for a return to phonics (sounding words out), Flesch was advocating a return to the teaching practices that had been largely discredited by reading research. In order to put a modern spin on this very old technique, Flesch introduced it as a more "scientific" approach to teaching reading. In the 1950s, an era often characterized by its emphasis on "modern living," the presumed scientific exactness of this method must have seemed very appealing to many people.

Since Flesch's time, other traditionalists, like Hirsch and the two Blooms, have been concerned not only with how schools teach but also with what they teach. Hirsch and the Blooms are convinced that the educational system is responsible for the perceived decline in literacy in America; as a remedy, they promote a return to the great books of the traditional canon. William Damon (1991), chair of the Department of Education at Brown University, accurately summarizes Hirsch's agenda: "Hirsch's belief is that . . . there is a specific set of facts that must retain a privileged position in our culture for both communicational and educational purposes" (p. 43). That "specific set of facts," according to Hirsch (and the Blooms), is found only in those books that have had the most profound effect on Western culture.

It is largely because of critics like these that we now have disagreeable terms such as *dumbing down* to explain how schools use uncomplicated texts with simple assignments in order to make knowledge more accessible to students. This trend, according to traditionalists, is responsible for what has come to be known as *grade inflation,* which means grades rise at every level of our educational system—from elementary to graduate school—despite apparent declines in performance.

While traditionalists like Hirsch, the Blooms, and Flesch advocate a return to the past, radical populists like John Taylor Gatto want to dismantle compulsory education altogether. *Dumbing Us Down: The Hidden Curriculum of Compulsory Schooling* (1993a) is a book written by this veteran New York schoolteacher and social critic. Writing in *Whole Earth Review* (1993b) under the title "We Need Less School, Not More," Gatto complained that schools are impersonal networks, and networks do not work; therefore, we should do away with compulsory mass schooling. According to Gatto, since mass education has failed to attain the ideal of literacy for everyone, schools should at the very least be scaled back. He writes, "A Massachusetts senator said a while ago that his state had a higher literacy rate before it adopted compulsory schooling than after. It's certainly an idea worth considering: schools reached their maximum efficiency long ago, and that 'more' for schools will make things worse, instead of better" (p. 62).

In the same issue that contained Gatto's article, *Whole Earth Review* provided a list of periodicals and books on everything from alternative schools to home schooling to how to quit ("rise out of") school. *The Teenage Liberation Handbook (How to Quit School and Get a Real Life and Education)* (Llewellyn, 1991), for example, gives advice to teenagers on why and how they should quit school. *Real Lives: Eleven Teenagers Who Don't Go to School* (Llewellyn, 1993) contains testimonials from teenagers who have quit school to go it on their own. The author of these books, like Gatto, offers radical solutions to what are perceived to be overwhelming problems in institutionalized education.

Unlike Gatto, Jonathan Kozol (*Illiterate America,* 1985) would much rather improve the current educational system than tear it down. Kozol, one of the most vocal critics of illiteracy in America, warns: "Twenty-five million American adults cannot read the poison warnings on a can of pesticide, a letter from their child's teacher, or the front page of a daily paper. An additional 35 million read only at a level which is less than equal to the full survival needs of our society.

"Together, these 60 million people represent more than one third of the entire adult population" (p. 4).

Even though the statistics he cites are suspect (for one thing, we wonder what criteria he is using to define literacy), Kozol has managed to confirm most Americans' fears about the extent of illiteracy. He attributes an astonishing array of social and economic problems to illiteracy, including crime, unwanted pregnancies, unemployment, industrial accidents, welfare costs, and drug and alcohol abuse.

Jonathan Kozol is one of the most vocal liberal opponents of illiteracy in America. However, Kozol's most serious charge is one that disturbs both radical populists like Gatto and traditionalists like Hirsch and the Blooms: "Democracy is a mendacious term when used by those who are prepared to countenance the forced exclusion of one-third of our electorate. So long as 60 million people are denied significant participation, the government is neither of, nor for, nor by, the people" (p. 23). Although the theory that literacy is essential to the democratic process is admirable, there is no evidence that literacy in the 3Rs can improve that process. For example, against their wishes and despite how literate they are, how many tens of millions of Americans are "denied significant participation" whenever a president decides to start a war without the approval of Congress?

Defining Literacy

The problem of how to maintain a literate and well-informed citizenry and voting force has occupied the minds of religious leaders, politicians, and educators in this country since America was first colonized. We believe discussion has been hampered by anxiety over the alleged ghastly state of the word. Even if we concede that Kozol's figure of a two-thirds literate society is correct, America has always had a large number—often far greater than one-third—of people who had trouble reading, writing, and ciphering. In fact, we see little evidence to conflict a counter-theory, that there are more literate people in America today than at any time in history. Furthermore, the idea that by simply teaching people to read, write, and cipher, we can somehow cure most of our nation's complicated economic and social ills is a naive assumption, which grows out of a narrow and misinformed understanding of literacy.

It is our contention that literacy in this society can no longer be defined so narrowly. These days, you can find books on computer literacy, political literacy, environmental literacy, historical literacy, science literacy, visual literacy, and just about any other type of literacy you can think of. We prefer to view literacy in a broader context, one that takes into account far more than literacy in the 3Rs, encompassing an individual's ability to interpret and create texts, to function capably in a vast array of settings, and to operate effectively in society.

Such expansion of a concept carries with it the danger of semantic generalization, in which, over time, the meanings of words become enlarged. A word like *rhetoric*, which the Greeks thought of as the art of persuasion or speech making, has come to take on both negative and positive denotations and connotations. For example, these days if you tell people they are being "rhetorical" in an argument, you are not complimenting them for being persuasive and convincing; you are criticizing them for being sneaky or crafty in their use of language. When words take on new meanings in this way, there is an increased abstraction of usage along with an increased loss of specificity. This, we believe, is the case with the word literacy. Therefore, we use three specific terms—*basic literacy, critical literacy,* and *dynamic literacy*—throughout this book in an attempt to be more precise in our analysis of literacy and literate citizens.

We define basic literacy in terms similar to the traditional meaning. It is the ability to decode and encode, to pick up a book and not only to call the words but also to say what they mean. Literacy in the 3Rs is closest to basic literacy. Critical literacy is the ability to move beyond literal meanings, to interpret texts, and to use writing not only to record facts but also to analyze, interpret, and explain. For example, when people discuss a film, argue over political issues, analyze complicated scientific data, or interpret a law brief or a contract, they are engaged in critical literacy. Further, writing an essay, poem, story, novel, scientific paper, or law brief is an aspect of critical literacy. Dynamic literacy goes beyond text (or film or video) to include the ability to act from the content and context of a text. Dynamic literacy also goes beyond words to include related skills: for example, the skills and abilities associated with science literacy, historical literacy, computer literacy, baseball literacy, plumbing literacy, and so forth. Since it usually encompasses both basic and critical literacy, dynamic literacy can be seen as using these other properties of literacy in practical situations.

We realize that one cannot clearly separate competencies from language, but we think *the word* must remain at the center of literacy. Further, it is not our intention to establish a hierarchy of literacies with dynamic literacy at the top. Rather, we see basic, critical, and dynamic literacy as three circles, each linked to the other, as illustrated in Figure 1.1. Each is necessary in our discussion of education and literacy and in our review of all the literacies a citizen might need to communicate today—oral literacies for engaging in conversation and discussions and for giving speeches; writing literacies for creating persuasive reports and essays, letters, and memos; reading literacies for understanding newspapers, books, plays, and poems; and technological literacies for operating televisions and VCRs, telephones, and computers (to name just a few).

With this three-ringed, pretzel-like view of literacy in mind, we will examine a few misconceptions about literacy.

Figure 1.1. Circles of Literacy.

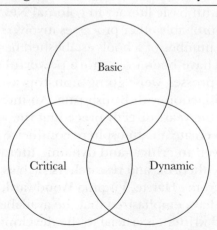

Literacy in America: A Few Misconceptions

According to historian Kenneth A. Lockridge (1974), the first colonial interest in literacy came about as a direct result of Protestantism, "perhaps the sole force which could rapidly increase literacy to high levels or bring the level of this skill to universality" (p. 5). By "universality," of course, Lockridge means near universal basic literacy for mostly white men, since few women and hardly any minority people were permitted the luxury of an education. Using the "signing" (making a signature) or "marking" (making an X) of wills as indicators of the ability or inability to read and write, Lockridge estimates "as of 1660 only 60 percent of men signed their will, whereas by 1710 the figure had risen to 70 percent and by 1760 it was up to 85 percent" (p. 13).

The biggest motivator for basic literacy during the colonial era appears to have had as much to do with people's fear of God as anything else. According to Lockridge, "Protestants were convinced that access to the Word would free men from superstition, and it seems that the gathered groups of devotees responded by providing for the education of their young" (p. 46). Lockridge also contends that "social concentration" in colonial New England made it easier for Protestants to put men in school (p. 62). Obviously, Protestants deserve some credit for their resourcefulness in setting up schools and laws pertaining to education in the colonies.

There is little doubt that religion and density of population had a lot to do with basic literacy in colonial New England; however, there were probably other processes involved as well. In addition to the large number of schools established because of Puritan laws, there may have been even more powerful social forces at work. Printing presses were going nonstop as a result of the colonists' dissatisfaction with British rule. An increase in reading material during the years directly preceding the war for independence helped to create an atmosphere conducive to basic literacy (and perhaps even to critical and dynamic literacy). Twentieth-century language theorists and researchers such as Jerome Bruner, L. S. Vygotsky, Jerome Harste, Virginia Woodward, Carolyn Burke, and Jane Torrey have emphasized that the availability of language, both spoken and written, is crucial to the development of literacy. Given the availability of printed material and the desire to understand it, there undoubtedly was also a great deal of literacy development occurring outside of the Protestant schools in colonial New England, especially in the years leading up to the war for independence from England.

Lockridge asks one of the more interesting questions about literacy during America's colonial era: "Yet is it correct to assume that eighteenth-century New England was a society in which a modernization of attitudes could occur, in which literacy enhanced these attitudes, and in which an increase in literacy swelled the tide of modern views?" (p. 32). Rightly, Lockridge questions the notion that somehow, through basic literacy, our early colonial ancestors were introduced to the principles that have come to be associated with this country—namely, individualism, enterprise, pragmatism, and optimism. If anything, these would have developed through what we refer to as critical and dynamic literacy.

Lockridge believes that in the seventeenth and eighteenth centuries, modernism—or liberalism—was never a goal of mass literacy movements: "The wills of the men in this sample tend to confirm the suspicion that no modernization of attitudes occurred in colonial New England. . . . Any modernization of attitudes did not show its activism, optimism, and wider consciousness in a heightened level of charitable concern" (p. 33). Lockridge discovered that learning to read and write did little to enhance our ancestors' charitableness, since records show literate citizens bequeathed hardly anything to charitable organizations in their wills. Neither, apparently, did basic literacy prepare the colonists for the speed at which their world was changing. Many New Englanders yearned for a return to the past: "Throughout the Revolution rural Americans complained of dark doings they could not understand, and pleaded for a return to a world without commercial mysteries" (pp. 37–38). The desire for a return to a kinder and gentler past seems to have been as strong in the seventeenth and eighteenth centuries as it is for many Americans today.

Historically, the goals of literacy in America have been driven by the religious and political forces manifest at the time. In the sixteenth, seventeenth, and eighteenth centuries, Protestantism was dominant, and while it still held sway in the nineteenth century, the economic force of capitalism was beginning to have a profound effect on education. Horace Mann (1796–1859), like Kozol in this century, was probably the most vocal proponent of universal basic literacy in the 1800s. As first secretary of the Massachusetts State Board of Education, Mann argued that an educated citizenry makes more money, is more informed, and is even more virtuous than an illiterate one. In his *Fifth Annual Report* (1867), Mann attempted to provide statistical proof that an educated citizen was better off morally and economically. Unfortunately, the statistics he provided to back up his claims have since proved to be highly suspect.

Historian Harvey J. Graff (1979) rejects Mann's figures. Mann sent questionnaires to manufacturers requesting specific information about the differences between those workers educated in common schools and those without an education. Two of the manufacturers even "attempted to estimate the wage differentials accruing to literate workmen" (p. 204). Using this data, Mann came up with a 50 percent wage differential between schooled and unschooled workers. Graff claims:

> There are grave problems with Mann's method of obtaining that figure and with his use of it. He apparently simply averaged the two extreme examples of wages—not the group averages—looking solely at atypical cases. Had he used the average wages reported to him, the result would have been less than half of his 50 percent differentials: 23 percent, far from such a huge variation, and still unreliable when based on a sample of only two firms. . . . In sum, we must agree with Maris Vinovskis, that "it is likely that Mann's figure of 50 percent for primary education greatly exaggerates the actual productivity of education during that period. A much more likely estimate would be in the range of 10–20 percent" [pp. 204–205].

Graff explains away even this 10–20 percent figure by emphasizing that the "cognitive skills" the workers gleaned from school had little to do with this slight raise in earnings. Citing Herbert Ginis, Graff explains "the noncognitive personality traits stressed in schools, such as subordination and discipline, have a more direct influence on worker earnings and productivity" (p. 205). In challenging Mann's figures, Graff uncovers another common misconception regarding basic literacy—it does not, in and of itself, improve earning power or enhance quality of life.

"The parallels and continuities between past and present discussions and concerns about the importance of literacy, its uses, and its quality are especially striking," Graff says. "How repetitive so many of the comments and observations seem" (p. 322). Today, the media assail the public with reports regarding the state of literacy in schools: America's test scores are lower than Japan's and Europe's; students are said to be unable to read, write, spell, divide, or multiply; and the dropout rate in high schools is disgraceful. Illiteracy, Americans are told, is like a disease, which must be treated, eradicated, and cured with doses of basic literacy.

We want the current outcry understood in historical perspective: there has never been a golden era of universal literacy in this country. In fact, we wonder if the rate of basic literacy in America—for all men and women of every religious and cultural persuasion—has ever been higher than it is right now. If this is so (and even if current levels of literacy may not seem to be good news to those who perceive universal literacy as the ideal), then it discredits the "old tyme" arguments of traditionalists like Flesch, the Blooms, and Hirsch; the defeatist attitudes of radical populists like Gatto; and even the suspicious statistics of liberal populists like Kozol.

Since the end of World War II, there have been several attempts in the United States to raise the rate of basic literacy, especially among adults. These projects have been sponsored by many different organizations, including state and federal governments, the military, and even private organizations like the American Library Association in conjunction with B. Dalton Booksellers. Most of these attempts have met with very little success, probably because, as Kozol and others point out, America, although committed to the idea of universal literacy, has never really been committed to the effort required to reach even basic literacy for every citizen.

It is also important to underscore the fact that basic literacy is not a panacea for America's economic and social ills. Poverty, crime, and unemployment are not caused by a lack of basic literacy in society; these are social and economic problems with far more complicated origins. Harvey Graff believes that "much more than literacy or education alone is required for cohesion, consciousness, and activity; social structural and economic factors, leadership and organization, psychology and motivation, numbers and opportunity are equally if not more important. Easier communication, which literacy can advance, may aid the process, but literacy is hardly the key variable" (p. 215).

If by literacy Graff means basic literacy, then we would agree that literacy merely facilitates communication. However, since Graff appears to broaden his definition by linking literacy generally to education, questions are then raised about literacy, education, and society. Does basic literacy necessarily lead to critical literacy and dynamic literacy? Does critical literacy influence people's social consciousness? Does dynamic literacy affect economic factors and the social structure within society? What would happen if all the schools in America began to see dynamic literacy and critical literacy as just as, or more, important than basic literacy? What would happen if this society placed less emphasis on what people do not know and more emphasis on what they do know? The answers to these and other questions move our society toward a broader definition of what it *could* mean to be literate in America.

Some Higher Aims for Schooling

Mihaly Csikszentmihalyi (1991), citing research done by social psychologist Teresa Amabile, sees serious problems in the way America perceives education: "Formal education thrives on external controls, evaluation, competition, and self-consciousness. Yet as long as this is so, it will be difficult for children to be motivated to learn spontaneously for the sake of learning" (p. 137). Earlier, we mentioned Lafer's concern about the "distorted message" often presented by the media and about the public's willingness to accept it. As a teacher, Lafer wonders if it is possible to teach, or in some way impart, the cognitive skills necessary for students to unravel the public rhetoric tendered by spin doctors in the media. Csikszentmihalyi sees serious problems in the prescriptive way educators present knowledge in school, while Lafer wonders whether students can learn to decipher public discourse in society. Given Csikszentmihalyi's worries about how students are being taught and Lafer's concerns about how they interpret what spin doctors are telling them in the real world, is it possible to teach students the critical skills necessary to function in a democratic society?

Some teachers and educators have managed to impart critical and dynamic literacy to their students simply by exposing them to new experiences. Educator Carol Edelsky makes a distinction between what she calls "hands-on" experience and "firsthand" experience For a hands-on experience, a teacher might set up a mock grocery store in a classroom, pass out play money, and have students buy things from the store. The purpose of the exercise could be to teach students how to use and count money. For a firsthand exercise, the teacher would take them to a real store and let them spend their own money (Carol Edelsky, interview with authors, Jan. 1995).

An example that shows how firsthand experience can be more effective than hands-on occurred in San Francisco. When a group of high school students, tough inner-city kids from Oakland, were taken to see Steven Spielberg's film about the Holocaust, *Schindler's List,* they thought it was so funny that they began laughing in the theater. The students laughed so hard that the projectionist stopped the film, and the students along with their teacher were shown to the street. The teacher explained that the same type of thing had happened right here in America to Native Americans and was still happening to urban kids caught up in gang violence. Because the teenagers had been given no context for the film, it was not real to them; therefore, they laughed. To remedy this situation, fast-thinking school administrators brought in Holocaust survivors to speak to the classes. In addition, they showed documentary films that depicted actual events and consequences of the Holocaust. They even took students to a museum and showed them artifacts from that horrible period.

When firsthand experience is reinforced by teachers who inspire students to seek their own paths to knowledge, the results can be surprising. In a speech to German college students, author Günter Grass (1990) talked about how, as a seventeen-year-old POW in America, he could not bring himself to believe the films about Auschwitz the Americans were showing him and his comrades. He, like the students in Oakland, had no context for it. His German people would never let this happen, he kept telling himself. Finally, after several years of being unable to deny the pictures and films that showed mounds of arms and heads and hair and bodies stacked like cordwood, he confronted his denial.

As a young man, Grass had believed most but not all of the Third Reich's rhetoric. One of the people whom he credits in his speech and essay "After Auschwitz" with preserving his connection to humanity was an art teacher who gave him much more than basic literacy. Writing about himself as a youth in the third person, Grass explained:

> Despite the shortness of his [Günter's] schooling he had a few teachers who taught him, more in secret than openly, aesthetic values, artistic sensibility. The woman sculptor, for example, assigned to teaching as her compulsory wartime service, who noticed the schoolboy constantly drawing and slipped him exhibition catalogs from the twenties. At considerable risk, she shocked and infected him with the work of Kirchner, Lehmbruck, Nolde, Beckmann. I clung to that. . . . In the face of such artistic provocations the certainty of this Hitler Youth began to waver, or, rather, it did not waver but softened in one spot [pp. 266–267].

Such literacy stories underscore the need for aims in schooling that go beyond basic literacy and mere competency in language. Jonathan Kozol worries about the effects of illiteracy, counting among them crime, drug and alcohol abuse, and unwanted pregnancies; yet he fails to explain how basic literacy can curtail these social problems. During an interview for this book, an elementary school teacher who had been diagnosed as HIV positive informed us that a lot of heterosexual teenagers were beginning to show up in his AIDS support group: "Before they were diagnosed as HIV positive, most of these kids thought they were immortal. They probably learned about sex in high school, but AIDS—they figured it could never happen to them." Obviously, basic literacy—even basic sexual literacy—is not going to give high school students the analytical aptitude needed to make healthy, responsible sexual decisions in a society that offers so many diverse opinions about sex.

The problems in society today are more far reaching and global than at any other time in history. Countries no longer can afford to isolate themselves from the rest of the world. The world is a global community faced with global problems—social, political, environmental, and economic—that affect everyone everywhere.

The existentialist philosopher Jean-Paul Sartre ([1948] 1973) wrote about the responsibility all men have to one another: "When we say that man is responsible for himself, we do not mean that he is responsible for his own individuality, but that he is responsible for all men. . . . Our responsibility is thus much greater than we had supposed, for it concerns mankind as a whole" (p. 29). Sartre believed deeply that when a war breaks out in one part of the world, all people in some way are responsible for that war. This philosophy seems especially true of the difficulties now facing the global society on the eve of the twenty-first century. Prevailing over problems as potentially catastrophic as the energy shortage, ozone depletion, and AIDS will require not only language and communication skills that transcend those possessed by the classic orators but also multiple literacies in many fields of knowledge. Therefore, it is important to use every educational tool available to further not just basic but critical and dynamic literacy as well.

We believe society's unwillingness to let go of traditional concepts of literacy impedes more enlightened approaches to schooling for a literate society. We are even more troubled by social critics like Gatto who want to give up on public schools altogether. His solution, if realized, would carry with it the most frightening repercussions for society—no more free education. In the film *Alien Nation,* a group of aliens from outer space flee their own dying planet, and the hospitable inhabitants of earth offer them a place to live on their planet. One night, a drunken alien cop tells his human partner why his own race has a love-hate relationship with earthlings: "We love you because you believe in the ideals of racial equality and harmony. We hate you because you cannot live up to these ideals." Like the alien, Gatto, the former New York schoolteacher, hates the fact that public schools cannot live up to his own idealized notions of education. In many ways, Gatto is no different from the traditionalist who sees education in terms of its failures rather than its successes.

The Evolving Word

We remain optimistic about education, and we hail and attend with awe the natural evolution of the American language. As soon as the first English settlers set foot in America, they began to perceive the world in new and different ways. Their first experiences in the New World—what they saw, what they smelled, what they heard, what they felt—changed the way they used their language. Those first settlers spoke a dialect that was close linguistically and grammatically to the English of the sixteenth and seventeenth centuries. Today, our Americanized English is so removed from even present-day British English that we pronounce and spell some of the same words differently than our British cousins do.

"Word meanings," Vygotsky (1986) states, "are dynamic rather than static formations" (p. 217). This is as true of written as it is of spoken language. The humanist philosopher Georges Gusdorf ([1953] 1965) says that "the established language must not be understood as a closed system. . . . Every attempt authoritatively to fix a tongue at any given moment in its evolution is doomed to failure" (p. 62). Language is always in a process of evolution. It is not a static absolute like mathematics; it is in a constant state of flux.

Language is also constantly adjusting to the needs of the individuals in society. Because of the importance modern society places on communication, language and discourse are inextricably connected to the cultural and social milieu of a community. Each new voice that joins society offers a fresh way of looking at the world, and each new form of communication, whether it is the printing press, the typewriter, the radio, the telephone, the television, or the computer, suggests a new means of transmitting human thoughts, views, and feelings to the rest of the world.

Vox Humana and the Power of Language

In an interview for the Public Broadcasting Service, Stevie Wonder once said, "The voice is eternal." We wish we could agree with his assertion. But even for a mass entertainer, that is not an altogether accurate notion. In fact, ordinary observation would suggest that the unaided human voice is puny and weak and therefore hardly everlasting. Occasionally there is a William Jennings Bryan, someone who took pride in reaching ten thousand people on the strength of his vocal cords alone. Yet, even with twentieth-century amplification systems, Adolf Hitler or Pope Paul or Stevie Wonder could reach, at best, multiple thousands live and in person. When the last amplified echoes have died down in the square or auditorium, that voice is gone.

Metaphors for the weakness of the human voice abound in conversation and literature—voices crying in the wilderness, shouting into a storm, hollering down a rain barrel. Resonant or thin, high or low, mellow or scratchy, the human voice is anything but eternal. In his Nobel prize speech of 1960, William Faulkner argued that on the very last day of earth, the human voice, puny but inexhaustible, will still be heard, still be crying out (1996). But the echoes of that voice certainly will not last beyond Armageddon.

Of course, Wonder did not literally mean to suggest that the sound waves produced by vocal cords are eternal. In that same interview, which reached our ears via radio, he "amplified" his remarks to say that it is the lyrics that last. As a composer-songwriter, he believes that he captures important truths in his works. Wonder writes about ideas that matter, and he preserves them for posterity through his work. His poetry, like any art, will outlast the moment of composition and the physical voice of its creator.

Moreover, Wonder uses the best of modern technology to preserve those words and the sound of his own voice—the recording. Until the recording-film-video-computer revolution, writing had served as humankind's most effective form of keeping records and recording speech. In writing, *voice* is what brings a flat black-and-white text to life.

In his novel *Slaughterhouse-Five*, Kurt Vonnegut, Jr., named a character *Vox Humana,* the human voice. It seems this person was in an air raid as a baby in Dresden during World War II. A church was bombed, and the character's mother was hit in the head with a fragment from the organ keyboard, a stop labeled Vox Humana. An organ, however, at best only imitates a human voice. Writing attempts to represent it. Since writing is an act of making meaning as well as transcribing speech, it makes sounds that remind us of the person who wrote it. Of course, at times the voice on the page is what the rhetorician calls the *persona* or *mask* and is not that of the writer at all. The normally cheery boss writes with a stern mask in discussing disciplinary problems or pending layoffs. The usually polysyllabic academic makes a point of using a few concise, folksy phrases in a paper to reveal his human side.

To have a closer look at this concept of voice, we will examine the writing of three contemporary citizens—three literate citizens—who took the time to write the local newspaper.

Eugenia Hutton (1994) wrote her local newspaper about the issue of public access to a trail that runs through private properties along a semipublic irrigation ditch. She writes:

Hikers, Bikers, and Pikers:

> You people that want to share the Steamboat Trail
> with the owners are dangerous! Isn't that called
> communism?
> I'd sooner have a herd of wild horses come
> through my property than you trespassers. At least the
> horses would leave behind something of value.

The letter clearly has that quality we call voice, resonant and clear. It is obviously designed for rhetorical effect, opening with its attention-grabbing, rhyming, "Hikers, Bikers, and Pikers." Bold and direct in its accusations, it asks a ringing rhetorical question of those who would take public control over private land: "Isn't that called communism?" The writer makes no bones about her opinion of the hiker-biker crowd and whatever it is they leave behind, whether footprints, bike tracks, or PowerBar wrappers.

As writing teachers, our first impulse on reading such a piece might be to make a few standard suggestions for revision. As one often does in academic settings, we might urge a bit of moderation by asking the writer: Don't you think your opening and closing would be more effective if you didn't insult the people you are trying to change?

We might question the logic of leaping from sharing a hiking-biking trail to the onslaught of communism, and we might point out that the indignant, unanswered question merely hints at a point rather than making a formal, well-reasoned connection.

On second glance, and putting away our academic red pencils, we have to say that Hutton's piece is genuinely effective in its own right. In the first place, she probably is not truly addressing the hikers and bikers; rather, she is voicing her support for fellow property owners. A great many of her readers would agree wholeheartedly. With her poetic and dramatic flair, she surely qualifies as a literate citizen. In fact, she reminds us of the people in the film *Network* who, urged on by a disgruntled newscaster, rush to their windows and shout, "I'm mad as hell, and I'm not going to take it anymore."

Such rhetoric may or may not be effective in civil discourse, say, in a meeting designed to get the hikers, bikers, and homeowners to negotiate a compromise. But in the spirit of involved citizenship, Hutton's letter surely sounds an alarm.

The next letter also sounds an alarm, but in a very different voice. J. D. Stempel (1994) writes:

> Daily, we are confronted with horrifying scenes: starvation, genocide or plagues or some combination in Somalia, Rwanda, Bosnia, East Timor, Haiti, etc. While corporate greed, unsustainable agriculture activities, corrupt and/or inept governments and the merchants of death tend to exaggerate the misery, common sense suggests that the root cause is overpopulation.
>
> Meanwhile, most of the world's political and religious leaders continue to be in denial, ignoring the obvious evidence of population pressures: deforestation, water, air and land pollution, loss of fisheries due to over-exploitation, loss of arable land due to erosion and soil exhaustion, increasing animal and plant extinctions mostly because of loss of habitat, and suicidal civil wars fought over increasingly scarce resources.
>
> Clearly the only rational solution is for a serious global effort to encourage birth control by all available means: education through the mass media, dropping all child subsidies (like the income tax deductions), and developing better methods of birth control.
>
> Opposition to birth control surely borders on madness.

In terms of politics and rhetoric, we like this letter more, so we must caution ourselves about judging discourse from too personal a perspective. In short, one should not like the rhetoric just because one agrees with the politics, for that leads to the sort of uncritical reading that takes things at face value. We happen to think Stempel is sensible in his view on the need for birth control, but as writers and teachers, we also have to admire the skill with which Stempel puts this brief piece together. The opening, like Hutton's, is meant to catch the eye or ear, which includes him in a long classical tradition of rhetoric. In that opening sentence, we are impressed by Stempel's catalogue of current world hot spots, establishing credentials (as did the ancient rhetoricians) by displaying knowledge of the topic. The writer uses similar long lists at several points in the letter, revealing a comprehensive and apparently detailed knowledge of world affairs.

Even as sympathetic readers, however, we would challenge Stempel's exaggeration and oversimplification of the traits of the world's corporate and political leaders (a tarring with a single brush similar to Hutton's lumping together of hikers and bikers as pikers), but we respect the synthesis that leads Stempel to argue that birth control is at the heart of these problems. We would challenge the writer (as we often do our students) to determine whether any other possible cause could be substituted for "overpopulation" in this letter. If one could plug in "the economy" or "Western indifference" or even "communism" in that same word slot and the letter still made sense, then perhaps the essay is reductionist.

Stempel's letter has a different voice from Hutton's, but like hers, it is strong, confident, and clear. The letter is, in our judgment, effective, though there is certainly a question of whether it would be successful with opponents of birth control, rather than with those of us who are already in sympathy with the idea. We would certainly put Stempel, with Hutton, in our list of literate citizens. Both are willing and able to make themselves heard.

What of the voice in this next letter? Jeannie Mascari (1994) responds to an editorial that called for more bilingual education programs in the schools:

> I am proud to be an American. My parents taught me to be proud. My father came to America from Italy in 1905. When he was settled he sent for my mother in 1906. In 1907 my brother Anthony was born. In 1909 I was born. Neither of my parents spoke English. When I was 7, I went to school. I did not speak English. There was no bilingual. I had to learn the English language. I think we need to tell people who come to America to

start knowing they are in America, learn the English
language as our early immigrants did. We should not
have to worry about bilingual teachers.

Mascari's opening, like the previous two, attracts one's attention and establishes voice. It is also effectively (though not necessarily deliberately) designed to capture the attention of precisely
those people who traditionally have been opposed to bilingual education: her rhetorical appeal to patriotism implies that anyone who
disagrees with her may, in fact, be less patriotic than she.

The syntax of this piece is plain, especially in contrast to the
grammatical complexity of a Stempel, but in its way, this letter
establishes a persona or voice even more clearly than Stempel's.
There are a couple of minor grammatical errors, which, coupled
with the effects of the syntax, lead one to conclude that even after
eighty years of speaking English, the writer is still not as fluent as
a native speaker might be. But the stylistic simplicity of the piece
is also part of its rhetorical effectiveness: this letter is, to us, highly
persuasive because this citizen is able to write effectively in a language that was not her original one.

Thus, we conclude that each of these writers succeeds in his or
her way. Each goes well beyond basic literacy to critique the world
through language and to try to control dynamically that world with
the use of language.

Despite what one reads or hears through the media, there is
no clear-cut line that separates the literate from the illiterate. Further, there is no end point to literacy learning, a time when one
can say, "That's it. I've got it. I'm literate for all time." It is in the
nature of language and humanity that we all—Morris and Tchudi;
Hutton, Stempel, and Mascari; and the readers of this book—
invariably fall short in our efforts.

The Disappearance of Voice

Unfortunately, there are times in writing and speaking when voice
becomes lost or murky or indistinct. For instance, in his classic
essay, "Politics and the English Language" (1948), George Orwell
warned us about the political misuse of language to cover up or
disguise intent.

A press conference with Admiral William A. Owens (Diamond, 1994) led to some utterances that Orwell certainly would have found appalling. While briefing the press on a new generation of military hardware, Owens explained that unmanned, computer-driven drone weapons will, in the future, allow the military "to reach out and touch an enemy meaningfully." As Owens put it, "If you see a large battlefield, 200 miles by 200 miles, and you can see surveillance reconnaissance so we know where all the relevant things are, can you imagine the power when you can take that knowledge . . . and now tie it together with all those weapons to do something that is smart in terms of eliminating that problem, that enemy? Then you can envision doing a lot of things more efficiently" (p. 2A).

As Orwell and today's watchdogs of doublespeak would be quick to point out, Owens has developed the use of euphemism to a high level. "To touch an enemy meaningfully" is, of course, to kill people, in this case with extremely powerful weaponry. To "envision doing a lot of things more efficiently" means to think up all sorts of ways of killing your enemy without putting your own soldiers in danger. Orwell claimed that military leaders employ euphemism because the public would be revolted at the reality of what is happening. Would Owens receive a positive response if he more explicitly and directly described the impact of these future weapons on human flesh?

We are especially interested in the significance of Owens's syntax in the extended quotation above. The sentence opens with an introductory dependent clause, an "if" clause that promises a declarative "then" statement. But part way into the sentence, the Admiral drops the straightforwardness of that approach and switches syntactical gears into a question, beginning, "can you imagine." Even within the question, however, a pronoun shift from "you" (the audience) to "we" (the military) is suggestive. "You" as the listener are *not* a member of the military, but as part of "we," you are involuntarily included in military thinking and perhaps share the responsibility for reaching out to touch the enemy meaningfully. But Owens's slip to the first person plural pronoun "we" may reveal a different position. It is the admiral and his colleagues who will, in fact, be making the crucial decisions. It is *they* who will be doing the killing, but if *we* buy into the admiral's rhetoric, *we-*

they must all assume responsibility. Somehow, in the middle of that extremely convoluted sentence, consciously or unconsciously, Owens catches himself and goes back to the second person, the finger-pointing pronoun, as "you" are invited to continue reflecting imaginatively on the results of high-tech military efficiency.

The result is classic doublespeak and a loss of voice. This is, as Orwell warned us, language that is intended as much to hide as to reveal. But a careful reader can ferret out the underlying meaning: military leaders are taking pleasure and satisfaction in long-distance extermination schemes.

Now, you, the reader, may object rightly that this is clearly a case in which Owens's informal, oral language was literally transcribed into writing, where it looks bad. This is speech recorded, not composed writing, and the admiral himself may have been horrified to read how his comments appeared when written down. Nevertheless, the case is instructive because we are convinced that this is not the admiral's normal mode of talking—it is not his vox humana. Does he sound like this when he is taking his kids or grandkids to Disneyland? Does he use these kinds of euphemisms when he is talking over weaponry in his own office with his peers? We suspect not. In this press conference, he drifted into a register of discourse recognizable long before even Orwell's time—using euphemism to disguise an unpleasant truth. It is a rhetorical technique that goes all the way back to the Sophists.

How did Owens learn this register? It probably was not something taught to him in school or college, although he may well have learned some of its characteristics in school if he had to fudge his way through an examination or term paper. More likely, he picked up this lingo on the job, hearing other officers handle press conferences and reading memoranda and reports written in military jargon. The false voice, we suspect, was assumed as a part of his position, due to his wish to be an integral part of the military community and due to the rhetorical context of the public situation.

Such artificiality of voice is typical not only of the military. Bernard Dixon (1994), editor of *Medical Science Research,* complains that the false voice is all too common in academic writing as well. He cites a sentence in a paper submitted to a professional journal he edits: "The mode of action of anti-lymphocytic serum has not yet been determined by research workers in this country or abroad" (p. B5).

As an editor, Dixon changed this to, "We don't know how ALS works" (p. B5). He replaced euphemisms with simple words and inserted the responsibility-taking pronoun "we."

Why do people write and speak in a false voice? Do these medical researchers go home and say, "It has been determined that the family unit might appropriately be transported to Disneyland for a holiday occasion"? Dixon opines that young scientists "are simply following the protocol established and maintained by an unconscious conspiracy of research supervisors and editors who, in turn, learnt these dreadful habits earlier in their careers" (p. B5).

There are theories in academia that the characteristics of this writing, most notably the passive voice and the avoidance of personal pronouns, result from a felt need to portray academic knowledge as more certain, solid, and Platonic than it really is. To say, "the researcher has hypothesized" sounds more confident than "I think." "The experiment was conducted" sounds more objective than "I did some lab work."

If challenged, most academics will quickly admit that they do not care for this stuffy, institutionalized voice, but the traditions carry on, and young professors start to believe that they will not get published unless they adopt the standard voice. Dixon concludes that a change in this writing will result only from more conscious reflection by writers on what they are doing, coupled with a breaking of the tradition by writers who have become firmly established. He cites the personal, chatty, yet fully scholarly writing of such people as Stephen Jay Gould, Peter Medawar, and Lewis Thomas as examples of those who are helping to break the mold.

Joseph Rogers (1977) has coined the term *decalang* for the voiceless writing that emerges when language becomes separated from the experience that generates it. He explains (pp. 22–27) that for the Greeks, language was centered in the real world, that Greek young people were educated following the ideal of "the sound mind in the sound body," tempering their study of classics with active engagement in sports, military exercises, and civic debate. The Romans, says Rogers, were a more bookish sort who lost track of these "dimensionalized" aspects of education—the real-world experiences that are the underpinnings of writing in reality. He argues that things became worse through the traditions of scholasticism in the Middle Ages, as illustrated by the classic, nondimensionalized debate over how many angels could dance on the head of a pin. Over time, Rogers concludes, schooling has become ever more bookish. The current cry for more hands-on and experiential learning over the past two decades suggests that others agree with Rogers.

The Literate Citizen

What we have been discussing, then, is the fascinating cycle of the interaction of experience and interpretation, of oral language and written language as they function for the literate citizen. Further, the relationships have become increasingly complicated in our own time. The national-standards project in English and language arts has observed (National Council of Teachers of English/International Reading Association, 1996, n.p.):

> As recently as one hundred years ago, "literacy" meant the ability to recall and recite from familiar texts and to write signatures. . . . Even twenty years ago, definitions of literacy were linked almost exclusively to print materials.

> Today, a full definition of literacy must include at least three significant additions:

> *Oral communication.* We have come to understand how much of our knowledge of language, acquisition of literate skills, and reflection on the work and worth of literacy occur in spoken language.
> *Visual texts.* Visual texts include items such as illustrations, photographs, film, and video. Although at one time they were dismissed as easy to read or only popular, these forms of text are now deemed critical for reading in contemporary life.
> *Technological displays.* The meteoric spread of microcomputer technology has changed the face of literacy. Increasingly, workplace participation depends on the ability of workers to learn symbolic languages. With equal speed, collegial work in science and technology depends on the Internet transfer

of data and analyses. In the humanities, on-line access to e-mail, computer-stored archives of images and texts, affects both the scope and currency of scholarly work.

So who is the literate citizen? Is there, in fact, such a person?

It seems important to us to recognize that despite the five billion and more different voices on the face of the planet, there are enough common characteristics to what we call literacy to discuss the idea of a literate citizen in the singular rather than the plural. Our literate citizen is not like the person W. H. Auden had in mind when he wrote "The Unknown Citizen," not simply a compilation of averages, of vocabulary, sentence length, and Scholastic Aptitude Test (SAT) verbal scores. Our view suggests that despite the great variance in literacies in society, there are certain traits that people we label literate have in common.

Inquiring about reasonable goals and expectations for language education for the twenty-first century, Carol Pope (1993) studied a number of national reports issued from such agencies as the Hudson Institute, the National Commission on Excellence in Education, and various studies from business. She identified five areas of proficiency "those who join the world of work will need" (pp. 38–41):

- The ability to communicate and work collaboratively
- The ability to work effectively in a multicultural society and work force
- The ability to adapt
- The ability to think critically
- The ability to use available technology

We propose one addition to her list:

- The ability to think and act creatively and imaginatively

By creatively, we do not necessarily mean the ability to write poems or paint pictures. Borrowing from David Holbrook (1967), we see creativity as people's ability to work with information and ideas and images that come to them and to make fresh and original (for them) formulations. Our concept of imagination is borrowed from Jacob Bronowski (1978), who sees it as the human ability, demonstrated in both the humanities and the sciences, to juxtapose ideas and images and symbols in ways that explore new possibilities. The literate citizen must be creative and imaginative, whether arguing for or against a bike trail, birth control, or bilingual education. He or she must be creative and imaginative in reading between the lines of a daily newspaper, a classic novel, or a set of instructions on hooking up the VCR.

Imagination and creativity (as well as the five criteria listed by Pope) are *language based* and *language bound.* That is where rhetoric comes in.

As we mentioned earlier in this chapter, in popular usage, rhetoric means political puffery and chicanery; it means the pitch of the used car salesman or the waitress or the guy who calls on the phone to sell you insurance or a trip to Bermuda. But rhetoric, our discipline, is more than such puffery. Academics, of course, have a habit of declaring their particular disciplines the center of the intellectual universe. The scientist says that the methods of science are at the essence of the universe; the mathematician points out that the world can be reduced to number; the historian warns both of them not to repeat the errors of history.

It is probably just as predictable that we see rhetoric at the heart of things. Rhetoric, at its best, is the study of discourse—language—and how it operates in a variety of contexts. Rhetoric thus subsumes the work and the language of the scientist and the mathematician; it examines the words and methods of the historian. It is equally effective for examining the medical jargon of a doctor, the pitch of a TV salesperson, or the love-letter prose of a Romeo to a Juliet. As we have discussed, one simply cannot separate ideas from the language in which they are composed, from the words in which they are written, spoken, broadcast, phoned, or faxed.

Having made that bold and fairly arrogant assertion about our own field as the center of all human understanding, we will back off a bit and simply reassert that rhetoric is, in fact, a central discipline to human affairs, that the question of what makes a literate citizen has implications that affect all aspects of life.

We adopt our approach in the coming chapters from a field known as "the rhetoric of inquiry." (Simons, 1990). We look at how people use their imaginations and their creativity to help them get along in their lives, and we examine the role that language plays in the process. We examine and reexamine the pretzel-like structure of basic, critical, and dynamic literacy.

Specifically, we look at six groups. First, we look into motivations for becoming literate in a group of people who came to reading and writing in surprising ways. Then we examine, in order, entrepreneurs and businesspeople, community activists, artists and writers, media people, and kids in school. By no means do we suppose that this is a complete canvas of the universe of discourse, but it allows us to present what a variety of interesting people do with words in their own lives—how they use language to solve problems, how they use it for aesthetic satisfaction, how they use it to generate and argue ideas both large and small.

By embarking on a search for the traits and operations of the literate citizen, we use a methodology based on *synthesis*. Many people are quick to judge others literate or illiterate on the criterion of basic literacy alone. As our terms critical and dynamic literacy imply, we do not view literacy in such a narrow context. And although we are looking at diverse literacies, we do not believe that every community has its own private language somehow learned in isolation. How literate citizens relate to others in a particular community of discourse may require terminology unique to that community, but they still use the same core language and the same global or generative processes of literacy. Therefore, we look for synthesis, for the characteristics of literacy that enable us to look at the language of the auto shop and of the English department as branches of the same phenomenon.

When we speak of this synthesis, we draw on the philosopher Georg Wilhelm Friedrich Hegel's use of the term, formulated in response to Immanuel Kant's theory of *thesis* and *antithesis*. Henry D. Aikin (1956) explains that for Hegel, both thesis and antithesis were "understood in a new light as imperfect expressions of a higher, more inclusive proposition which contains what is significant in both of them" (p. 74). Too often, however, the original Hegelian idea is misinterpreted to mean compromise, a benign blending or lopping off of the contradictory parts of contradictory ideas leading to a simplistic union. Timothy Crusius laments in *Discourse: A Critique and Synthesis of Major Theories* (1989), "Surely there is something better than all parts and no whole or an all-encompassing vacuity, something better than no rigor or a self-defeating overrigorousness. The something better is creative synthesis, closely akin as I think of it to the kind of synthesis Hegel espoused" (p. 108). Crusius is referring here to the creative synthesis of pedagogical theories in composition, but his statement is easily applied to the way we are looking at literacy in this book.

The Hegelian dialectic is a means whereby one idea or belief and an opposing or contrary idea or belief are analyzed to form a third idea or belief. This third idea, which Hegel referred to as *the Triad,* is more comprehensive (or truer) than either the original or the contrary. For Hegel, this is a continuous process in which, as C.E.M. Joad (1957) reminds us, "The mind is driven . . . to ever wider and more comprehensive formulations of the truth" (p. 403). Obviously, we do not use Hegel's dialectic to chase an infinite truth. Instead, we use it to find small but earnest truths—practical and imaginative, concrete and abstract, experiential and hypothetical—in the diverse literacy stories we glean from literate citizens. These truths, in turn, inform our discussion of schooling for a literate society.

Chapter Two

Reading, Writing, and Motivation

If you ever talk to anyone who has reading and writing problems (and from about the tenth grade on I considered myself semi-illiterate, which means I can read and get along, but with great difficulty), they tell you that their lives have been governed by the fact that they have a literacy problem. I can think critically. I ponder both sides of a story. I look at it and am open to new ideas. But you can't show that because everybody wants you to write it down.
—STANLEY C.

In this chapter, we move to the heart of the matter—our interviews with a range of literate citizens. Before we examine other people's stories about their motivation to read and write, we want to share a childhood story of our own. Although this anecdote does not pertain directly to literacy, it does illustrate how easy it is to thwart a child's (or an adult's) natural desire to learn. When Paul Morris was ten or twelve years old, he was invited up from the Peewee League to a Little League baseball team. His sudden elevation into the big leagues inspired him. On his Peewee League team, he had been a fairly good pitcher, but in Little League he became a very good shortstop and hitter. Then, halfway through the season, he was beaned by a pitcher with a wild fastball. The incident so unnerved him that his batting began to suffer. To make matters worse, the coach, who had been so supportive of him when he was playing well, began to berate him. Eventually, Paul lost all confidence in himself as a ballplayer. His fielding began to suffer, and his teammates began making fun of him. Paul's team won the pennant that year, but he spent the last quarter of the season on the bench. Whenever he was allowed out on the ball field, he felt so demoralized that he usually made an error or two and was quickly taken out of the game.

We do not believe this experience is all that unique. In fact, just recently a friend told Paul a similar story over dinner. Stacey was in college when his baseball coach decided that every member of the team should hit exactly like Atlanta Braves' star Dale Murphy. The coach told them that if they could not learn the batting techniques of this professional baseball player, they would not be allowed to play. Stacey, who had been hitting .350 using his own batting style, began hitting below .100. Eventually, discouraged and frustrated by his coach's demands, he quit the team. We believe most people can recount similar incidents from childhood, times when an authority figure like a coach or a teacher encouraged or discouraged performance, whether on the playing field or in the classroom.

At the 1992 Conference on College Composition and Communication, writing teacher Susan Reed-Jones presented a paper on "'Faith in the Reality of Belonging': The Story of Alonzo A." Reed-Jones first met Alonzo after he entered the work furlough program where she was a caseworker for the Department of Corrections in a large Western state. She relates how Alonzo, an ex-convict and gang member and a recovering alcohol and drug addict, "always felt left out" at school—"full of shame that he lived with his grandparents, and they only spoke Spanish." Alonzo told Reed-Jones that in school nobody "cared . . . whether he could read or write"; therefore, he "left school in the eighth grade and joined a neighborhood gang" (p. 5).

When Reed-Jones was introduced to Alonzo, he could neither read nor write. Later, through her encouragement, Alonzo started attending Alcoholics Anonymous (AA) meetings. At these meetings, Alonzo found the motivation and reassurance that had been lacking in his eight years of schooling. As Reed-Jones explains, "Much literacy theory functions on the tacit assumption that literacy itself is meaningful, transcendent of culture and individual motivation. Alonzo's story refutes this assumption. His desire to become literate emerged from his desire to be a part of A.A., a fully contributing member of a literate community. His first real exposure to written texts was his exposure to A.A. texts, the encoded values of the A.A. community. Alonzo internalized these values; they became the focal point of his life" (p. 11). Because of the encouragement he first received in AA, Alonzo "began taking adult education classes at night, improving his reading skills and learning to write" (p. 7). Reed-Jones explains that Alonzo's primary goal was simple; as he said, "I wanted to be a part of A.A." (p. 7). Eventually, Alonzo became not only a part of AA but a literate member of society as well.

Although Alonzo's story has an optimistic ending, many people are never able to overcome the damage done, very often in a school setting, to their self-confidence in childhood. Reed-Jones's essay contains a message for educators about the importance of "a feeling of belonging, of being a necessary part of the group" (p. 10).

The idea that *how* students are taught is just as important as *what* they are taught is not a new one. The Brazilian educator Paulo Freire ([1973] 1992) has been a frequent critic of educational techniques that "transform people into 'things' and negate their existence as beings who transform the world" (p. 95). In the preface to his book *Lives on the Boundary* (1990), Mike Rose criticizes America for being a "nation obsessed with evaluating our children" (p. ix). At the heart of Paul's and Stacey's disheartening experiences with baseball is an accent on errors and corrections rather than on risk taking. Furthermore, Paul's Little League coach was insensitive to his player's problems because the coach was unable to see beyond his own single-minded goal of winning the pennant.

It is a similar emphasis on an end product and on evaluation that discourages so many people from learning to read and write. If schools ever want to counter this attitude, it is important that teachers and administrators try to understand what it is that motivates an Alonzo's entrance into what psycholinguist Frank Smith (1988) calls the "literacy club" (p. 8).

The following case histories examine the literacy patterns of both highly literate and at-risk individuals. The need for studies that explore why and how such people become literate is obvious: there are thousands, some say millions, of people in America who have problems with reading and writing. Susan Reed-Jones attributes many of these problems to "our beleaguered educational system['s]" failure to "acknowledge the experience of the individual and . . . how that experience is valuable to the larger community" (p. 8). In the case of Alonzo, Reed-Jones believes "the educational system" was unable to "provide Alonzo with a sense of belonging and personal value" (p. 8). By studying the motivations behind the individual's desire to be literate, it is possible that teachers can use this knowledge to encourage and inspire students in schools now.

Jeanie, Ellen, and Maggie: A Love Affair with Words

Jeanie

Jeanie F. is a college English teacher. Her mother went to college for three years, and her father, who attended school as far as the sixth grade, is, according to Jeanie, "partially literate": "He did go to school some of the time, but not a lot because he was the oldest son, and he ended up doing the farm work with his dad." Because Jeanie's father had problems with reading and writing, some might assume Jeanie also had problems in these areas; however, this was not the case.

The idea that illiteracy can be passed down from a mother or father to a son or daughter was challenged over twenty years ago by researchers like Jane Torrey. In the article "Learning to Read Without a Teacher: A Case Study" (1973), Torrey questions the myth that all so-called illiterates have illiterate parents. Torrey describes her subject John, who was born to parents with very limited educations: "According to most predictions, John should have reading problems all through his school career. But John is one of the thousands of children who somehow learn to read in much the same way that millions of children learn to speak—before they arrive at school, without the help of a teacher, and without very much in the way of obvious instruction from parents or other adults. Like many other precocious readers, John taught himself to read with the aid of labels and television" (p. 147).

Because Jeanie's mother was highly literate and her father had barely finished the sixth grade, there was a "funny kind of split emphasis" in the family home between "doing things and reading and writing and school." According to Jeanie, her mother loved to read and write, "but my father could care less about those things." In spite of his own lack of interest in the written word, Jeanie's father helped to reinforce his children's early literacy patterns:

> I'm the oldest child in my family. And when I was born, my mother immediately started reading to me and talking to me and singing to me. She was thirty-two when I was born. She was thrilled to have a baby, and she spent enormous amounts of time with me. My dad would come home, would sit down and also read to me. But he wasn't really reading. He had memorized the books when my mom had read them to me. But by the time I was two, if he made a mistake, I would correct him because I also had them memorized.

Jeanie was encouraged to read by both her mother and her father. Jeanie's father "recognized that [his children] needed what he didn't have" and wanted them, "especially his two daughters," to have more.

Language development theorists recognize the importance of reading and talking to a child at a very young age. No matter how precocious children are, the benefits of reading to our children are manifest. Sociolinguist M.A.K. Halliday asserts in the introduction to his book *Language as Social Semiotic: The Social Interpretation of Language and Meaning* (1978), "Language arises in the life of the individual through an ongoing exchange of meaning with significant others. A child creates, first his child tongue then his mother tongue" (p. 1).

Jeanie's mother sang and read the Bible to her. As a result, Jeanie was reading the Bible on her own by the time she was seven years old: "I can remember being outside reading the Book of Job and thinking, This is neat. It was the language in the King James. It fascinated me. The stories fascinated me."

Jeanie has always seen her father as a doer rather than a reader, and because of his limitations as a reader, there was more emphasis on the oral than the written in the house. She recalls, "It was different in my family than it is for people who grew up with two parents who can read and write. But not everyone who grows up in a nonliterate household is illiterate. The older children in my father's family were all storytellers. My dad always told stories; everything in our family is narration. This whole pattern of telling stories is strong, and we were indoctrinated with it when we were children."

Jeanie sees less of an emphasis on oral communication in her own family now that she is married and has two children of her own: "We write notes to each other. We couldn't do this when I was growing up with my father." The emphasis on stories and narrative in her childhood had a profound effect on Jeanie's love of reading. As a child, Jeanie read everything she could get her hands on: "There was never any money to buy books, but my mother's sister would buy books and send them to me. I read everything they would let me read from the school library. After I went through all the books there, then Mom would take me to town for books at the county library."

When Jeanie was a baby, her mother used to sing to her. This, Jeanie suspects, is one of the many ways her mother "nourished" her love for words and stories: "Mom had a beautiful singing voice, and I can remember her singing hymns and old folk songs to me. And that's poetry. This is as beautiful as you can make words."

It is interesting that Jeanie's fascination with storytelling turned into a love affair with the written word. The connection between an oral tradition and the written word was emphasized by her father's reading and writing limitations. The stories that her father and aunts and uncles told her introduced Jeanie to new and exciting versions of the world. Later, Jeanie would discover that reading could do the same thing (Jeanie F., interview with authors, Mar. 1994).

James Britton (1978), the English educator and researcher, says that "as soon as we bring words into our reflection of experience, the image [our fantasy] takes one step towards the idea." He goes on to say, "Culture, the common pool of humanity, offers the young child witches and fairy godmothers, symbols which may embody and work upon the hate and love that are part of a close, dependent relationship; he will read of witches and tell stories of his own that arise directly from his needs. In doing so, he performs an assimilative task, working towards a more harmonious relationship between inner needs and external demands" (p. 47).

By reading to children, by telling them stories, parents and teachers are offering them not merely words, but new ways to look at and elaborate on their own worldviews. This rudimentary social interaction lays the foundation for basic, critical, and even dynamic literacy.

Ellen

Ellen L., another teacher, also a graduate student in composition and rhetoric, remembers "being read to quite a bit." She says, "I think one reason I remember this so well is because occasionally my father will remind me that he read to me, he and my mother. But he especially read to me." Ellen's father is an English professor, and her mother has a doctorate in botany. She recalls his "telling me when I was in high school that one reason I was a good writer was because they, my parents, read to me a lot when I was growing up. I think what he meant was that I got the rhythm or the flow of the language in my head through his reading to me as a child."

By the time she was seven or eight years old, Ellen spent long stretches of time reading in the car on the long trips to the family's summer cabin:

> We would make the seven-hour drive to the cabin a couple times a year, and I always remember how my brother and I both read while my father drove and my mother knitted. It sounds like such an horrendously nuclear family, and I guess it was. In spite of the fact that my father and mother were sitting right there in the front seat, there was never any sharing of what I was reading. It wasn't important to me; my book was all I needed. I was absorbed in it.

Even though Ellen never discussed what she was reading with her parents on these trips, an important aspect of the literacy patterns of both Ellen and Jeanie is the sharing of books from one generation with the next. Ellen recalls, "I had a couple of Nancy Drew mysteries that my mother had given me because she had them from her childhood. We still have them. They were wonderful—peeling parchment, wartime paper, but beautiful."

It is interesting that this was also a common practice in Jeanie's family when she was growing up. Jeanie has since passed on the books she received from her aunt to her daughter: "My daughter loves to read. She's becoming as voracious a reader as I am."

Although the passing on of texts to children does not necessarily guarantee critical or dynamic literacy later on, here the exchange of knowledge between mother and child follows the literacy patterns suggested by cognitive psychologist Jerome Bruner in *Actual Minds, Possible Worlds* (1986): "Vygotsky himself remarks that the acquisition of language provides the paradigm case for what he is talking about, for it is in the nature of things that the aspirant speaker must 'borrow' the knowledge and consciousness of the tutor to enter a language. . . . It is the mother who establishes little 'formats' or rituals in which language is used: 'book reading' routines with picture books, request patterns, little games, and so on. She plays her part in them with striking regularity" (pp. 76–77).

Although family members play an extremely important role in early language development and literacy patterns, few people have good enough memories to recall their first reading or writing experiences before starting school. Most can remember, however, not only their first experiences reading and writing in school but also the teachers who had the most profound effects on them. Ellen remembers getting comments like, "You're a good writer" or "good story" on her grade school papers, but she "assumed they [the teachers] were writing that on everyone's paper." It was not until high school, when one of her teachers went out of her way to praise her work, that Ellen realized she might actually be good at reading and writing. "I had a history teacher who said, 'I really enjoyed reading your papers, Ellen. That skill will really be valuable to you in the future.' I knew immediately that she meant my writing." Ellen says it was around this same time that she began working especially hard at trying to please her teachers. "I always remember wanting to be liked by my teachers," she told us. "That's always been important to me, and it still is. I think I seized on this idea of teachers liking my writing or saying I was a good writer as a way of pleasing my teachers, and therefore making them like me."

For highly motivated readers and writers like Ellen and Jeanie, with families who support their reading and writing efforts before and during school, the classroom can become a special place for engaging in many different types of literacy activities. These activities can be influenced by teachers, peers, or even by authors representing new worlds through books. Frank Smith (1988) believes most people learn about language through collaboration with other writers and readers: "Mutual engagement in literate activities leads to an even deeper form of collaboration in which children learn with readers and writers who are not present. . . . I am referring of course to the authors who show children how written language is produced, helping them to become both readers and writers" (pp. 66–67).

These "deeper forms of collaboration" are responsible for what Rose calls critical literacy: "framing an argument or taking someone else's argument apart, systematically inspecting a document, an issue, or an event, synthesizing different points of view, [and] applying a theory to disparate phenomena" (p. 188). Further, in the social context of the academic community, complex literacy activities like the ones Rose mentions are responsible for "shared concepts and orientations" like "alienation, authoritarian personality, the social construction of the self, determinism, hegemony, equilibrium, intentionality, recursion, reinforcement, and so on" (p. 192).

These concepts represent exactly the kinds of sophisticated literacy activities—critical and dynamic—referred to in Chapter One. It is important to note, however, that neither Ellen's nor Jeanie's motivation to be critically literate grew out of anything as abstract as a desire to be a critical thinker. Children are, Smith reminds us, "skilled and practiced thinkers" before they ever enter school. It was Ellen's need to please her teachers and to be rewarded for her writing and Jeanie's fascination with stories and storytelling that precipitated and encouraged their desire to do well in school. Further, it was the sustaining social influences at home and in school and their own need to be members of a particular literate community—in this case the academic community—that helped Ellen and Jeanie make a place for themselves and find acceptance among their peers and teachers. As the worldviews of Ellen and Jeanie became even more sophisticated, they paved the way for more involved social relationships reflective of the standards and values of academic discourse, making it possible for Ellen and Jeanie to become extraordinarily adept at complicated reading and writing tasks (Ellen L., interview with authors, Mar. 1994).

Maggie

We have looked at two adults and their memories of childhood literacy. Now we go directly to the source. Seven-year-old Maggie B.'s enthusiasm for language is just as strong as Ellen's and Jeanie's. Like Ellen, Maggie has parents, Bridgett and Dennis, who are both teachers. Bridgett teaches college English, and Dennis teaches math and science in high school. Bridgett says she has "boxes and boxes" of Maggie's writing. Bridgett's mother also kept boxes of her daughter's writing, and she shared her knowledge of books with Bridgett, just as Bridgett does with Maggie: "My mother did the same things with me that I do with Maggie. Maggie gets a magazine every month. My mom made sure that I got certain books. She talked to me about the plots. I remember my mom doing that with me when I was in the third or fourth grade. I do that with Maggie, too."

As with Ellen and Jeanie, we see a heritage of encouragement and confidence building. The collecting and archiving of Maggie's past and present creative efforts is a kind of publication and validation of her development as a writer and reader. We believe that affirmation and support of this sort is essential for the development of literacy—basic, critical, and dynamic—in readers and writers of all ages. Someday, should Maggie ever decide to have children, she quite probably will do the same kinds of things with them.

Bridgett still remembers when Maggie crawled into bed with her one morning and began reading to her for the first time: "It was before she was in kindergarten when I was on sabbatical. She had just turned five and Dennis was at work. She got in bed with me with this book. She didn't know all the words, but she just faked those to keep the story going. I could see her turning the pages at the right times. I had read the story to her many times, but I knew she was reading it because she said the mother 'bath-ed' rather than 'bathed' the baby in the story."

There have always been encouragement and plenty of books around the house for Maggie. Language researchers Jerome Harste, Virginia Woodward, and Carolyn Burke (1984) say in *Language Stories and Literacy Lessons* "all children at this age seem to have an almost natural affinity for books and for paper and pencil activities if the environment makes these things available" (p. 44).

However, Maggie's interest in learning to read and write seems to go beyond the instinctive curiosity that Harste, Woodward, and Burke allude to. For her, there seems to be a much more powerful incentive, one which Georges Gusdorf ([1953] 1965) associates with "the struggle for style . . . the struggle for consciousness." According to Gusdorf, "Each of us is charged with realizing himself in a language, a personal echo of the language of all which represents his contribution to the human world" (p. 76). Maggie yearns to tell her own stories, to announce her own versions of the world to the world. "Language and arts," says teacher-researcher Glenda Bissex in *Gnys at Work* (1980), "are not only culturally transmitted; they are also reinvented by children, who increasingly shape their inventions to cultural forms" (p. 203).

Through words, Maggie designs her own worlds; furthermore, she sees this type of creation as its own reward: "Because when you're all done it makes like a whole new book that you've created. You do the hard part, which is writing and thinking up a story. And when you're done, you're like, Wow! I just created a whole new thing."

Maggie's creative writing does more than just develop her own unique worldview. It also facilitates, as Australian researcher Jack Thomson suggests in *Understanding Teenagers' Reading* (1987), understanding of other storytellers like oneself: "Writing and reading in the spectator role are mutually supportive activities. Constructing their own stories and poems serves to make students very conscious that other people's stories and poems are constructs, products of choices and linguistic mechanisms that can be manipulated to achieve one's own purposes" (p. 111). Maggie has been creating her own worlds for some time now, and though she may not be as sophisticated or knowledgeable as Ellen and Jeanie, through this process, she is already on her way to becoming a critically literate member of society.

Maggie is in the first grade now. She enjoys school, and according to her mother, Maggie and her closest friends, Cristen and Sara, are doing very well in their class. But Maggie says not all students in the class are doing as well: "Sara writes a little more than me, and Kim only writes a few lines. Sara writes these neat stories, but she kind of spells the words wrong. But she goes on even if she does make a mistake. She just likes to write. Kim doesn't like to write. When she reads it [out loud], she gets embarrassed because she writes so sloppy and she can't read so well. She always has to go back to her seat and write it over again."

According to Maggie, Sara never corrects her mistakes, and the teacher seldom makes her go back to correct them. The teacher seems to support Sara's emphasis on storytelling by allowing her to take more risks technically. Kim, by Maggie's account, has problems creatively as well as technically, and the emphasis on mechanics like neatness and spelling could be doing her harm. Although Maggie likes her first-grade teacher very much, it is this emphasis on neatness and the technical aspects of writing rather than the story making itself that bothers her mother:

> Maggie is already hung up on correcting mistakes. When she has a pencil, she'll make sure she has an eraser. When she's writing in ink, she wants me to get the bottle of whiteout. Part of that's fine because some of that is important; she will be judged on all that. But when it gets to the point where I can see she's losing her train of thought because she's asking how to spell every other word, I tell her, "Go ahead and write it. We'll figure it out later."

The emphasis on correctness in the classroom is especially disturbing because it tends to inhibit a child's creative impulses. Harste, Woodward, and Burke have researched the importance of risk taking in early language users. Most children learn to read and write through a kind of trial-and-error social process and not by having mechanical errors constantly brought to their attention. They point out, "The perception that when one writes one must spell correctly appears to be the single biggest constraint which 5- and 6-year-old children see as the reason why they can't engage in the process. Given the attention spelling is given by teachers and parents, this perception is understandable, but nonetheless dysfunctional to growth in literacy" (p. 131).

Recently, Maggie came home from school upset because she was marked down on one of her papers for sloppiness. According to her mother, Maggie almost always receives O's (for outstanding) on her papers, but this time she received an O- (outstanding minus) for creativity and an S- (satisfactory minus) for neatness. Bridgett told us, "Her teacher writes stuff on the board, and they have to copy it down. But Maggie copied the wrong sentence on one page, so she erased it and wrote down the right sentence. Maggie made the correction, but she didn't make it neatly." Maggie was so disturbed by her teacher's comments on the exercise that she used a heart-shaped sticker to cover up the word "messy" written in the top corner. Bridgett also worries that she and her husband may be transmitting their own concerns with correctness and order and organization to Maggie. Maggie has watched her mother respond to student essays and has asked what "sp" (spelling) means when Bridgett writes it on a student's paper.

Bridgett still has painful memories of her own father's critical intolerance. Her father, a physicist, had little patience with his daughter's limited math abilities. She still remembers, "My dad was hypercritical of me, and that's what I'm afraid of transmitting to Maggie. When I see her doing the correcting and stuff like that, I sometimes think I've transmitted it to my daughter. Somewhere she's getting it, and I don't want her to go through what I went through in terms of self-esteem problems, where no matter what you do it's not good enough."

As we suggested earlier, most people can still remember instances, like the one Bridgett mentions here, when their performance was judged harshly. Ellen remembers being "mystified and troubled" by the "odd" teacher who "was hard to please" and did not care for her writing. Fortunately for Ellen, her desire to please and her love of words sustained her; she was able to transcend their disapproval with a minimum amount of damage to her self-esteem. Maggie, with the help and support of her parents and more informed teachers, will undoubtedly do the same (Maggie B., interview with authors, Apr. 1994; personal observations of authors, Jan. to Mar. 1994; Bridgett B., interview with authors, Apr. 1994).

There are many more people who are not as fortunate as Maggie and Ellen and Jeanie. We will discuss how two of these people, like Alonzo, were able to regain their self-confidence and become literate members of society.

Harold and Stanley: Literacy with a Sense of Purpose

Harold

Harold P. is in his fifties and drives a street sweeper for the city. Today he can read and write, but this was not always so. He grew up in San Francisco during the fifties where he lived with his mother and siblings:

> I was the baby of the family. My mother worked at night, and I was on the street all the time. No one was there to help me with my reading like they do today. My family was always on the go, doing something, and my father took off when I was real young. When I was in school, I used to be embarrassed if they asked me to read in front of anybody. I would just say no and make all kinds of excuses, like I'd say I had to go to the bathroom or something. When everyone else was learning vowels and pronouns and all that, I had a problem with it. The words were too big, and the teacher didn't have the time.

Harold shoulders a lot of the blame for his problems with reading and writing: "I've been thinking if I really asked for help, I'd have got it. But I always sat in the back of the room and didn't get involved." Certainly Harold's lone-wolf attitude did not help him very much; however, there were undoubtedly several other factors working against him.

From junior high school and beyond, Harold enjoyed sports, math, and mechanical drawing classes, but he "avoided learning anything when it came to reading. It was really boring," he says, "like history and stuff. Who wanted to know about what happened three hundred years ago? I wanted to know what was going on now." Harold was bored with the books he was given to read in school, and obviously there were few teachers in the San Francisco public school system during the fifties willing to ask Harold what he wanted to read. Harold says, "The teachers were old, and they were like baby-sitters. I guess they kind of gave up on everybody." Not surprisingly, Harold never did any homework that had anything to do with reading and writing. He constantly worried about his spelling, probably because it was emphasized more than anything else. Dictionaries only made matters worse and confused him, since once he found a definition, he "had to go look for the words they were trying to explain in there," too. Finally, Harold "decided it was a waste of time to read a sentence if I couldn't understand it."

Like many people who have trouble with reading and writing, Harold got along very well in society for many years: "I was a good bullshitter. I was streetwise. I'd never let anyone know my weaknesses, and I'd never ask for help. I'd always work out a way to get around things. When I took the test to get into the Air Force, it was a true and false thing. To me that was simple. You either get it right or wrong. I guess I was lucky because I got more right than I did wrong. I'd use common sense."

One of the myths promulgated about people with reading and writing problems is that they are unintelligent. Jeanie believes her father has been able to survive in the world because he is strong and "extraordinarily intelligent. It's his incredible memory, the ability to hear something once and remember it." Jeanie's father has always been able to decipher complicated oral instructions and carry them out perfectly.

Harold remembers, "I could figure problems out if the teacher did it on the board. But if I had to read it out of a book, I couldn't do it. If the teacher went up to the board and showed me how to do it there, I could figure that out and get good grades." In fact, Harold learned the skills required for just about every job he has ever held through on-the-job training. These jobs included such complicated and technical skills as meat cutting and nursing. "If I'd had to go to school to learn anything," Harold said, "I'd be out of luck. If you had given me a book that had all the directions on how to do something, I couldn't have done it. But if you showed me how to do something, I'd pick it up right away. And I'd be good at it."

Harold, like Jeanie's father, was a doer. Once a woman he was dating took Harold home to meet her father. "He had a library in one room," he told us. "One day he said to me, 'You see all these books here. I read them all.' And I thought, big deal, I done most of these things myself in real life. I'd rather do things than read about them. I thought, you're reading about them. I'm doing them. I go out and do them."

The only thing Harold needed books for was to copy out of them. When he was a meat cutter and owned two meat markets, Harold copied the advertisements out of the newspaper and used them for his stores: "I'd get all the newspapers and copy Safeway and other ads. That's how I did a lot of writing. I'd copy out of papers and books and other things." Harold was using an age-old learning technique, imitation and representation, to its fullest rhetorical advantage to further himself economically in society. We would argue that Harold, without any real knowledge of what we have defined as basic literacy, was quite capable of performing critical and dynamic literacy activities.

Unfortunately, Harold's propensity for "doing" also got him into a lot of trouble in school and later with the police. Harold started drinking heavily when he was in junior high school. Once, after coming back drunk from lunch, he beat up one of his teachers and thereafter received A's on all his class work. Harold's antisocial behavior while drinking as an adult, however, was not rewarded so charitably. Eventually Harold, like Alonzo, ended up in several jails and hospitals (Harold P., interview with authors, Apr. 1994).

Stanley

Stanley C., a machinist for a major airline, began to have disciplinary problems when he was in elementary school. Stanley believes he was "functionally illiterate" up to the time he entered high school. Now in his forties, Stanley recently passed all the English classes required for his admittance to a college English class. Like Harold, Stanley remembers unhappier times in his childhood. He says his father was a "very literate person," even though he dropped out of school in the sixth grade: "He never read any books or anything, but he wrote and could read very well." His mother dropped out of high school in the eleventh grade because of what Stanley refers to as "learning disabilities." He believes, "If there's any learning disabilities in the family, they come from my mother's side, especially with reading."

When Stanley was in the third grade, his father became very sick, and Stanley began to act out: "The first time I knew I had any problems was in the third grade. The problems were more disciplinary than anything else. My mother later told me that my third-grade teacher insinuated I might be retarded. I remember getting in trouble and my mom coming down to the school. Later, she took me to a children's hospital to have me tested—IQ test and such. The doctor who tested me said there was nothing wrong with me."

Stanley's problems with reading and writing could undoubtedly have been remedied with a little more help at school and at home. The damage done to him by his teacher's insinuation would have been (and was) much harder to deal with. This, coupled with the fact that he never received any help at school or at home, ensured that Stanley would be placed in what he refers to as "the dummy classes."

After his father died, Stanley's mother put him in a Catholic boarding school where the brothers brutalized him:

> I felt like a refugee. I was twelve, and I felt like my mom was abandoning me. I had some pretty traumatic things happen to me, like getting slapped around because I wouldn't read. I was afraid the other kids would laugh at me. I was in the fifth grade, and in the classroom, there was a stage where the teacher had his desk and a podium. Everyone had to come up and read something out of this book. We had both the fourth and the fifth grade there. I went up there with my first-grade book, and when I started to read, the other kids laughed, so I stopped reading. The teacher told me to read, but I wouldn't. That's when he slapped me. He slapped me some more, but I wasn't going to read because I'd rather get a beating than be ridiculed by the other kids. You know, I was never a POW during the war, but I felt like one then.

Later, in a public junior high school, Stanley remembers doing "pretty good in math and art." It is possible, according to Stanley, that even at this point "it wasn't too late" for him to get some help: "But nobody knew how to help me. I was one of those kids who they thought was bright but just didn't know how to apply himself." So Stanley "got passed along" from one remedial class to another.

In high school, Stanley flunked freshman English: "They put me in a remedial class, and I did well in it. I could read books and answer questions." Stanley says he could never spell well enough for his teachers ("still can't"). He also had a lot of difficulty processing information when he read: "Sometimes I don't hear things. And sometimes when I read things, they don't register in my brain exactly the way they should, and I have to read them two or three times." He believes this affected his ability to take tests on the information he had read. We suspect, however, that most people have similar problems with reading and listening in school, especially when reading texts or listening to lectures is associated with dry dissemination of information rather than with dynamic participatory knowledge-making processes.

Stanley remembers doing well on certain tests, especially in subjects in which he had an interest, like history. In fact, Stanley's interest in history seems to have been influenced by his history teacher as much as anything else. According to Stanley, there were three different levels of history classes at his high school: "This one teacher I had was a history teacher. He was a Mormon who went to Brigham Young University. They gave him three history classes to teach with the best, the middle, and the worst students. I was in the worst." Not only did this history teacher exhibit a concern for Stanley as a student but he also read history books aloud to the class:

> He never required us to read. He did all the reading, and then he'd hand out these mimeographed pages and help us fill them out. Then we'd go home and study these things. I would always get B's on those tests because I liked history. When he would read, it would be like seeing a movie. I would just close my eyes and see this movie going on in my head. I now know that that's what happens when you're reading a book. That teacher never required us to read, but I learned because I loved history. . . . He never corrected our spelling.

Stanley did well on these tests (multiple choice and fill-in-the-blanks). In fact, he did so well that he "aced a test once," and his history teacher called him into his office to congratulate him. Later, this teacher spent more time with Stanley, encouraging and praising him: "He would call me in about once a month after

Boyer
story

school. It would be like having a father again. He'd tell me how bright I was. And he would wonder why I couldn't read or spell."

Most people can remember a teacher like Stanley's history teacher, who gave them confidence and support. Ellen still remembers the teacher in high school who praised her writing skills. Jerome Bruner gives credit to a Miss Orcutt who "was a human event, not a transmission device" (p. 126).

Stanley's history teacher brought the past alive for his students by reading it to them. Thomson emphasizes how it is as vital "for English teachers to spend time reading stories to secondary students as it is for parents to read stories to pre-school children." It is easy to see the significance of this for Stanley—his history teacher was the first person to read aloud to him. Stanley cannot remember his mother or his father ever reading to him when he was a child.

In spite of his problems with reading and writing, Stanley, like Harold, managed to do well in most of the things he set out to do. In high school, he did well in an industrial arts program for the same reason he did well in history—the teacher sat in front of the class and read the technical manuals on diesel mechanics to his students: "We kind of read along and looked at the diagrams and pictures. It was just like in my history class." Later, in the service, he failed the Navy entrance test three times, so he went into the Marines: "I never finished a test. Even when I took my SATs, I never finished them. I know I did well on what I did, but I never got them done. I could never make the time." Stanley thinks his processing problems were the culprit: "I'd read the story, consider the questions, read the story, consider the questions, and all of a sudden my time was up."

However, the reliability of timed tests, especially when used to judge a person's writing ability, is highly suspect. We believe that the unnatural time restrictions presented to students during timed tests are particularly unfavorable for the writing process. No professional writers that we know give themselves one hour (or even two, three, or four) to complete the whole writing process from the initial idea to a completed manuscript. In fact, we suspect the reliability of any examination that tests for particular information without also testing for ability to synthesize and make new knowledge.

It is interesting that Stanley credits his stint in the service as more useful for building his self-confidence than school was: "In the service, there's some guy up there telling you how to do it and showing you how to do it. Then there's a guy helping you do it, while another guy's making you do it. But in the end, you learn how to do it." With this method, Stanley may not have been finishing the tests they gave him in the Marines, but he was passing them.

Again, like Jeanie's father and Harold, Stanley was able to get by and do well mainly because of his intelligence. "Most people who have literacy problems overcompensate in other ways," Stanley said. "I listen real well and I remember what I hear. I'm constantly flying by the seat of my pants. I catch enough facts and enough information to go out there and put a good show on. I just work it out as I go along."

When he got out of the service, Stanley got a job as a mechanic, where he "wasn't required to do a lot of reading." But he wanted more, so he applied to go to school to be a machinist's apprentice and was accepted. "There was going to be a lot of reading and theory and stuff," he said. "A lot of it was hands-on type stuff, but I still had to pass the tests. And I did for the first couple of years. Then I got into drugs and alcohol real heavy and learned how to cheat the last year of school. That way, I didn't have to worry about reading theory."

Stanley's dependence on alcohol and drugs had begun in the service. As with Harold and Alonzo, it got the better of him, and he, too, started going to jail for his behavior while under the influence (Stanley C., interview with authors, Apr. 1994).

Overcoming the Stigma of Illiteracy

Although Stanley and Harold eventually quit drinking, they still had to overcome the disgrace associated with their reading and writing problems. Part of the stigma in our society of being labeled illiterate involves the unreasonable shame associated with it. Reed-Jones makes reference to this in her story of Alonzo: "All his life, Alonzo had feared that when people found out he couldn't read or write they would reject him, thinking him stupid" (p. 6). The tendency in this society, with free compulsory education for everybody, is immediately to assume that if you cannot read or write, first, you must be stupid, and second, it is your fault and not that of your home environment or the school system.

Reed-Jones's story about Alonzo's experience parallels the experiences of Harold and Stanley with AA and the subsequent desire to improve their reading and writing. Harold and Stanley now go to AA, and each has been sober for over a decade. Their stories, like Alonzo's, are compelling, particularly because they demonstrate the impact that social relationships have on our literacy patterns. When Harold and Stanley joined AA, they were accepted into the group along with all their problems—substance abuse, behavioral, reading, writing, and so forth. For individuals suffering diminished self-confidence, the acceptance into any group has a profound effect not only on their self-esteem but also on their sense of purpose. Reed-Jones refers to this in her story about Alonzo: "Alonzo's change in attitude after joining A.A. is striking. This change in attitude stems, at least in part, from Alonzo's feeling of belonging, of being a necessary part of the group. And the development of literacy, I believe, is a very important component of this sense of belonging" (p. 10).

Once Harold decided he needed help for his drinking problem and joined AA, he realized that the way people stayed sober in AA was by following certain guidelines. Since these guidelines are printed in the book *Alcoholics Anonymous* and Harold wanted to remain sober more than anything else, he had to admit to someone that he could not read very well. For Harold, with his streetwise, I-don't-need-anyone attitude, this particular disclosure to a sponsor in AA was "really humbling," but also liberating: "He [Harold's AA sponsor] told me they had tapes for all these books. So I went down and got the tapes. What I'd do is listen to the words on the tape and follow along in the book—kind of sing along with Mitch, you know."

A year later, Harold enrolled in an adult literacy program, so he could learn to read more AA literature. He also bought more tapes of this literature, so he could read along with it. At one meeting, called a Big Book Study Group, the members took turns reading aloud from the text *Alcoholics Anonymous:* "I did more listening to the tapes and started going to a Big Book study where everybody gets a chance to read. When it came to me, I would pass, but I'd read along with everybody else. I picked up a lot of reading that way." One day, Harold joined "a class for people with reading problems" and met a woman who worked as a news broadcaster: "I worked with her for a few months. After I dropped out of that, we had a test at work for a promotion, so I called her up and asked her for help. I'd never taken a test before except for true and false. We met at the library, and she went over how to take the test. She brushed me up on my math. She said to read the question twice and then answer it. She gave me hints on how to do things."

To receive the promotion, Harold had to pass the written test along with "an oral and a practical test on the equipment." He was the last person to finish his written test, but "out of the whole thing, I ranked number one and got the promotion." This was not enough for Harold. Recently he took the test for his GED—the high school equivalency test—and now has the equivalent of a high school diploma.

Stanley, who could read and write a little better than Harold, was laid off nine months after he quit drinking and joined AA, because he "wasn't skilled enough to use the new computerized machines." He credits two people in AA, his sponsor and a woman friend, for inspiring and encouraging him to go to college and get his associate of arts degree. Stanley watched his sponsor and his friend achieve their career goals after they became sober and decided, "If they could do it, I could." As he put it, "Well, I figured it was a little too late to go for a Ph.D. in marine biology or whatever. When I started school, I was two years sober. But I wanted to get a degree just to say that I did it after all these years. Even though I had a good brain, I couldn't show it to you. So I started going to school and took my aptitude test and passed it good enough for freshman English 101 [a developmental English class]."

But college has not been easy for Stanley. In his first English class, the teacher rejected his first writing attempt because it had too many spelling errors. Stanley had written a story about his experience in Vietnam, and the teacher told him, "Your spelling is atrocious. In fact, it's worse than atrocious. It's horrible." He described how it felt:

> She might as well have kicked me in the balls. I wrote her this beautiful little story about how you'd hear the drone of helicopters, and you'd look up and see cobras coming. It would be like you were

scuba diving on the bottom of the ocean looking at sharks swim-
ming over your head. A cobra gunship looks just like a shark with
its mouth hanging open. It was a neat little story, but I must have
misspelled about twenty-five or thirty words. She discouraged the
hell out of me.

As a result, Stanley returned to machinists' school "to make up
for all the cheating" he had done before: "My essays weren't very
good because of my proofreading skills. But there was a lot of copying and quoting in my technical papers, which you can do."

Eventually, like Harold, Stanley found someone to help him
out. One of his college psychology professors tested him and discovered that Stanley had a writing-processing deficiency. Regardless of the validity of this type of psychological testing, the results
obtained by this professor were liberating for Stanley. He remembered all the times his mother had yelled at him and called him
lazy because he had done poorly in school. He remembered the
teacher in the third grade who had labeled him as retarded and
the Catholic school brothers who had tried to beat literacy into
him. He remembered all the students who had ridiculed him and
called him stupid. Stanley realized he was not to blame for his poor
performance in school: "If the guy at the Catholic school had
helped me out for an hour every day instead of slapping me in the
face and instead of letting the kids make fun of me, I'd have been
better off."

Stanley went into a lower English class in college, wrote his
paper, and had it placed in a publication put out by the Bay Area
Writing Project. He has since gone on to pass the English 101 class.
He told us, "I took a 102 class that was for more detailed writing—
how to use structure and research in a paper. But the teacher
insisted that my papers be typed, and I don't know how to type, so
I dropped out of that class. But technically I can take English 1A
[college-level English] now if I want."

After a short layoff, Stanley is now getting ready to return to
school. Today he owns a word processor and has much more confidence in himself as a reader and a writer.

Motivation and Collaboration Within a Community

The experiences discussed in this chapter highlight the significance of social influences on individuals' becoming accomplished

readers and writers. At the heart of the literacy stories of Harold and Stanley and of Jeanie and Ellen and Maggie is the encouragement and the help they received from others as well as their own aspirations to be a part of a larger literate community. What Harold and Stanley have done in response to their reading and writing problems, while inspiring, is not unique. In *Lives on the Boundary*, Rose relates his own struggles and successes with reading and writing and devotes the rest of the book to the failures and triumphs of people just like Harold and Stanley and Alonzo. Human beings are remarkably resilient and adaptable creatures, but nobody exists in a vacuum. Humans are, above everything else, social beings, and their abilities to use and manipulate language grow out of that reality. At the same time, as developmental psychologist Margaret Donaldson (1978) reminds, "We do not just sit and wait for the world to impinge on us. We try actively to interpret it, to make sense of it. We grapple with it, we construe it intellectually, *we represent it to ourselves*" (p. 67, emphasis added).

For Jeanie, Ellen, Maggie, Harold, and Stanley, the need for literacy is both different and the same. Whether they did it for a job, for membership in AA, or simply to please a teacher, the underlying theme in each of their literacy stories is the desire to be literate reading and writing members of society. Jeanie's mother and father encouraged and nurtured her love of stories through an oral language tradition. Bissex (1980), quoting Russian researcher Kornei Chukosvsky, saw the inherent propensity for literacy in her son Paul, growing "miraculously" out of "the same methods, processes, and peculiarities of word construction which were used by [our] . . . very distant ancestors in building the language" (p. 203). Ellen's penchant for writing grew out of a need to please her teachers. Her interest in reading emerged from a wish to escape into children's adventure stories: "I remember that I didn't want to stop reading children's books. Even as an older child, I remember not wanting to stray from the children's section of the library. I knew that those books would be interesting and they wouldn't let me down." Both Maggie and Ellen read books that their mothers and grandmothers had passed on to them just as Jeanie's father passed oral narratives on to her. Further, the stories that Maggie and Ellen and Jeanie have written elaborate on these passed-down stories and narratives, expanding and developing their own worldviews as well as influencing the views of those who will someday read their stories. Harold and Stanley learned how to stay sober and read and write by listening to and reading stories about other people who were literate and sober members of society. They, in turn, helped others with their narratives.

It is this social aspect of literacy that is most fascinating in terms of its effect on language users and learners in our society. Harold and Stanley and Alonzo sought help to improve their reading and writing only after they joined a community in which, as Reed-Jones puts it, their "experience was considered valuable, [their] contributions important" (p. 8). Similarly, the desire of Ellen and Jeanie to become members of the academic community clearly grew because of the encouragement and support from other participants in that community. And if young Maggie's passion for creating books is to be fostered, she must see that her knowledge and experience is important and valued by others—not just at home but in the classroom.

Unfortunately, it is these motivating influences that many traditional teaching techniques tend to disregard. Each of these people—Jeanie, Ellen, Maggie, Harold, and Stanley—is a unique individual. Yet each has been through an educational system that places more emphasis on letter grades than on written evaluations of a student's progress, more emphasis on testing for particular informational knowledge than on developing a synthesis of the learner's experience and his or her comprehension of that knowledge, and more emphasis on error and correction than on risk taking.

Elementary schoolteacher Linda Dinan (1994) insists on the importance of risk taking for early language users. She says, "Teachers often find it difficult to support risk-taking in writing because" of an emphasis on "mispronunciations" and "misspellings," and so forth. "Teachers and parents must respond to children's written approximations the same way they respond to children's first words, with praise and encouragement. It is decidedly unhelpful to demand error-free writing" (p. 135). An overconcern with errors and corrections helps to produce the sort of anxious adult writers Lynn Bloom talks about in "Anxious Writers in Context: Graduate School and Beyond" (1985). In her essay, Bloom gives credit to "Mina Shaughnessy's pioneering work, *Errors and Expectations* (1977)," then argues that "error cannot be accurately understood without an understanding of the student's history and current environment" (p. 120). Bloom describes how one of her subjects, Sarah, came up with an interesting solution for her own writer's block: "With two others struggling to finish their dissertations, she formed a support group (another type of [social] context), an informal 'Dissertations Anonymous.' They met weekly to chart their progress, reinforce their writing goals, and encourage each other" (p. 127).

Social psychologist Claude Steele (1992) believes this same type of group support might be helpful for African Americans in higher education. Steele says that "70 percent of all black Americans at four-year colleges" drop out "compared with 45 percent of whites" (pp. 69–70). The statistics for African Americans in high school in most large cities are even worse. These alarming statistics arise in part from the fact that many African American students have problems "identifying with school." Steele calls this process "disidentification." He makes the point that "doing well in school requires a belief that school achievement can be a promising basis of self-esteem, and that belief needs constant affirmation even for advantaged children. Tragically, I believe, the lives of black Americans are still haunted by a specter that threatens this belief and the identification that derives from it at every level of schooling" (p. 72).

Steele extends this assessment not only to African Americans but to other disenfranchised groups in our society, including "lower-class whites, Hispanics, and women in male-dominated fields" (p. 75). The development of workshops like University of California, Berkeley's Mathematics Workshop Program has helped some students: "Working together, students soon understand that everyone knows something and nobody knows everything, and learning is speeded through shared understanding" (p. 75).

There is no doubt that more collaborative efforts like the one Steele mentions, which underscore the social aspects of learning, are needed to promote reading and writing in schools. Teacher-researcher Russell Hunt (1989) advocates joint research-writing projects in which students create knowledge together in groups. Hunt believes that two very important things happen when students work together on essays. First, the traditional method of student evaluation (teacher as sole bearer of reading and writing standards), which is reinforced by students writing individual themes, is deemphasized as the students themselves take on the task of measuring one another's work. Second, writing takes on a more authentic social function in the classroom. Hunt believes that "the most important change might be characterized as finding ways to make writing more instrumental, attempting, if you will, to make it 'real,' and thus whole. The most effective way to do this is to create situations in which student writing—and the teacher's own—is read for its meaning, for what it has to say, rather than as an example of a student theme to be 'assessed' or 'evaluated'" (p. 95).

Hunt's elaborate process for a "whole" approach to reading and writing involves "research, writing, and publication" by the students themselves. Further, he suggests that "any subject about which someone might want to learn, and which it is possible to divide up into separate questions or issues" is adaptable to this process (pp. 96–97).

Rose recommends the same sort of procedures for students with reading and writing problems, the so-called remedial students:

> Provide some context, break them into groups or work with the whole class, involving everyone. Let them see what, collectively, they do know, and students will, together, begin to generate meaning and make connections. One person once read something else about big bang . . . and his knowledge helps a second person understand the nuclear processes in paragraph two, and that second person then asks a question that remained ill-formed in the mind of a third. And the teacher darts in and out of the conversation, clarifying, questioning, repeating, looping back to link one student's observation to another's. And so it is that the students, labeled "remedial," read and talk and write their way toward understanding [pp. 145–146].

In groups and classrooms such as these, students are engaged in a dialogue in which real learning takes place; furthermore, they can find the encouragement and motivation necessary to become critically and dynamically literate. Every person in this society must be extended the opportunity to join the literacy club. Before this can happen, such innovative notions as open-admission policies must be implemented in more colleges. Further, public schools need to confront and invalidate the disgrace associated with reading and writing problems.

While we wonder whether anybody can really explain what motivates people to be literate, it is relatively easy to study and document where teaching techniques have hindered rather than helped encourage literacy in our society. "We are," according to Rose, "in the middle of an extraordinary social experiment: the attempt to provide education for all members of a vast pluralistic democracy," and in order to make this grand experiment work, "we'll need a guiding set of principles that do not encourage us to retreat from, but move us closer to, an understanding of the rich mix of speech and ritual and story that is America" (p. 238). Our hope is that every adult and child in America one day will get a chance to add his or her literacy story to this immense democratic utterance.

Part Two

The Universe of Discourse

Chapter Three

Entrepreneurs and Rhetorical Inventors

Life is what happens while you're passing time in school.
—HIGH SCHOOL CLASS MOTTO,
  RENO GAZETTE-JOURNAL

A common charge against the public schools is that they fail to prepare students for the real world—for life in general and literacy skills for business in particular. Executives regularly complain that new employees lack a range of skills, from the fundamental ability of spelling correctly to the sophisticated ability of writing effective reports. In attempting to rebut such charges, educators point out that it is not the primary task of the schools to teach job-specific skills, that the job market is changing so rapidly that skills taught today are often obsolete tomorrow, and that it is naive to suppose that general public education can prepare students for the intricacies and vagaries of the job market.

The issue is complicated, we believe, by the fact that the expectations and parameters of business literacy are not altogether clear. In striving to meet demands—real or imagined—teachers annually give lessons in business-letter form, such as where to place the return address, how to write the recipient's address, how to open and close. They have their students write mock letters of application or mock memoranda. But as T. S. Eliot's Prufrock says, "That is not it at all, / That is not what I meant, at all" (1936, p. 97), for the art of business literacy cannot be encapsulated in matters of form. In fact, such instruction is rendered fairly moot by books and computer programs that offer 101 models for business letters, where the writer merely plugs in the text of the message. Such formula writing, we argue, is far removed from meaningful business literacy. We are not certain that very many people even write business letters anymore, not with phones and faxes available, although even with these technologies, the form matters less than the quality of literate communication.

From time to time, universities survey businesspeople to find out what skills they want in a college graduate. Whether prodded by the interviewer or desiring to shake off the image of the money-driven capitalist, many executives reply that they are not necessarily looking for a student with a degree in business and a broad array of economics courses. Rather, they frequently say they are looking for traditional liberal arts skills—the abilities to think creatively, to work on common problems and solutions with other people, and of course, to express oneself clearly in speech and writing. When asked if that means they want to hire English majors in preference to business majors, the executives typically demur but say that given a choice between an English major with good literacy skills and a business major who cannot read and write, they will opt for the English major.

Sifting through all the conflicting demands, both for business skills and literacy skills, some people present the argument that the school–real-world dichotomy is a false one, that schools teach skills that are important for life as well as for the economy and that the traditional aims of a liberal education are, in fact, to prepare students not just to read Shakespeare and Shelley but also to function practically and effectively outside the schoolhouse walls.

In this chapter, we examine these relationships. We talked to people we call "entrepreneurs and rhetorical inventors," people who are forging careers for themselves in a variety of fields. Most of them are freelancers in one way or another. These are not the employees of firms on the Fortune 500 list but rather folks working for and sometimes creating small businesses. We found that they are not only inventing businesses but also discovering, inventing, and reinventing the rhetoric of their areas of expertise. They are critically and dynamically literate, and their literacies, as we discovered, go far beyond the business letter and make some surprising connections with the aims of traditional liberal education.

Bob: Professional Hobbyist

Bob W. has worked for a package delivery service for almost twenty years. Bob works the night shift as a supervisor on the loading dock. He oversees the operation that handles the incoming packages—getting them out of trucks and into the sorting area, organizing the outgoing packages, and distributing them to the proper vehicles. After that, they are transported to homes, businesses, and out-of-town locations. In his late forties, Bob has about five years to go before he is eligible for his pension, at which time he plans to retire and pursue his other interests.

But even now, Bob finds his job ideal because it lets him pursue those interests: "I don't have to think about my work at home," he explained. "I can leave it at 'the office.'"

What he pursues in his spare daylight and evening hours and what he will do full-time once his pension comes through is to buy and sell collectibles, everything from antique Coca-Cola vending machines to Miller beer neon bar signs, from Budweiser baseball caps to Hires root beer pens.

During the interview, Bob was thirty-five thousand feet in the air, on his way to a collectors' convention. He was flying at his own expense. "I'm not going to display my stuff," he explained. "This trip, I want to see what's happening in the industry, what's hot." He explained that to save on shipping costs, he exhibits his own stuff only regionally, hauling it himself.

"What kind of stuff?" we asked. He told us the big-ticket items are the antique soft drink machines, which, even after the seller deducts shipping costs, can bring a profit of several hundred dollars.

"A lot of them are going out of the country," he said, and that worries him. "The Japanese like to collect them and are buying them up and shipping them home."

Bob also buys and sells items that are not antiques, including many newly manufactured items and items designed to be collectible. He described a recently manufactured item, a miniature slot machine with a small corporate logo. He bought fifty of them for $50 apiece, hauled them to his rented storage space, trailered them to a show, and sold off the lot for $150 each.

"You can't always tell what people want to buy," he explained, "but I've got a good sense of it. That's why I go to these conferences, to learn what people want. If I could buy a hundred of those slot machines at, say, $150 today, I could sell them off for maybe $200, $250 within a month."

As we discussed in Chapter One, we are reluctant to frame literacy in a context that is independent of its connections with language, but if we view it metaphorically, it is clear to us that Bob has a high degree of *memorabilia literacy,* exhibited by his ability to "read" the market and to "read" the value of various kinds of machines. Bob told us that early on, he learned not to be too much of a purist about buying and selling. He recognizes that selling some of the contemporary memorabilia and pseudocollectibles, stuff that as a collector he does not respect at all, helps support the lower volume dealing in antiques.

We quizzed him about the literacy of his business. Bob does little writing; in fact, his writing is limited almost entirely to the basic literacy of record keeping—jotting down transactions, sending bills, and the like. However, oral literacy plays an important role in his work. "In selling," he said, "the important things are done face-to-face, or maybe on the phone." He explained how negotiating deals requires a great deal of skilled talk: "Basically, you've gotta be there; the other guy has to be there; the piece has to be there for you both to look at."

What he described next is the critical literacy of the skilled negotiator, the salesperson, and the buyer—somebody who has something for sale and wants to sell it for as much as possible and somebody who wants it but wants to pay as little as possible. He illustrated the point with a story:

> So I'll walk up to a guy who has this logo cooler for sale at a show, and to get it started I'll ask, Is this authentic? 'Sure,' says this guy, and right away, I know I've got him, because of this logo down on the bottom. I know that it comes from a cooler from a different model and year. Somebody has switched the logo. So I push a little. What about this logo? Is this authentic? And the guy says, 'That's exactly the way it came to me.' Now that's important, because when he says that's the way he got it, he isn't really telling me it's authentic at all. Somebody could have yanked that logo off another machine and bolted it on two minutes before the sale.

"So this means you've really got to be careful about what the words mean?" we asked.

"Exactly," Bob replied. "Like 'authentic,' it can mean a lot of things. It can mean taken off a different cooler. Some people will even use that word to describe a reproduction item, like an 'authentic copy' of an original part."

We saw in Bob a good general semanticist, one who knows that words are slippery things, that definitions go soft in the heat of discussion and negotiation, and that one has to probe critically beneath the surface structures of language to find out what is really going on.

Bob went on to describe his negotiating techniques and strategies at great length, stressing his own desire to make it clear to his buyers that he is authentic as a dealer.

> I don't cover up things with spray paint the way a lot of guys do. You can slip in a fake part, give it a nice paint job, and nobody will know the difference. Or you can take apart things like bar signs and put the logo from one with the frame of another and still claim it's authentic, but I have to persuade my customers that it's the real thing that I'm giving them. I guarantee my stuff that way. People have to have confidence in me that I'm authentic.

That is not to say that Bob does not use a sophisticated array of persuasive strategies. He thinks about how to price items, what to throw in for free, even about when to offer loss leaders, small items that he will sell below his own cost in order to get people into his exhibit.

He went on to tell us how reading fits into his work:
"You have to be able to read in this business, too," he explained. "You find a lot of good items in the daily paper, but you have to be able to read." He looked in the airplane seat pocket for a newspaper and seeing none, continued, "If we had an ad here, I could show you what it means. If you read it yourself, you'd have no idea whether this was the real thing or not. I get a lot of my stuff by reading."

His detailed explanations left us with the strong feeling that we would be better off either to stay out of the collectibles business or to take a highly literate collector like Bob with us to a show. We realized that here was a man skilled in a great many strategies of classical rhetoric: the abilities to see through apparently persuasive arguments, to phrase an argument in a way that presents the truth in the most favorable light possible, and to examine and incorporate another's position into one's own thinking.

Bob did not feel that his education had prepared him particularly well for this sort of work, a theme to be repeated throughout this chapter, but he did not attack the schools either. He thought that his college education was fairly satisfactory in a general sort of way, although he was not able to apply much of what he had learned in his major, business, to the entrepreneurial world of memorabilia. This gave us pause, since business courses are always said to be practical and real world, whereas the humanities are seen as impractical and ivory tower. Bob's experience was quite similar to what we find in a number of adults who have learned to write. As he put it, "I had to pick it up on my own."

We asked him about teaching writing: "If you had our jobs, teaching students at the university to write, what would you tell them; what would you teach them?"

Bob thought for a bit and said, "Teach them the meaning of the word *authentic*." What Bob would choose to teach is precisely what we have called critical literacy—the ability to create and analyze precise meanings beyond the dictionary definitions of the words. Moreover, he clearly is skilled at and favors dynamic literacy, the on-the-spot, real-world ability to size up a situation, make sense of it, and use words precisely and crisply to convey ideas and present a positive impression of oneself and one's ideas. In particular, he would teach semantics, the subtleties of denotation and connotation, abstraction and concreteness. Perhaps it is not surprising that Bob's view of the world and his business led us directly back to some of the traditional aims of liberal or general education.

We are not business bashers any more than we are school bashers, and we have deep respect for people like Bob who have forged an entrepreneurial enterprise for themselves. At the same time, we need to look critically at the dynamics of the relationship between school and work. It is currently fashionable to talk about school-to-work programs for children (a gloomy phrase that is only slightly improved by the euphemism school-to-career). It is clear that the schools cannot prepare students for careers in antique sales (and for Bob, this is a career, not a job). But it is just as clear that we can improve the kind of education that underlies that literacy. All too many adults nowadays say they had to learn their literacies on the job, but we think schools can teach critical and dynamic literacy in ways that will change that, so a guy like Bob might say: sure, my schooling got me ready, got me to the point that I could figure things out for myself. We might call this sort of thing *entrepreneurial literacy* (Bob W., interview with authors, Aug. 1994).

Ron: Ex-Cop

Whereas Bob emphasized authenticity in his dealings with others, for Ron P. the word is *clarity,* a variation of authenticity. Now in his forties, Ron has given up work as a police officer and has gone back to school.

The amount of writing he did as a Paiute police officer was considerable, "huge narratives," as he put it. He learned that clarity and detail matter in police reports. "You're basically writing for the prosecuting attorney, and you have to include everything needed to try the case," he told us. "It's like a story, like a book." He cited an example: "On ____ (day), ____ (date) at ____ (time), I was driving south on Main Street when I observed a white '94 Chevy driving erratically."

He stopped and corrected himself, "No, you can't say 'erratically,' because that gives an opinion. You have to say, 'I observed the vehicle drifting across the dotted line or changing lanes,' or, 'I looked in the window and saw this guy eating a sandwich and fiddling with a bag of chips,' or," he corrected himself again, "not 'guy'; 'the subject was consuming a sandwich and opening a bag of chips.'" He stressed that accuracy and neutrality are critical because "anything is public record," and everybody will want to know, "Was the arrest proper?"

Ron learned the police-report style rather quickly. He just started doing the paperwork. The first day on the job he made a few mistakes, "and my sarge chewed me out pretty good for that." Ron had failed to put his own dialogue within quotations marks, so the sergeant marked these with a pen and said, "Do it again." Apparently, this mild tongue-lashing pushed Ron to make certain his writing followed standard forms of correctness. He was also pushed toward correctness by the fact that he worked on a typewriter, making four carbons. An error would look "unprofessional," and correcting all those carbons was a lot of work. We see the same phenomenon with young writers who allegedly cannot spell or "do" grammar. When their writing is published, however, they make surprising and successful efforts at getting it in spit-spot shape for an audience.

We expressed some surprise that Ron had not received training in report writing from the police, yet it had come to him so naturally. Then he recalled a workshop conducted by an officer from the Los Angeles Police Department. This officer was teaching how to write arrest reports in bullet-style, a common format for public documents, wherein each item is placed in a bulleted or dotted paragraph, making it easy for the prosecutor to read. Ron felt that the style was awkward and broke up the report unnaturally. He did not use it for his own reports, sticking with his natural storytelling style, and none of his superiors objected.

We asked him how he learned this. How had he learned to tell a straight story? If he did not follow the form taught to him and wrote using his own style, didn't he get in hot water for it? Where had his style come from? "I guess I just had it in me," he reported, beginning to mull over how he had learned writing.

We pushed him, not wanting to settle for a vague answer: "What do you mean by 'it,' Ron? What's the 'it' that made you a competent writer?" He was not sure. "What about school? What did you learn there?" We heard a story that makes Ron another of our literacy surprises.

"I absolutely hated English," he said. "In fact, I refused to do the work." This rebellion began during his junior high school years, shortly before he dropped out of school. He reported that he had actually enjoyed elementary school. We talked about the possibility that his sudden dislike of English was related to a general adolescent rebellion, what every parent recognizes as the "terrible teens." Ron nodded, adding that he had been part of the early sixties dropout trend, all of the typical stuff—rock 'n'roll, *Easy Rider*, marijuana, a latter-day lost generation.

But Ron was unwilling simply to accept adolescence as the culprit in his bouts with schooling. He blamed English in particular: "In school, English was the worst." Ron felt he could "speak it fine" and "write it in sentences fine," but the grammar and usage work was of no help.

There was that "it" word again. We pushed further to learn more about the "it" of his literacy, what it was and where it came from. "If you could speak and write 'it' okay at that point," we observed, "you must have picked 'it' up someplace else."

Ron thought for a bit and from his memory banks came up with some interesting anecdotes: "I used to write comic book stories. You know the Sergeant Rock comics?" We did not, but we remembered Maggie, described in Chapter Two, who did, and we could recall drawing some comic stories of our own as kids. Ron went on, "Well, they're war stories and I used to read a lot of them. And then, probably at the sixth grade, out of school, I would write three- and four-page stories."

"With drawings?"

"No, I can't draw at all. These were just stories. And my mom read them. She was surprised that they were so long and said they were good. There were a few problems with commas, and she would help out with that, but basically she would just read them."

We pushed a bit more. "How about before that? Can you remember other things your mother did for you?"

Ron lit up: "I haven't thought about this in years," he said, "but she used to read to us all the time. We had a stack of Dr. Seuss books about two feet high that she read. We were fanatics. *Cat in the Hat* and books like that." He recalled another tale: "The first day of school they gave us those readers, like Dick and Jane. I learned to read and came home and showed my mom. She flipped!"

We flipped, too, for Ron's mom, apparently intuitively, was doing precisely what virtually all the literacy experts tell parents to do at home: *Read with and to your children. Respond to and praise their writing.* Now, we are not prepared to argue that it was exclusively Ron's home environment that gave "it"—some sort of baseline language skill—to him. He was a military kid who traveled a lot, and to this day, he shows a kind of independence and tenacity that makes him an energetic, entrepreneurial person, which is probably what got him in trouble during his formal schooling. Nevertheless, Ron's mind is clear on the points that first, he had and has "it" and, second, "it" came from places other than school. His experience is consistent with those of Bridgett, Jeanie, Ellen, Stanley, and Harold in the previous chapter in this respect: the motivation and drive for literacy grew in the context of an engaged and supportive community.

Ron is a literacy surprise because he never went back to public school. The odds against his going to college were high. He worked for sixteen years as a filing clerk (requiring a certain kind of basic literacy, and probably dynamic and critical as well), completed his GED, got his job with the police, and finally, no longer satisfied with police work, enrolled in the university where he is seeking new options, including studying Japanese and taking an intermediate writing course. On the side, he harvests firewood with a national forest permit, hauling and selling enough to pay his expenses. He is, clearly, an entrepreneurial type.

Of the teaching of writing at the university level, he had strong opinions, and here, too, he is a surprise and a success story. Although Ron felt and feels that he has pretty good writing skills, he was apprehensive about college writing. He voluntarily enrolled in a remedial freshman English course. From the start, his instructor was convinced that Ron had been placed too low, but as is typical of many adult literates, Ron fretted about his lack of "grammar," a word used to describe a vast array of writing problems.

He worked his way into the main track of the required writing course by impressing the instructor with his powerful storytelling. Ron attributes his success, in part, to his background in police writing because the emphasis on clarity that he learned "fits with stuff in academic work." As a writer, Ron works methodically: he outlines his work (using the roman numeral system he was taught somewhere in school), figures out how he wants to organize his paragraphs, and writes, "though sometimes as I write, I find that my thesis will change."

He likes instructors who give him some choice of directions, who say, "Let's do what you want," although he can respect the instructor who (like his old sarge) says, "It's gotta be done this way." He rebels, however, at one writing instructor whom he describes as a "butcher," a teacher who collected papers and put them on the overhead "just to ream you out." That is the kind of person "who makes you afraid to write."

Ron is obviously a teachable student, despite his run-ins with teachers of yesteryear. He tries to learn from his instructors. In our experience, for example, very few students are able or willing to use the formal roman numeral outline as they write. Most learned it in school, and as soon as the teacher did not require it, they used their own, idiosyncratic system of organizing (just as we do). But Ron also uses his imaginative skills—his entrepreneurial literacy—to push the limits, to negotiate the boundaries. Although he is willing to respond to instruction, what he really wants from teachers is support and freedom to explore ideas. For Ron, a teacher should be a guide and a catalyst, not a traffic cop.

Ron impressed us particularly with his deep sense of purpose. We discovered at the end of the interview that he had a Japanese exam the next hour, a language he was learning "because it seems interesting," not because he thought it would bring him any practical benefits or even a potential job: Ron is not going to join IBM and move to Tokyo. Ron politely answered our questions but pulled out the Japanese book as we stood to go. We looked over our shoulders as we left to wave goodbye, but Ron had his head in the book, pursuing yet another kind of literacy (Ron P., interview with authors, Oct. 1994).

John: Fisher-Writer

For John J., what a teacher needs to offer is *encouragement,* a word that came up six times during our conversation. At age fifty, John is a fly fisherman who has recently developed his own river-guide business. Moreover, he has just published his first book, a volume on the art of fly-fishing, and he is under contract to write a second book on how to manage a drift boat on the rivers. Along with writing and river guiding, John is in the process of setting up a fly-fishing shop. All three parts of his professional life are thus integrated, and he told us his writing is integral to his business. For over fifteen years, he has been writing a weekly column on fishing for a local newspaper. He has lost count but estimates that he has written some four to five hundred columns. He observed: "Sure, the column lets me promote myself." However, he does not use it directly to promote his guide business. Rather, "It lets me write about what is important to me."

In school, John was not encouraged about his writing. As an elementary and secondary student, he did "very poorly," with an almost "dyslexic" inability to spot errors in his work, what he called "the seeming illiterate aspects." His teachers were generally "not looking for content that much," focusing on structure and surface errors. Only one teacher in his recollection, a high school English teacher, "saw what I was trying to say" and encouraged him in his writing. But overall, his school grades were "poor," and the trend continued in college, where freshman English proved to be especially frustrating.

John dropped out of college, and after working for a while selling advertisements for a radio station, he joined the Army, which, in its curious way, turned out to be a successful teacher of literacy: "I signed up for clerk school," he said. This was the Vietnam era, and "clerks were usually stationed someplace other than the front lines." He told of spending long days learning to type while copying pages from *Time* magazine, and he thinks that at least some of his present writing ability can be traced directly to the effects of that immersion in professional writing.

He was sent to Vietnam, and then the "goofy Army picked up on my ability to type" and turned him into a combat reporter, for which he felt he was "completely unsuited." He ended up much closer to the front than he had hoped. He learned a lot of things fast, including both writing and photography, and he discovered that he enjoyed writing for the Army newspapers and magazines. His assignments were not "war stories" but human interest material. He wrote about a medical civil action patrol unit that "brought care to remote areas" and about the time when "Weyerhaeuser sent elephants to pull lumber, [which would] develop the economy, [and win] the hearts and minds of the people" and "about the aboriginal, Montagnard tribesman," a "mountain man type Vietnamese" who worked with the U.S. doctors, became an Army nurse, and eventually went on to U.S. medical school.

How did John learn to write so successfully so quickly?

"Well, for one thing, now I had an editor who could push material into shape, clean up the errors." But more important, the military encouraged him, "showed me that there was some talent." In fact, John mused, "It was *always* there."

We asked about that elusive "it," apparently the same kind of "it" that Ron P. always had. "It was a natural talent," John explained. "You have a story to tell. The *realization* that there was a story to tell. I write the way I talk, and writing is a very verbal thing for me. You just try to tell a story."

We were pleased to hear this, since it parallels a piece of advice we often give novice writers, "Write the way you talk." Of course, we realize (as John knows) that this does not mean to put down a literal transcription of one's speech but rather to maintain the voice and fluency one has in conversation.

After the service, John spent about ten years working at ski areas in Colorado as a resort chef in the summers before moving to Oregon where his interest in fishing blossomed. From his Army journalism, he now "had confidence" in his writing, so he drafted a couple of fishing columns and took them to the editor of the local paper, who not only bought them but also encouraged him to continue and develop the weekly column.

The more he fished, the more John became concerned about environmental issues. He became an advocate of "catch-and-release" fishing. He became concerned about what was happening to "managed" rivers in the West and became convinced that fat, well-fed, and lazy hatchery trout were driving out native wild fish from the streams. He became a researcher and a public advocate on these issues, studying government reports, observing the streams. John can now tell you far more than a nonfisher would ever want to know about nymph hatches in the springtime and how the native fish hang out behind logs and natural debris that should not be cleared from the river. Above all, he articulately describes the cycle by which the hatchery trout—which the Department of Conservation maintains improve the river for sports fishers—create a hothouse situation detrimental to the fish that are born, live, and die in their own habitat. He has put together a slide show about his favorite river and has presented the case for the native fish to various legislative groups. He takes groups of schoolchildren to the river to see how it works. He has won over some of the state conservation people and has helped them write management plans for the river. He has written and self-published a booklet that presents his views on the river, obviously a trial run for his present commercial writing. John has even written a novel based on his experiences with the river, and he suffered when the novel and his computer were destroyed in a fire.

John joined a writers' group for a while, but found that people were just too critical of one another's work: "They would slaughter each other." He enrolled in a seminar for writers about fly-fishing and found encouragement there. Now, he shares his works in progress with only a very few people, those whom he trusts to respond to his work and to critique it appropriately. Especially helpful was a veteran outdoor writer who, listening to some of his ideas, encouraged John to develop them as a book proposal. As we have seen, this type of encouragement seems essential to writers of all ages. The friend helped John find a publisher who was interested in the project and eventually published the fly-fishing book. A second publisher issued a contract for the book on drift boats. John is now sifting through his newspaper columns, exploring ways to bring them out as a collection. His aim for the future is to run his guide business and fishing shop in the summers and to hole up and write books in the winter.

We remarked that he seems to have integrated his interests in writing and fishing quite successfully. "I seem to have hit a good chord," he said. "By having a voice, I teach myself more about fishing," which summed up his view neatly.

John provides important lessons about the role of personal experience in writing. We often tell our students to "write about what you know." John J. shows us that with encouragement, one can come to know through writing, come to learn from it. It is also important to observe that his is a literacy not taught in the schools. Nobody taught him how to teach school kids about the river; nobody gave him public relations lessons on how to deal with the Department of Conservation. His experiences and aims provided an energy that, in turn, took him in the direction of being a literacy entrepreneur, figuring out how to write human interest stories and engaging newspaper columns. This energy motivated him to learn to read and research relevant topics, to learn to read bureaucratic documents, to study entomology texts to learn the habits of the flies he ties. As we will discuss, both centering phenomena—experience-into-words and experience-out-of-words—appear to be crucial to the development of the literate citizen (John J., interview with authors, Nov. 1994).

Joan: Social Worker–Writer

Joan S. opened our interview by asking us to tell her what this book is all about, if it would not skew the interview too much to do so. When we explained our interest in school and community literacy, she said, "I see the connection. A lot of what I do is concerned with helping young people bridge the gap between community and school." Joan works thirty hours per week for a large county school district in Title V, Indian Education. Her office runs tutoring programs for at-risk elementary and secondary Native American students. "My job is to help people," she explained, "to help them learn to solve problems, to learn to write."

The Title V programs could use Joan much more than thirty hours a week. The demand and the need are such that the district probably could use a half-dozen full-time people. But funds are tight, and thirty hours is all it can offer. Joan does not seem to worry about the part-time nature of her work, for she also runs a freelance writing business out of her home. On top of that, she is working seriously to become a creative writer of fiction or poetry.

Meaningful is the word that turns up most frequently in Joan's conversation. She feels that her work must be significant not only for the people she serves but for her as well. Having graduated with a college degree in social work, Joan spent about ten years as an "underpaid and overworked" human services employee, dealing primarily with health-prevention programs for the elderly. As part of her work, she developed some writing skills: she learned to put together a newsletter and to write a variety of grant proposals. But she "burned out," finding that in addition to the long hours, she mostly was working with and for healthy people, keeping them that way. This was not meaningful to her. She needed to have greater and more immediate impact on her clients.

She left that line of social work and more or less simultaneously found herself living in a rural area with virtually no employment possibilities. She began to expand on her writing interests and became a freelance writer. She worked for a variety of local organizations—an arts council that needed a proposal written, an organization seeking funds for Hispanic children and other children from low-income families. This "satisfied my need to write," she explained, and it kept her in touch with her roots in social work.

She took each writing job as a challenge. "I think anything can be made creative," she explained, "even proposal writing. I came to realize that I could really write for any damn organization I wanted to." How did that work, we wanted to know? There must be great differences between writing for an arts council and a social agency helping kids. "It's not that difficult," Joan explained, and she admitted that she often learned the necessary skills of writing for different agencies only after she had landed the job. "I would say that I could do it for some clients," she said matter-of-factly, "and then I got the job and figured out how to do it."

She would read a number of general books and materials on fundraising. Once on the job, she would survey previously written proposals to learn the language and get a sense of the rhetoric and buzz words. She would carefully read what was called for in the request for proposals (RFPs) from the funding agency and would "plug in to" what she thought the funders wanted. She did a good deal of listening. "Listen to what people are saying around the office," she advised. "Talk with your funder." Her skill as a writer, then, came in part from her ability to do a rhetorical analysis of the situation, to figure out audience and purpose, to master the style and language of the particular field. "I seemed to have a facility for pleasing my audience."

Joan added that she has a deep commitment to doing a quality job for her clients, and that enhances her ability to write for diverse groups. She also finds the process creative: "There's always a little room to make a grant proposal special."

We asked about her school and college background. Did she master these skills through school? Joan thought hard and came up empty. In school, she said, she was a "nervous" writer; her writing was "laborious," "painstaking," "difficult." Although she had received "some strokes" for her writing in school, she had no recollection of finding writing instruction particularly helpful.

She began to talk about the Native American kids she works with now, and she was highly critical of how they are taught—or not taught—the skills of literacy in school: "I can't believe that most of the kids I work with can write at all. Your feelings? 'To hell with that!' say their teachers. 'Do the homework. Write the 500 words.'" Joan firmly believes that one cannot simply cut to the chase of abstract school-related writing; you cannot leave the human part of yourself outside the schoolroom.

The students coming to her program were writing very little, and most of that was ordinary schoolhouse stuff. As we have seen with other interviewees—Ron and John, in particular—many teachers seem to focus their attention on superficial or external structures, not on ideas, not on kids' feelings.

We discussed the idea that in school, writing is often done for its own sake or for the teacher's sake or to earn a grade or to prepare for the alleged demands of college or the world of business. We talked with Joan about how, in the real world, the writing actually becomes secondary or even invisible in the task of reaching an audience, getting a grant, satisfying a client. "You can't write if you're under stress about writing," Joan said. She said that as a freelancer, she has found she can actually relax about her writing, even though there is the stress of completing jobs successfully and on time.

At some point in her freelance work, she explained, "my writing sort of blossomed." In addition to cranking out proposals, she began to freelance with some area weekly newspapers. Her newsletter and press release writing flowed naturally into newspaper writing, and she found this new work meaningful, "being able to write about substantive issues—land use, workers." She was highly successful at this work, although none of the papers was willing to put her on full-time. We observed that she seems to be cursed by her need to do meaningful work, and that nobody seems to want to pay people to do meaningful work full-time in the social arena. "That's what society wants," Joan said bluntly. She recognizes that the work she finds important and meaningful is not that which pays big bucks. There is a trade-off.

Although Joan was happy with the writing life she had worked out as a freelancer, she also "needed a little more," and after a dozen years of this, she "grew tired of marketing myself." She "wanted to grow." Someone suggested that she do some imaginative writing as a kind of therapy, to seek integration in her life. "Tell your story," was the advice, so in her free time, she began to explore imaginative writing. She perceived her own story writing as "unwieldy." She struggled over manipulating time and place in her stories. To overcome that, she enrolled in the local university and began taking creative writing courses—fiction, nonfiction, and poetry. Highly critical of her own work, Joan nonetheless finds this to be satisfying. She sees it as literally connecting her life and her work. She wants to be a good writer, would like to be published, but finds significance in just telling a good story. "I would like to be satisfied with my writing," she explained.

Joan is especially articulate in describing what she called *integrative literacy*, akin to what we call dynamic literacy. Coupling her idealism about doing meaningful work with her practical ability to master new fields, Joan has neatly bridged the gap between the world of creative writing and the world of business and industry. Like the others in this chapter, with her entrepreneurial spirit and interests, and her drive to make even the mundane assignment creative, Joan exemplifies the holistic nature of dynamic literacy, the ebb and flow between world and idea, between idea and language (Joan S., interview with authors, Nov. 1994).

Jane: Jane of Many Trades

Jane W. is something of a rarity among former college English majors—she does something other than teach English. After receiving a literature degree in the 1970s, Jane went to work for a solar energy cooperative. She conducted workshops on passive solar design; wrote brochures, pamphlets, and instructional leaflets on solar techniques and strategies; and designed and installed solar window shades. In the 1980s, she went to work for a computer software firm and wrote instructional manuals. Now, in the 1990s, she is employed by the Port of Portland, Oregon, as a reader and writer of grants and contracts. Each of these areas required her to master new languages and rhetorics, each far removed from her college training in reading and writing about Beowulf and Virginia Woolf. She is also a skilled craftsperson and hobbyist: she weaves; she repairs and redesigns tools and equipment around the house; she builds; she grows things.

Whereas several of our interviewees describe their mastery of entrepreneurial literacy as a process of stumbling or feeling their way, Jane views her development as an analytical process. "I like to understand how things work," she explained. She is interested in machinery, in organizational processes, and in books, and she approaches her understanding of all three in similar ways. She learns from reading, tracing her technical expertise back to the solar cooperative, where she became "interested in reading about how to do things in general." She wondered why some books on how to do things, such as design a passive solar greenhouse or insulate that greenhouse, "worked" and others did not. What was it that the writers included or left out that made a difference? She asked similar questions about instructional videos. Why did some offer clear and articulate directions, while others seemed to have left crucial information on the cutting-room floor? This analysis developed concurrently with her assignment to teach workshops for the solar cooperative, and she extended her analytical skills to her teaching. She wanted to know how to teach well, and she started connecting her own perceived teaching successes and failures with her growing understanding of what worked and what failed in other written and visual material. She began to develop the ability to "find the holes," in her reading, her teaching, her own writing.

Did her English literature background help her with these skills? Not much, she mused, although reading literature is "a major personal activity" for her today. She does not see strong connections between the sort of reading and writing she does today and her background in "artistic and expressive writing." We suspect there may be more of a connection than she acknowledges, as evidenced by the ease with which Jane shifts in her conversation from nuts-and-bolts matters—her work, her writing, her gardening—to large and abstract social, political, and intellectual issues. Perhaps her skill goes back even further, although she does not see much connection between her family background and her literacy.

Jane acknowledges that she came from a family that was "interested in reading and talked about reading." But she was a "solitary kid" who used reading as a way of "entertaining" herself, especially when surrounded by some "nasty ugly brothers." So whether or not there was a direct impact on her more recent workaday reading and writing, Jane clearly came from a highly literate background and was richly experienced with books and conversation.

This may help explain why, despite the considerable differences in her three occupations—in solar design, computers, and grants and contracts—she reports that she could "almost immediately" figure out a new subject area and learn its rhetoric. In fact, she delights in entering into "a variety of subject matters," each "with its own language," its own "arrays of terminology." In her present work with the port authority, she has mastered the languages of the grain elevator business, airport administration, commercial public arts (including purchasing statuary for the airport), and shipping. She especially enjoys the shipyard aspect of her job. She has seen "complex machines on a scale I've never been involved with," and she likes the fact that the shippers cling to older nautical language: "They actually talk about 'scuppers,'" she noted with a laugh. To master a new language, she listens to people talk, goes on tours, sits in on conferences with contractors and granting agencies, and as she says, rather quickly masters the language, a process similar to that described by Joan S. in the previous interview.

Jane's port authority work involves much more reading than writing, and the reading leads to some interesting observations about organizational prose. Much of the writing that comes across her desk is "hierarchical," commissioned by somebody to get a job done, the writing itself serving as a contract or set of specifications. In fact, a considerable amount of the writing is actually done by someone other than the actual contractor or granting agency—that is, contractors often use stock phrasing or even purchase written material from central agencies that specialize in, say, writing proposals in architecture or engineering. Reading such material, she says, is tricky. "In fact, we have to make certain that they aren't simply selling us our own words," for frequently contractors will pick up the language of a set of specifications and parrot it back to the contracting agency. (We know from our own grant writing experience that this is standard practice: you quote the agency to itself to prove to them you will, in fact, be meeting the job specifications.) However, as Jane noted, simply reciting the language of the RFP does not guarantee that a contractor will do the job. Jane does a great deal of reading between the lines and interpreting the language to make certain the job will be done.

Much of her time is spent policing documents, looking for unauthorized changes. Having a computer background, Jane realizes that word processing, with its ease of revision, can lead to documents of muddled authorship. She recalls thinking about this when she worked for the software company. Standardized or stock letters were put into a master computer file and were used and revised by many different people over time. These letters evolved to the point that no person could actually be identified as a letter's author. She finds this trend "disturbing," for it "diminishes the significance of individual contributions," including her own. Nevertheless, Jane finds her work quite satisfying. The more complex the task, the better she likes it, "getting to know the parts, making certain the references are correct."

The voiceless, faceless prose that concerns Jane results from the pressure for productivity in the business. Why should contractors write something from scratch if they can purchase or acquire or recycle language, especially given the ease of transfer of large chunks of information through word processing? Jane recalls an important discovery she made while reading a contract for an overhaul of the airport's steam heating system. Somewhere she had learned that Oregon's seismic codes had been upgraded, calling for stronger anti-earthquake engineering. The proposal for the steam system came in, and she realized that all the language came from older codes. She notified others of the error, and appropriate changes were made. Again, she attributes this sort of reading skill to her interest in how to do things: it is her understanding of the way things are put together that makes her a good reader and writer.

However, Jane said, "What I do doesn't make you a better writer," and she is thinking about finding ways to spend her time that will allow her to read and write in "a more heartfelt gear." That metaphor, with its interesting mix of the affective and the mechanical, appropriately describes Jane's unique traits as a literate person (Jane W., interview with authors, Nov. 1994).

The Entrepreneurial Rhetoric

On the surface, these rhetorical entrepreneurs do not seem to have a great deal in common. Further, we do not cite them as representing a particular population, certainly not the total world of business and industry. If anything, they help show the idiosyncratic nature of business literacy, and in the process, they both reveal and complicate the issues of schooling for a literate society. Can one conceivably develop a school program that somehow could prepare people as diverse as Bob, Ron, John, Joan, and Jane for the reading and writing experiences of their lives? (In a later chapter, we will argue that the answer to that question is yes.) Obviously, the schools cannot teach the specifics of the rhetorics of fly-fishing, grant writing, memorabilia analysis, personal narrative, and the myriad other forms that these and other entrepreneurs have mastered and will master.

Yet, there were some surprising commonalities and unexpected themes that emerged in their accounts. For example, we were interested to find that most of them feel a certain ease and even pleasure in rhetorical invention. They report that learning a new language or a new discourse form, whether reading or writing, is, in fact, no big deal and even enjoyable or at least engaging. Faced with a new form to write or read—the police report, the arts council proposal, the steam generator specifications—the literate citizen has strategies for figuring out the new vocabulary, the new structure. Literate people talk to others; they read; they study models. They find their way to a successful literacy venture through careful experimentation. How does this happen? Consider Alec Hinchliffe's model of literacy learning (1968, p. 38):

Skill getting ↔ Skill using
Need to express ↔ Need for literacy

Hinchliffe felt that unlike many fields or disciplines, reading and writing provide their own instructional strategies. The literate person knows—mostly subconsciously—how to figure out new literacy problems. Linguist Noam Chomsky even has argued that human beings come equipped with, as Steven Pinker (1994) calls it, "the language instinct." It is as if people are somehow programmed to generalize from specific instances of language usage to very complex rules of grammars. Although the question of whether this ability is innate (genetic) or social (experiential) is subject to great debate, we think it is arguable that this human ability applies to rhetoric as well. Human beings catch on to language conventions with amazing agility. They do this through imitation, through trial and error, through the experiences of reading and writing. The result is that even as people are learning to use language, they are picking up certain entrepreneurial strategies that allow them to move to the next level, the next challenge. This is not to say that people do not need teaching—or, as our interviewees show us, support, encouragement, and coaching—but it does suggest that there is less need for direct instruction in literacy skills than one might suppose.

The previous chapter demonstrated the importance of motivation. Clearly, occasion and purpose power literacy development as well. Learning new strategies, forms, and genres does not happen in a vacuum. People learn new approaches to problems as they face new challenges and as they themselves set aims and goals they want to achieve. Rhetoricians have always recognized that purpose is part of the rhetorical act, that a speaker or writer needs to describe his or her purpose carefully before developing a text.

However, the subjects in this chapter give a slightly different meaning to the word *purpose*. For them, it is not only the aims and goals of the text itself but also their own aims as individuals. To some extent, learning a new discourse comes about as a by-product of occasion. The Forest Service needs a pamphlet on wild fish? Okay, I'll learn to write that form. I need to review a set of specifications for bronze statuary? Okay, I'll learn to read about the technical side of metal casting.

This leads us to suggest that literacy is catalyzed by *curiosity* and *need*. Entrepreneurship and rhetorical invention are closely linked. The entrepreneurial spirit often requires characteristics we value in general education—to think critically, to analyze and deconstruct, to reconstruct or create, to synthesize. These are also the hallmarks of analytical and critical literacy. But few people are analytical or critical just for the hell or the fun of it. The interviewees for this chapter all were rich in intellectual curiosity, which is linked to a desire and a drive to make things happen, a practical or functional sense of getting the job done. Literacy thus becomes a tool in their intellectual arsenals, not a trait to be developed solely for its own sake.

More important, based on the admittedly small sample here, we see the phenomenon of literacy as linked to the personal, the human, the individual side of life. We were surprised by the number of times the subjects mentioned such ideas as "personal satisfaction," "meaningfulness," and "integrating one's life." We had supposed that many of them would describe a workaday attitude toward reading and writing, as something simply to get the job done or to be done with. Rather, they showed us that they regard even the most mundane job as an opportunity for creativity and significance and that they see their work and their literacies as part of a larger, dynamic picture. In this respect, several of them saw an easy flow and connectivity between practical or job-oriented reading and writing and imaginative literacy. We are not seeing a two-culture gap between functional literacy and creative literacy, between job and personal life, between work and imagination.

All of this leads us to conclude that well meaning as it may be, teaching young people to write business letters and résumés is not a route that will lead to the integration of school and a literate society. The people we interviewed offer powerful evidence of the need for educators to push the concept of school literacy beyond pseudopractical applications and beyond the limiting paradigm that school, business, and general life literacies are somehow separate from one another. These people are all part of that quintessentially entrepreneurial activity—living one's life to the fullest.

Chapter Four

The Politically Literate

A little vagueness goes a long way in this business.
—FORMER CALIFORNIA GOVERNOR EDMUND BROWN
(QUOTED IN LEWIS, 1980)

Governor Brown reminds us how, from classical times to the present, politicians have traditionally given rhetoric a bad name: it is seen as a tool of those who propose to shape, control, and direct public opinion. If you ask the typical citizen to define rhetoric, you will often get a pejorative description of people in the public sector—those who generate mere words, lies and smoke screens, or utter pettifoggery.

As we were writing this book, biennial elections were being held, and it was clear that the citizens of the United States were sick of rhetorical pettifoggery on the part of their leaders. In an election whose results were most commonly described in the press as "resounding," voters turned a number of incumbents out of office and changed the balance of power in both the House of Representatives and the Senate. The electorate passed a variety of regional and state ballot measures, including term limitation acts, that demonstrated a desire to wrest control from the big business of government and return it to the people. Measures for new taxes were routed, and several states (including ours, Nevada) passed propositions that require anything from a two-thirds to a three-quarters majority to raise taxes.

Reading the results of the election was no easy task. The victorious party, of course, interpreted the vote as a repudiation of the opposition party and its policies and as a call for new forms of action and direction. The losing party, chastened, but not totally exhausted of rhetoric, read the vote not as repudiation but as a modest course change toward centrism. Political commentators were inclined to see the results as a warning to all politicians that voters were impatient with political officeholders generally. It may have been that voters were not so much voting for or against a particular philosophy as they were voting to voice frustration at the perceived failures and lies of the politicos. This was an election of rejection, on the part of both the voters and the many who chose not to vote at all.

It was perhaps no coincidence that the political campaigns were perceived by the press and the public as the most negative in electoral history. Public relations operatives combed the records of opposing candidates for evidence, not so much of wrongdoing (although there was a fair amount of that to be uncovered), but of the slightest hints of impropriety that could be puffed up into a negative advertisement. Thus, a politician who once went to China on a trade mission was described as a "puppet" of the communists, of serving "foreign interests," and of being a freeloader touring the world at public expense. A senator who once had served on a parole panel was portrayed as having opened the jailhouse door to set rapists and murderers free to commit their nefarious deeds once again. The most positive statements of the campaign—positive in a perverse sense—were boasts by candidates that they were willing to throw the electric chair switch. Of course, politicians who were pro-choice on abortion were portrayed as baby killers, often by the very candidates who were so eager to put convicted criminals to death.

The rhetoric of this campaign was mostly small-time, filled with quibbles and innuendo instead of bold claims and rich argumentation. There were no Marc Antonys to galvanize public imagination and turn the crowd around to their ways of seeing the truth. There was no Adolf Hitler either, although his name was invoked from time to time in an attempt to tar and feather an opponent.

One of our colleagues at the university, historian Neal Ferguson, teaches a course called "Where Have All the Heroes Gone?" Reflecting on these current events, he notes that in the late twentieth century, the dominant figure has largely disappeared from the public arena. We have no Teddy or Franklin or Eleanor Roosevelt, no Dwight Eisenhower, to embody hero status. Leaders have brief moments of glory and power, but due to so much scrutiny by the press and public, their flaws are quickly detected, and they soon fall from power. Andy Warhol's claim that each of us gets fifteen minutes of fame during his or her lifetime may apply to the public leader as an outside limit, metaphorically that is. In an era of sound bites and public relations image makers, a politician has just a few opportunities to look good and many to look bad. Nowadays, everybody has feet of clay.

Moreover, there is increasing recognition that public and political change is a slow process of negotiation, debate, and consensus. We never again will have a New Deal, and it seems unlikely that we will ever again have patriotic unanimity about going to war.

In this chapter, we are concerned not with the center stage politicians but with a quieter, less-public group of people, those folks who work, mostly behind the scenes, as community activists. These are literate citizens who in ancient Greece and Rome would have been perceived as citizen-leaders. If one can take school curriculum guides—and their rhetoric about building citizenship—at face value, these are people who have genuinely learned the lessons of responsible citizenship in a democracy. In classical times, rhetoricians studying leaders' speeches examined their motives and their strategies, their ethics and their appeals to passion. They questioned a leader's education to determine: Is this a knowledgeable rhetor? What are the speaker's beliefs regarding truth and justice?

We will ask those questions, too, and we will go on to look at the subtle variations of education, rhetoric, and literacy, for we have discovered that like heroism, public activism has changed in the twentieth century. The person today who would change public opinion works in a variety of subtle ways and seldom sees dramatic results. People toil patiently or impatiently, advocating causes, working for what they think is important. We found people who negotiate and politic, who lobby and beseech, who question and challenge, who act and react, who inform and slant. These people tirelessly interpret and reinterpret, monitor and strategize, seek loopholes and push for new laws; they frustrate others and are frustrated in return. We found people who read a great deal, who talk a great deal more, who do some writing, and who make full use of electronic media both to send and to receive ideas.

Interestingly enough, we found that contrary to the stereotypical perception of the public rhetor as lacking in ethics, citizen-activists are often deeply committed to the public good. They engage in world activities because they feel it is important to do so, and they know how to use rhetoric to their advantage. These people hardly fit the notion of the rhetorician as sophist or trickster, seeking to make the worse appear the better cause.

Dennis: Nuclear Watchdog

In previous chapters, we observed that many of our subjects do not think their education had contributed directly or particularly to their skills as literate citizens. Thus, it is important to acknowledge and even celebrate the fact that Dennis B. gives considerable credit to his teachers, although only at the graduate school level. The idea of writing as a career "hadn't jelled" in his mind during his high school years in the 1960s, but as an undergraduate at University of California, Los Angeles (UCLA), Dennis B. said, "I decided I wanted to write." He enrolled in film school and discovered that he had a "good ear for dialogue." But he decided not to continue in film and instead went on for a master's degree in journalism, where he encountered some "dynamite instructors." These professors were, in fact, professional journalists, including a book reviewer for the *Los Angeles Times* and a "hotshot" Associated Press reporter. The training they offered was of a real-world, hands-on variety. Dennis worked on the university's laboratory newspaper, learning the skills of writing and editing as well as production. As a result of that, coupled with his street training, he felt "ready to do it" when he left school. (Note once again that the pronoun "it" has emerged as a general descriptor of literacy skills.) The limited credit Dennis gives to his education, then, is hardly a mandate for K–12 public education.

Later, Dennis did graduate work in mass communications at the University of Minnesota, but he eventually dropped the doctoral program, discovering, "I didn't want the Ph.D. all that bad." In contrast to his journalism work at UCLA, he found doctoral research and study dull, too remote from the action.

In the 1970s, he found employment in a series of jobs that directly used his journalism abilities: he covered the police department, the federal court, and the gaming and legislative beats for the *Las Vegas Review-Journal;* almost single-handedly, he ran a twice-weekly California newspaper; and he served as a speechwriter and executive assistant for a Nevada governor.

In 1989, Dennis took the job that first brought him to our attention, public affairs manager for the Nevada Nuclear Waste Project Office. This state government office is funded—about $5 million a year—by a surcharge to the nuclear power industry throughout the country, at the rate of one mil per kilowatt hour generated by every nuclear power plant in the United States. The funds, a staggering amount nationwide, are mandated by federal law for use in areas impacted by the nuclear industry.

The industry is not happy with the way those funds are spent in Nevada. The Nevada Nuclear Waste Project Office has vigorously opposed federal plans to place a nuclear waste repository at Yucca Mountain, a desert site north of Las Vegas. The office has also found itself at odds with the Department of Energy (DOE), which, in its own way, serves as a nuclear industry watchdog. "We weren't always anti-DOE," Dennis explained. "It took two years for DOE to piss everybody off."

As the staff at the Nevada Nuclear Waste Project Office carefully studied what was happening in the nationwide search for dump sites, they became convinced that the DOE already had selected Nevada as the primary and only site and was merely going through the motions of reviewing other locations. They became further convinced that the nuclear industry believed Nevada would "roll over" because of the positive financial benefits from the dump site—employment for Nevadans, in particular.

Lobbyists for the nuclear industry introduced bills in the Nevada legislature "late in the session" to get approval for the dump; the DOE made it difficult for the Nevada Nuclear Waste Project Office to get its federal funding; crucial documents on site evaluation were "lost." At the project office, they looked at how the DOE had managed nuclear projects at Hanford, Washington, and other sites and concluded that DOE "had a really bad track record."

As public affairs manager, Dennis now engages in a range of activities that draw on his skills as a journalist and that have moved him into new areas of literacy. He reads an enormous amount of technical material as the DOE conducts feasibility studies at Yucca Mountain. Not directly trained in science, Dennis spends a lot of time in his office "bullshitting with the technical types" to master their language. In his mind, the distinction between the DOE scientists and their "managers"—the public relations people—has become somewhat blurred. Scientific data about the feasibility studies are always filtered through the DOE front offices. Because of this, Dennis said, he has come to distrust scientists. Then he corrected himself and explained that "scientists don't make the decisions," that the DOE managers express scientific findings in terms favorable to the perceived needs of political rhetoric, "which is disheartening to someone who trusts scientists." (He added parenthetically that he used to trust lawyers until he covered them as a federal court reporter.)

Much of his job consists of sifting through materials put out by the DOE, looking for evidence of what is really happening at the Yucca Mountain site. He observes, for example, that the DOE once reported "test drilling" into the soil to determine whether the land is strong enough to support the planned structure of the dump. A close reading revealed that the diameter of the test holes was much larger than required, so large, in fact, that "they were actually building the project while claiming to be just testing."

He carefully analyzes the rhetoric of both the DOE and the nuclear power industry. The DOE, he claims, is "out to create a sense of urgency, that nuclear materials must be moved from reactor sites all over the country right away." His own reading of the literature, which he freely admits is biased by his own antidump beliefs, suggests that most nuclear materials, which at present are placed in storage ponds and in dry cask modular units at the reactor sites, are secure where they are for now and that the DOE need not rush the Yucca Mountain project. Moreover, he says, the real reason for the urgency is that several states have passed laws prohibiting the building of any new nuclear facilities until the old waste is cleaned up. It is not a matter of science or technology that pushes the Yucca Mountain project forward but rather the fiscal interests of the nuclear power industry.

He is a watchdog of the rhetoric coming from the nuclear industry–public relations offices. He discovered, for example, that a "grassroots" group claiming membership of 15,000 Nevadans was actually just reporting the size of its self-developed mailing list and was, in fact, founded and supported solely by the nuclear power industry. He studied a series of TV commercials done for the industry by a former Las Vegas sportscaster, a man with no science background, who spoke reassuringly on camera of the safeguards and research into the safety of the project. "At one point," Dennis said, making a pinch with his fingers, "this sportscaster holds a mock nuclear waste pellet up to the camera to show that it's safe, a pellet that would actually kill a person if it truly contained radioactive materials." Dennis studied the claims of the engineers who favor the dump, people that think they can "engineer around anything, which, I'm convinced, they cannot."

Dennis's reading and research is translated into language and flows from the project office in a variety of forms. A newsletter takes an unabashedly antinuclear stance and is broadly distributed throughout the state. Dennis writes frequent press releases, sometimes when there is hot news, sometimes just to keep up general awareness of the project office. "Some newspapers," he reports, "will print anything you send them."

Dennis goes on the road frequently, speaking at schools and universities and at public gatherings. One of his trips was a tour through Midwestern states in an effort to gain alliance with Nevada. He argued that states willing enough to dump their waste in Nevada should think twice, knowing that "nuclear stuff is going to pass through your backyard, 145,000 truck shipments over the coming twenty-eight to thirty years; that's a shipment every one hour and forty-five minutes, with an average trip of 2,200 miles." Dennis, obviously, is not opposed to creating a sense of urgency himself or of using carefully selected and dramatic statistics of his own.

His line of argument takes two directions. On the one hand, he and the Nevada office argue that the nation's long-range nuclear waste disposal policy must be overhauled. The short-range plan, however, is to seek delays through lawsuits, catch the DOE in technicalities, and raise doubts in the minds of the public about the value of the project. "We stall," he admitted. The office does not feel compelled to offer constructive alternatives, but simply says, "not now, not until you have something better."

"If I do my job properly," Dennis remarked, "I am out of a job." He is not at all certain of the probability of success in this venture, but he is clearly and deeply committed to the task: "I pause and think, Am I doing the right thing?" As we spoke, he paused, thought again, and said, "I think I'm right on this. This may sound like B.S. but what I do has to mean something to me."

The question of the rightness of causes and the rationale for using rhetoric to promote them is as old as the field of rhetoric itself. There is no doubt that Dennis uses information selectively and dramatically. There is no doubt the nuclear power industry tries to downplay the problems and uses rhetoric to try to soothe those who would be affected by the Yucca Mountain repository. Plato might dismiss both sides as sophists, arguing in favor of a search for the truth of the matter. But something like Yucca Mountain clearly illustrates the postmodern view of truth as a matter of perspective as well as of evidence. Scientific data can be interpreted in multiple ways; the scientific truths and the social needs of affected people may well conflict. Ironically, since some of the material to be deposited at Yucca has a half-life of 24,000 years and the storage facility is designed to last 10,000 years, no person presently on the face of the earth will be around to know which side was right. This is not, then, the rhetoric of debate class; nor is it the neat, two-value wrong and right of the ethics class. There are real, immediate, and long-range consequences. Even so, the strategies mastered and used by both Dennis and the nuclear power industry have a distinctly classical look to them. The nature of the appeals and the manner of using evidence can be characterized by the classical rhetorical terms, *argumentum ad hominem*, appealing to prejudices and simply arguing against an opponent, and *argumentum ad populum*, appealing to the people's passions. Dennis's use of language, then, both validates classical rhetoric and shows how complicated it has become in our time. It offers no easy or comfortable answers about schooling for a literate society (Dennis B., interview with authors, Nov. 1994).

Janet: Healthy Living Through Writing

Like Dennis, Janet B. is deeply committed to the meaningfulness of her work, but unlike Dennis, she was not trained as a professional writer.

In fact, "scary" was the first word out of Janet's mouth when we asked her to begin talking about writing. She reads widely and writes "a ton of stuff" as the health-promotions director of an area hospital. We looked over her press releases, public service announcements, and informational pieces and thought they were quite good, but Janet's vague apprehension about the writing process remains and goes back to her childhood. "My sister is the scholar," she explains. "I was the athlete in the family, who couldn't stand to read a book. She was the great writer, and I sort of had to kick sand at her to get her to do anything."

Janet's sister went on to the University of Michigan (UM) to study English, where she was the winner of UM's prestigious Hopwood Award for creative writing; she is currently a Middle East correspondent for the *San Francisco Examiner*. She is also fluent in four or five languages, including Hebrew. In fact, to hear Janet tell it, her sister's only bad time with literacy came after the family moved from Michigan to Kentucky. Suddenly, her sister's spelling grades dropped. When the family investigated, it turned out that the sister was transcribing the teacher's dialect, spelling words in Kentucky English—as she heard them pronounced—rather than using standard spelling.

For her part, Janet wanted to coach and maybe teach from the start. No low achiever herself, Janet was a highly competitive track-and-field athlete with Olympic possibilities. Her obvious successes triggered our suspicion. "So you were raised pretty much in affluent, well-educated communities. Your sister was this high achiever, and so were you. Did your parents drive you and your sister toward this kind of success?"

"Not really," Janet replied after thinking it over. Her father was a business executive and a "great writer" who "checked over our papers" from time to time. But Janet kept returning to the topic of competition with her sister and the fact that in Janet's mind, her sister is the scholar-writer.

"I can write a sentence well," Janet said, "and I write great letters." She reports that she wrote a good deal in junior high school, voluntarily—letters to girlfriends, love letters and such—and she "did a lot of journaling" in high school and college, a practice she continues today and recommends to others. But Janet, like so many literate adults, feels vaguely that her "grammar skills" are weak, and she wishes that she had "paid more attention" to her schoolteachers when they covered "the basics."

At the same time, her nostalgia for such instruction is limited. "They didn't light your fire," she says of her high school English teachers. And she recalls a college literature professor who "asked people to write about poems" and then "told them they were wrong." Frustrated by this particular professor, Janet sent a poem and assignment to her sister, the scholar, who wrote an analysis. Janet turned in the interpretation of the award-winning English major. The professor trashed her sister's work as well, making Janet totally distrustful of college literacy experts.

She contrasts her own school experience to those of her husband's students. He teaches sixth grade and has his kids make videotapes on current issues and problems. His students identify problems that interest them, take cameras out of school, interview people, and make video reports. This strikes Janet as preferable to and far more effective than the schooling she received. "It's a lot better than" (and here she raised her voice and nasalized it in imitation of either a stereotypical schoolmarm or the Wicked Witch of the West) "do these exercises in the book!"

Yet, as we pointed out to her, here she is a writer, a professional writer, so busy that she has a "hard time keeping up with it now." We puzzled aloud over how this turnaround had happened. Janet told us how she first became involved in writing about public health issues. After college, she had taken a teaching-coaching job at a high school in Idaho. As the health teacher, she was concerned with coaching the "whole person," an element of her ethic that continues today. She did not want to teach just athletes, and she did not want to be just a coach. She wanted her students to be concerned about stress levels, food quality, and physical and mental well-being (completely in keeping, we observed, with the Greek ideal of the sound mind in the sound body). She started a before-school workout program for kids, and soon teachers were participating as well. Then she began writing some columns for the school paper, "funny columns." The style of those columns was obviously more closely related to her personal letters and journals than to her academic writing. Nevertheless she worried: "What if it's not grammatically correct?" She feared being perceived as "the coach that doesn't have any brains." Her efforts at writing brought no negative effects and considerable positive response from students and the faculty. She feels she was successful in "modeling a health curriculum" at the Idaho school.

Time passed: Janet did some work in graduate school; she coached university track and field; she did some teaching, always including journal writing as a technique for helping students link their physical and mental health. She became a health and recreation director at a private club and wrote columns for its newsletter, picking up most of her skills on the job (like the literacy entrepreneurs in the previous chapter).

Then she moved into her present position at the hospital, where she is responsible for developing a wide variety of public courses, programs, and workshops, from toning the tummy to heart disease recovery. She writes countless informational pieces about the hospital's services to raise its visibility in the public eye.

As we have noted, Janet had never taken a course in public relations writing, never done work in journalism. She simply plunged in and "learned to fly by the seat of my pants." She explained, "I just kinda did it." She talked with her dad about his business writing, but mainly she shared stories and problems with other department managers at the hospital, picking up techniques "by osmosis." Like Dennis, she learned a great deal about language from the people around her. This osmotic process, we discovered, has turned Janet into a sophisticated rhetorician, despite the fact that she finds the writing "still stressful."

Before writing anything, she spends a considerable amount of time focusing on the audience, trying to figure out precisely who reads her materials and why (just as classical rhetoricians would have her do). For a time, she wrote a weekly column for a local newspaper, but her manager felt that the paper was reaching too few people. Now the hospital publishes *Health Scene,* a monthly digest. Many of the articles about national health trends are written by a commercial newsletter service. Janet writes the local material, which is plugged into blank spots in *Health Scene.* The result is a highly professional, even slick digest with considerable local material. It is delivered to every home in the hospital district, theoretically guaranteeing a 100 percent audience. Hospital marketing surveys suggest that realistically the readership is lower, but *Health Scene* probably has a greater readership than did her articles in the local paper. Janet is distrustful of the sampling procedures, however, and relies on her own seat-of-the-pants measurements. For example, whenever she is at the post office following publication of an issue, she looks on the floor and in the trash baskets to see how many copies of *Health Scene* have been thrown away. She also monitors community response. To her surprise, some people think she writes the whole paper, not just the inserts, which suggests that she has successfully integrated her own writing style with that of the "canned" copy.

Janet's writing has brought about some loss of anonymity. When she is doing her own shopping, people sometimes stop her and ask her to do a variation of the hospital's "grocery tour," which shows how to shop healthfully. Or, she adds, "They see me coming and try to hide what's in their carts, making excuses for what they've bought, which suggests that they did at least read the paper."

Her audience is incredibly diverse. We discussed a column she had recently written on the use of sunscreen for winter sports activities. The audience for this piece, she reported, could range from middle-aged tourists coming up to their condos for a weekend on the ski slopes to thirty-year-old "ski bums" who are "contemptuous" of skin block and think the article is a marketing ploy for the suntan industry rather than a piece of health information.

Obviously, Janet is not only concerned about sunscreen but also with holistic issues of health and wellness. Warming to discussing her audience, she asked, "How do we write to convert those who are not already converted? How do we capture an audience? How do we know where they are in their lives?" For example, she questions how she can "preach" parenting skills to "a newly divorced mom who is in 'crisis' mode or 'survival' mode." We can "plant a seed," she observed, "but it has to be put in the right soil at precisely the right time." People's lives are changing so rapidly that the health-promotions person hardly knows quite where to target her writing. There are no protocols as in nursing, no standard operating procedures. You have to "constantly reexamine what you're doing and how you're doing it, how to be there at the right moment."

Janet's analysis of audience is clearly sophisticated, far more complex than simply bean counting the number of readers reached. Yet, with her obviously deep and ethical commitment to preventive and holistic medicine, her rhetoric is also influenced by fiscal considerations. The task of the health-promotions department is to "break even or show a profit." That means the sum total of Janet's work—setting up and publicizing workshops, health screenings, health fairs, and the like—should make money or "at least not lose too much." She describes problems with fee splitting: if one of her columns brings new patients into the hospital for a lab screening, who gets credit for the money generated, the lab or the health-promotions division? Every decision she makes concerning community needs and reaching individual people must be tempered by whether there is sufficient money being generated. She is optimistic about proposed new state legislation that would require tax-supported hospitals to provide a certain amount of services and educational programs to the community regardless of profit and loss. Such law would allow her to put on more free workshops—for example, health-awareness activities in the schools—rather than having to wonder whether a particular project will pay its way. Hers, then, is a practical rhetoric, driven by a vision and commitment, yet tempered by the fiscal realities of the medical world.

In our discussion, Janet returned to the role of writing in people's lives, again advocating the use of journals as a technique. She laughed about a paper she had written for a course in her master's degree program. Students were to write reports on areas of the community that needed particular services or programs. Looking around the class, she saw graduate students who were "stressed out," holding down health-care jobs, running families, trying to complete their assignments for an advanced degree. She did her report on the health of health-care professionals.

"Journaling," she repeated, "is a great medium for health." In advocating journals, Janet is part of a coterie across the curriculum who have found journal writing, which is essentially a response to one's own experiences, to be a healthful and instructive form of literacy. In English classes, our colleagues, like Janet's teachers, use it as a way to strengthen a writer's voice and build fluency. We find that when students write on self-selected topics, without the pressure of editing, correcting, and grading, they often write better than they do for formal class assignments. Janet uses the journal both in her personal and professional lives, although for different purposes. Janet says she does not care if the journal helps people write better. She is concerned that it help them *live* better, with the writing only an ancillary tool.

We think Janet's view of journal writing offers some solid clues about and implications for schooling for a literate society. Literacy is most often successful when it is invisible, that is, when people read and write for their own purposes rather than to complete an assignment. Of course, one must be a good enough reader and writer to be able to use the language comfortably and unconsciously, but a growing number of teachers have found that even for the youngest students, purposeful, integrative writing and reading are possible. The kids may misspell or mispronounce words, and they may even make mistakes of content in reading and writing, but they become increasingly adept at using language when it functions in the ways that Janet B. describes.

She is an especially articulate speaker about literacy, and her experience has important implications for teaching. Janet's school and college English teachers were not, on the whole, bad people or bad teachers. With the exception of the college poetry professor, none of them actually made her feel stupid about her writing. She reported no experiences (as many others do) of being humiliated because of her alleged lack of writing skills. It is clear that she was mistaught in some ways, though, in particular being told that grammar is a problem for her, because it is not now and we suspect it never was. Like most literate people, she may make an occasional usage error or struggle for the right word, but these are not sins of grammar. Moreover, it is clear that like many of our subjects, Janet mastered literacy as a kid. She would not have written journals and diaries and love letters if she were illiterate.

We believe that as an adult, she picked up on those literacy skills from her youth and skillfully and successfully employed them in pursuit of important ends—her commitment to holistic health and medicine and her commitment to providing services to people when they need them (Janet B., interview with authors, Dec. 1994).

Once again, we have seen the particulars of a critical, dynamic literacy driven by on-the-job learning. It is often a struggle, and it often involves the feeling that one is just barely getting by, learning by hook or by crook. Yet, despite the thin ice quality of this practical literacy, we continue to return to the notion of generalized literacy skills. These are the skills that enable a writer, even while feeling insecure, to discover and master the rhetoric of everything from the adolescent love letter to the article on tummy toning to the public health curriculum for an entire community.

Margaret: Lawyer-Writer-Citizen

In some ways, Margaret S. could be Janet B.'s sister, the academic achiever. Margaret, too, was "always a high achiever." In high school, she got top grades, and she continued that course in college. Yet she dropped out of a small women's college, in part, because she discovered that she "couldn't apply anything" she had learned. She explained, "I could close my eyes in a test and recite the page in history. That's the kind of student I was." Acknowledging that she is "a very analytical type," she nonetheless "couldn't get on top" of her college studies. She could learn the basics and the facts, but she struggled with larger implications, bigger issues, and applications of the facts.

Nevertheless, after time off from college, she used her academic powers to get into law school without an undergraduate degree. In three years, she earned her law degree at the top of her class, all as a single mother working full-time. "You learn how to juggle," she explained simply. While Margaret has little use for the education offered by the lower schools (and for that offered to her children, which seems to her little different from her own), she says that law school opened up her mind and her thinking abilities. Law school, she explained, teaches one "how to use language differently." Furthermore, "it teaches you how to think in a different way."

We asked how that happened and what she meant by a "different" way, for we had always heard that law school involved a great deal of drudgery—plowing through cases, memorizing precedents, copying down citations. Margaret's legal education, we discovered, did not fit our stereotype at all. She received her training through what she calls the Socratic method. The students would read three or four cases and come to class to discuss them, mainly to "stretch them beyond the central theme." The professor, their

Socrates, would extend the implications of judgments to different settings. If the topic was the responsibility of a mother for the health of an unborn child, for example, the professor would ask: "Here's Judy, who has a drink, knowing she is pregnant. What is the law here?" Or "Suppose she goes into a room that she knows has secondhand smoke?"

You "learn to read between the lines" in law school, Margaret said. You learn to "twist the facts to fit your case," to "find flaws." Twist? We remarked that this sounded a little like Socrates's indictment of the Sophists, using rhetoric to make the worse appear the better cause. Margaret would not buy that reasoning and said that the best teachers in law school "let you argue a point."

She talked about learning the techniques of legal language. We asked her what that meant. Did her professors teach formulas or strategies? Did they deliberately teach lawyers-to-be to skew the facts or alter the truth? Musing on this, she referred again to Socratic or discovery learning. It was in struggling with and broadening ideas and cases that one learned to think, so that her idea of technique really meant broad processes of arguing, not application of specific paradigms or rubrics.

Margaret's description of her education reminded us of Dennis B.'s account of his training. We thought it significant that the two subjects who found their schooling to have taught them something they actually wanted to know both referred to meaningful education at the graduate school level—Dennis through his journalism professors who got their students out on the streets, Margaret through her law professors who used the case study method. Both Dennis and Margaret emphasized that one learns the processes and procedures of a field this way rather than through hard-and-fast rules. Both emphasized the importance of teachers as mentors, models, and gadflies rather than as presenters of algorithms.

In real life, Margaret explained, law practice involves "having the balls to go in and do it without knowing everything in the case." (She apologized for saying "balls," but she mentioned that she did mean men, mostly.) Lawyers cannot and do not know everything, she said, and she likened the law to a game of strategy. As she moved into legal practice herself and observed her colleagues at work, she concluded that men "love the game" but women prepare better for it. Men—and she quickly acknowledged that she was overgeneralizing to make the point—are "impressed with hearing themselves argue and feel they can argue off the cuff." Women, by contrast, do not feel they need to have the "balls" to do that and instead, do more homework. "It's a learned process," she explained, learned mostly on the job. Trial judges, she claimed, generally agree that women lawyers come to court better prepared than men.

Margaret played the lawyer game well but tired of it. She then cranked up her academic skills, went back to graduate school, and knocked off a master's degree in English with a straight 4.0 grade point average. As she finished her degree, a job opened up that allowed her to draw on her legal skills, and she is presently the legal counsel for the governor of Nevada, a position that obviously puts her directly among the political movers and shakers and in a new rhetorical game.

In this job, she works on a vast array of issues, including human services, the prison system, the state's industrial insurance system, the gaming industry, and the state's relations with the business community. For a time, her primary work was dealing with constituents' complaints, putting citizens in touch with the appropriate agencies. More recently, she has turned much of that work over to a paralegal. She now concentrates most of her attention on policy issues, advising the governor, and helping to draft legislation. This involves her in a range of interdisciplinary issues and, in contrast to what works in the courtroom, requires more than strategy and bluffs.

For instance, she recently found herself in the midst of a debate over a mandate for 800-megahertz emergency radio systems. Confessing that she knew nothing about the technology at first, she had to "learn from scratch" to discover that some of the state agencies were ignoring federal mandates and developing incompatible systems. She studied the issues and, wielding the clout of the governor's office, told the agencies to get it together: "You will do what we say." In sharp contrast to her previous career, which necessitated making legal argument, much of her work now involves reaching conclusions and enforcing them, more the role of judge than lawyer.

But effecting such top-down change is rare, she reports, and much of her work involves meetings, discussions, negotiations, and problem solving. She works with county and state officials to help them figure out how to meet unfunded mandates, how to solve problems effectively. She studies legislative proposals, translates them into budget figures, and writes the drafts of laws that the governor will put forward.

Although she reads voluminously, she has been required to fashion a self-education that follows the pattern we have seen for Dennis and Janet: go to the experts and let them talk. Margaret added, "I always ask, who are the experts? Can I trust them?" Then she sets up meetings and "lets them talk." She explained, "Through this job, I learned a strength I didn't know I had. I sit in a room, bring the discussion together, summarize and synthesize." She has, in short, mastered the kind of thinking that she feels her early education left out.

We reminded Margaret of our interest in the implications of her work for a literate society. "You cannot have a democracy without a literate society," she said flatly, but she expressed her fears that today's voters are learning about public issues "through the sound bite, through *USA Today*." There is little in-depth analysis on the media, she said, and "that's how the public is learning to vote." Furthermore, legislators are shifting their positions to accommodate the style of media reporting. You "speak in short sentences," and if the media ask you a question you do not want to answer, "You put in a mild expletive to make certain they won't show you on TV."

The trend toward short and quick answers, she continued, has also influenced her work. Recent elections had undercut the governor's support in the legislature, so "we have to pull it in," modifying programs to make certain they are not rejected outright, a task of negotiation and compromise. "But we want to proceed." She explained that hers is "more than just a job; we believe in the social programs." She is particularly concerned that media reportage and election concerns have encouraged lawmakers to focus on a "crisis orientation," responding to the most obvious needs, usually with short-term solutions.

The electorate must come to demand long-range solutions, she believes, and literacy education must "teach people how to think," or "there's not much hope." She repeated that her own early education did not help her along these lines, merely teaching her to regurgitate facts, and she thinks the schools must do more "horizontal teaching," not just "Columbus discovered America in 1492," but education that asks what was happening in science, religion, and art in 1492 and "how this relates." "How were women treated in 1 B.C.?" she asked, giving another hypothetical example, "and what does this have to do with the role of women in the church today?" "Nothing happens in a vacuum," she concluded. "Let's broaden our perspective."

Yet the question of how to do that remains a troubling one. In particular, we have seen in this chapter's first three interviewees, and will see in the following one, a pattern by which perspective and inquiry develop in adulthood. Is it possible that the schools have problems because they start too soon? Does one have to reach maturity to be able to develop and enrich critical thinking skills? We would like to think not, and we can point to some evidence (the students of Janet's husband, for instance, or the children of the following subject) that young people can develop sophisticated insights into the world of issues and arguments and ethics. The challenge is to make that happen in the classroom (Margaret S., interview with authors, Nov. 1994).

Grace: Citizen-Troublemaker

"Why me?" asked Grace B. when we approached her about interviewing her for this project. "I have no college education." As if that made a difference. We know that collegiate education is neither a mark nor a guarantee of knowledge or of research ability. Grace is legendary in our area as a writer and researcher for Citizen Alert, a public watchdog group. She is also a writer and researcher for the Rural Alliance for Military Accountability. Grace had previously spoken to one of our classes about her work.

Whereas several of this chapter's interviewees rely heavily on conversation and listening to acquire background information, Grace reads—voraciously, carefully, and critically, and she reads some of the most boring and difficult literature in the world—government documents.

She reads to keep track of new plans and developments in the military, which operates large training centers in Nevada and owns a huge chunk of the state to use as bombing ranges and military practice areas. Interested in public affairs since she was in high school, Grace was mobilized into activism over a decade ago when she was "buzzed" by a military jet flying at low altitude. Her car wound up in a ditch and she and her infant daughter were "terrified." That is all it took, and the military has probably regretted that buzzing—whether deliberate or accidental—ever since. "We created Grace," a military official once lamented.

"It's all there in the documents," Grace said of the information needed for her current project, which is keeping track of military efforts to test a laser bombsight. She is convinced that the testing is a threat to the health of citizens, that people can be blinded by intense lasers being fired from planes. "If you can read," she said easily, "you can find what you need to be a threat." It is difficult reading, not only because of its technical content but because of the specialized language. "You open one of these documents up," she explained, "and there's four pages of acronyms." But she wades through it, sifts through it, and often finds what she is looking for. In the case of the laser sights, she located a government document prepared in North Carolina that did, in fact, confirm the danger. It took her over two years to find what she needed: "You need lots of patience in this business," but she was able to stop the military from testing those sights in Nevada.

Grace's rhetorical strategy is one of quoting the government to itself. "I'm nobody," she said. "They won't listen to Grace talking. But if you have a document to back it up, they can't brush you off." She believes in having a document to support every claim. "You talk with a document to back you up," and "you have to have your p's and q's in order." Rich background knowledge is essential if one is to be effective. Her own writing bristles with facts, and she makes her claims quietly but firmly after she has laid out all the evidence.

She has high praise for the Freedom of Information Act. Although much government information is top secret and excluded from the act, an enormous and surprising amount is available to any citizen who files a request. In fact, she notes, the United States is ahead of many European countries. She knows of researcher-activists from other countries who use the U.S. Freedom of Information Act to keep track of the activities of their own governments. "And they have to respond to you," she explained. "If you request it, they have to provide it." The process can be slow, and again she urges patience for the citizen-activist. Sometimes the documents arrive slowly, and sometimes a document does not contain the information needed or sends one off on a new search, but often the very evidence she needs will be found, and you "jump up and down when you get it." She adds, "It's fun," a phrase that she repeated several times during our interview.

Among the successful campaigns she has participated in are defeating the MX missile system, changing military flight paths in her area, defeating electronic battlefield plans in eastern Nevada, defeating a bombing-range plan in Idaho, and enacting laws on the Bravo 16 laser sight. "I have a few notches on my belt," she said, with a hint of a chuckle. "But you can't claim victory. You never can tell exactly what it is you've stopped."

Apart from the buzzing episode, we wondered how Grace got into the activism business, which is quite obviously the literacy business as well. She told us that she comes from a family for whom reading and discussion were always important and that she was "always a reader." Her mother was a voracious reader, putting away two books a week. Grace picked up her mother's habits. She emphasizes that her own reading is by no means limited to government documents. "I read everything," she said, "autobiography, romance, mystery. I believe that you can learn something from even the stupidest books." (We wonder what E. D. Hirsch and the two culturally conservative Blooms would say to that!)

A product of a Catholic high school in New Jersey, Grace liked history most of all. She giggled when she said to us, thinking of history, "it's fun." She sees the study of history as a way of avoiding the mistakes of the past. Reflecting on the history she studied and the history her own children study, she argues that school history needs a broader perspective, a global perspective, not simply American.

She was deeply impressed by a high school geography and political science teacher she had in the 1970s. "I remember every word that man taught me." But he was influential more because of his actions than his disciplinary knowledge. A priest, he was "kicked out of school" for being too radical. Toward the end of the Vietnam War, the students wanted a day off to march against the war, and the priest supported them. The march was never held, but the kids wound up spending the day in the school halls protesting the firing of the priest.

Grace thinks that her own children, now twelve and fourteen, will likely pick up on her interests and values. She recalls a fifth-grade teacher who "taught me how to pick out a message in a book or article," and she says she has passed on that skill to her daughter, who, she reports, "will be a big troublemaker." The daughter is already involved in her own set of issues, mostly environmental and ecological. Grace's teenaged son is interested in nuclear waste disposal issues, and she says he "chewed my butt" for not going to a recent set of hearings on nuclear issues.

She closed our interview by once again repeating her educational advice, "Read and be patient." "In the darkest hours, things may be going the best. You never quite know what you have started," Grace told us (Grace B., interview with authors, Dec. 1994).

The Rhetoric of Activism

Getting things started is what being an activist is all about. Many people dream of shaking things up in society, of bringing about major and dramatic changes, but few people do it. From the presidency on down, it is a phenomenally difficult and rare task. For every Abraham Lincoln who shook up the country to its roots, there are a dozen like Jimmy Carter, Bill Clinton, Rutherford B. Hayes, or Herbert Hoover, whose long-range effects have been modest or even have been erased. Grace is right: "You never quite know what you have started," and that includes the possibility that what you have started may not produce long-range change at all.

As we reviewed our interview sample, we found some common characteristics, all with important implications for schooling. For example, we saw that public literacy requires ethical and emotional commitment. These subjects were a lively lot. As we reviewed our interview notes, we realized that our ordinarily bad handwriting was even worse than usual, scrawled, with large numbers of abbreviations, a sure sign that the subject was pouring out ideas at an energetic rate. One would not become an activist without deep ethical and emotional commitment to a cause. Dennis, the veteran journalist, impressed upon us that he works long hours on the nuclear issue because he believes deeply in it. Margaret, whose interview was difficult to schedule because of her wall-to-wall appointments, emphasized her commitment to the governor's social agenda as a driving force behind her day-to-day negotiating.

Where does that commitment come from? How can the schools assist young people in finding causes and commitments they can see as valuable (without, of course, the school trying to dictate ethics and directions)? Is it even the business of the schools to concern themselves with such matters at all? Most of the evidence from researching this chapter indicates that causes and commitments tend to emerge independently of school. Grace B.'s political science teacher is the only example we saw of school-inspired activism, and it grew from an incidental event rather than from education directly. Possibly, commitments of these sorts are adult concerns that simply will not develop during the adolescent years, but then again, we have the example of Grace B.'s kids and their propensity for troublemaking (or one might say activism), as well as the example of kids nationwide who have become attached to causes while still in public school.

The key point, and one that should not be lost in the values question, concerns what we call *public literacy,* the act of getting out the word. This literacy is powered by beliefs and commitments. Our interviewees are not the stereotyped Sophists of Plato's *Gorgias,* attaching themselves to any old cause. Indeed, in the case of Margaret S., it was the perceived sophistry of the legal business that helped lead her out of the courtroom and into the public arena of change through legislation.

Moreover, general education and learning from others provide background for learning specific arguments and strategies. On the face of it, few people can be knowledgeable enough in their own right to argue and present successfully in the public arena. One can become a specialist in a particular issue—like Grace and the military, for example—but often the activist must be something of a generalist, sometimes operating on technical information prepared by specialists—like Dennis and nuclear science—or be adept at brokering a wide range of related information—like Janet and a plethora of health issues. All of our subjects are skilled and dedicated readers, who demonstrate the maxim that "if you can read, you can learn just about anything." But they also are skilled informal interviewers and listeners. To educate yourself on an issue or cause, you go to the people who know and either listen to what they have to say or engage them in conversation to learn it. With the exception of Grace, who found her study of history fun and instructional, our movers and shakers made little reference to background knowledge and understanding picked up in school. Rather, they seemed to agree with Janet, commenting on her and her husband's teaching through video: "Teach kids resources, where you can go for help."

A crucial issue for education, we think, is how to give kids access to these resources, human and others, given the constraints of the school day. How can kids bump up against people in the know other than their teachers? How can we get them outside the classroom digging up resources in the manner of a real-world mover and shaker? Occasional field trips will not do the trick; nor will the occasional guest speaker. If school is to offer genuine learning experiences, new ways to break down the classroom walls will have to be found.

We see, too, that movers and shakers often draw on mentors and role models. Dennis B.'s positive experiences in journalism school came from real-world practicing journalists; Margaret's "learning to think" was fostered by professors who modeled alternative ways of thinking about a problem; Grace had the priest who was fired and her mother to inspire her; Janet had her father, her sister, and her husband. Is it the job of the schools to provide role models beyond the teachers? If so—and we certainly think the answer to that question must be yes—how can this be done?

As we saw previously with the rhetorical entrepreneurs, mastering a new language does not present great difficulties for the literate citizen. The folks we have interviewed are quick to pick up on a new set of terms and to assimilate the rhetoric of a new field. The languages of specialized fields are not foreign languages. If one reads the documents and hangs out with people who know, the literate person *can* crack the code and learn how to use it him or herself.

It also appears that literacy is an invisible tool. Few people set out to learn to read and write (or take photographs or use a computer or a fax machine) solely for the sake of mastering a language or a technology. People master language because it helps them get a job done—moving, shaking, jostling, nudging. The people in this chapter were all literate in traditional ways—writing notes on pads, reading books—and in newer, electronic ways—calling on cellular phones, doing desktop publishing, compiling electronic archives. Their skills were mostly picked up *on* the job, *in* the job, in *medias res*, in the thick of things.

It is important to note that many of the concerns of classical rhetoric emerged in these discussions: these people are concerned with invention (figuring out tools and sources for persuasion), audience, strategic structuring of discourse, and the like. Some of their appeals to audience are quite classic in shape and form, including such old ploys as the *red herring*, which draws your opponent off the scent, and the *rhetorical question,* asked but not answered. At the same time, these interviewees are in the thick of modern rhetoric, both in creating new discourse for new settings and in seeking to put forth their visions of the best possible truth in a less-than-perfect world.

We left the interview with Janet B. thinking about the role of literacy in her holistic health scheme. We began to wonder, "What would it mean to talk about *holistic literacy?*" At chapter end, we are ready to suggest that literacy is a holistic skill, driven by motives and ethics, developed in large measure by osmosis within a literate community, functioning best when writers-speakers-faxers keep their eyes on the target—the audience, the action—rather than focusing on the literacy skills themselves. The challenge, as we see it, is to develop literacy within school systems that have traditionally been atomistic, where learning has been fragmented into disciplines, classes or periods, textbooks, tests. Without increased concern for holism of this sort, we think literacy instruction may be forever doomed to be like a shadow on Plato's cave wall, a mere hint of the real thing, imitation rather than substance.

Chapter Five

Writers, Artists, and Musicians

People who write or create, no matter whether it's dance, theater, whatever, it's the same thing. We all create in the language or voice in which we want to be heard.
—MICHAEL S.

In the song "No More Heroes," the Stranglers (1977), a punk rock group, bemoan what they perceive to be a serious shortage of heroes like William Shakespeare and Leon Trotsky in the modern world. The Stranglers are convinced that today's society literally has no heroes of this quality, and they wonder why this is so. We have heard people complain that there are no Shakespeares being created in the schools of the twentieth century. The implication is that if schools were suddenly to revert back to the schooling techniques of Shakespeare's sixteenth-century England, more writers and poets of the Bard's caliber would emerge. Putting aside the issues involved in choosing Shakespeare as the greatest writer over, say, Virginia Woolf or James Baldwin or even Raymond Carver, we would argue, as we have done throughout, that a return to the teaching practices of some bygone era would be naive and romantic and probably ineffective. Although there is evidence that he was well schooled, there is no evidence that Shakespeare's ability was a systematic by-product of the schools. And if it was, even the Renaissance schools only produced one Shakespeare.

The schools in Renaissance England and Europe were mostly for boys and men from the aristocracy and the growing mercantile class. Very few citizens of either sex from the lower classes attended school. The schools emphasized variation and imitation of different forms and styles in writing as well as in music, painting, and other fine arts. Most Renaissance "grammar schools" were, according to Don Paul Abbott (1990) "directly inspired" by the philosopher-monk Desiderius Erasmus (1469–1536) and his book *De Copia: Foundations of the Abundant Style.* "There is nothing terribly original about Erasmus's *De Copia*" (p. 95), says Abbott in his essay "Rhetoric and Writing in Renaissance Europe and England." "The work is based on broad readings in the classics, a knowledge of rhetorical theory, and great practice in composition" (p. 95). In *De Copia,* Erasmus states that any serious student of rhetoric should read extensively on all subjects. Not only would a student be expected to read everything published (an insurmountable task then as now), but he would also be required to do his papers in Latin or possibly even Greek, languages thought to be superior to the Italian, French, or English vernacular of the time. Further, given the examples of child abuse portrayed in Charles Dickens's novels of the nineteenth century, is there any reason to believe that schoolmasters in the sixteenth century were any more humane in their treatment of students? Probably not. Corporal punishment was, no doubt, seen as an important component of any teacher's pedagogy in Shakespeare's time.

There are at least three reasons more compelling than the quality of the schools to explain why Shakespeare's creative genius developed during the Renaissance. He was, first of all, a product of the humanistic ideals of his time. Humanism honored the human spirit and the capacity for self-realization through creativity. Second, the English language in sixteenth-century England had not been fully stabilized. Third, the idea that English was somehow inferior to Latin was not shared by everyone. Thomas Wilson (1523–1581) wrote the first English rhetoric textbook, *The Arte of Rhetorique* ([1553] 1962), in which he emphasized the vernacular over the ancient languages. This must have been a very exciting time for the English language. Modern English was in its infancy; creative spelling and punctuation and even the invention of new words can be seen throughout the literature of the English Renaissance. The times and the intellectual climate probably had much more to do with Shakespeare's creative outburst than any school he attended.

Still, we do not want to dismiss altogether another implication inherent in the question: why aren't we turning out more creative language users from our schools in this century? Asking the question at least attempts to validate the importance of connecting schools and literacy to imagination and inventiveness rather than to imitation. Shakespeare aside, we will turn that one question into several. Is there a connection between schooling and creativity? Can our present schools enhance a student's desire to be more creative and imaginative? Finally, if the schools cannot do it now, how can we change them?

To begin to explore these questions, we turn to French author Albert Camus, who died in a car accident in 1960. Scholar William Drozdiak (1994, p. 5) has discussed the previously undiscovered novel, *The First Man,* which was found in "a briefcase lying in the mud a few yards away" from Camus's mangled sports car. The manuscript remained unpublished until recently, when Camus's daughter released it for publication. According to Drozdiak, the novel is significant because of its autobiographical nature. "[Camus] embarks on a kind of meandering psychological journey to explore his roots," says Drozdiak. "Until now, little has been known about Camus's thoughts on growing up without a father in a poor Algiers suburb, his upbringing by a deaf and illiterate mother, and his intellectual salvation by an inspirational teacher." Despite the obvious handicap of growing up in a home where there was probably no reading or writing, Camus went on to become a very famous writer, with the help and encouragement of a schoolteacher named Louis Germain. Drozdiak explains that Catherine Camus finally "decided to publish the unfinished book because it provided such rare insights into the character and background of her father."

It was with an eye toward uncovering some insights of our own that we interviewed the five people in this chapter. Our sample includes two writers—a poet and a novelist—two painters, and a musician. All have received recognition for their work through performance, publication, monetary rewards, or awards, but you will not find their work in *Rolling Stone* or *Art Forum* or the *New Yorker* (at least not yet). Nor are the members of this group meant to be a comprehensive cross section of writers and artists, but they are hardworking, creative people who represent a range of experiences and thus a range of possible answers to our questions about the connections between schooling and creativity.

Obviously, what most intrigues us about Camus is how the schoolteacher Germain was able to fire the young Camus's imagination and creative drive. Therefore, we asked these artists and writers to explain how and why they became what they are and what they believe should be done in our schools to turn out more creative people. Since several of them teach to support their work, they had plenty of advice on that score. Finally, using our Hegelian methodology, we synthesized their ideas with our own knowledge of pedagogical theory in an attempt to discover what schools need to do to produce not giants like Shakespeare or Woolf but plain old literate citizens who have an emancipated, imaginative use of language.

Wes: A Practical Poet

Recipe for Tea
Sunlight on her back is the first
ingredient and she lingers there
in the garden, among her vices,
the herbs and flowers and mint
growing faster than she can bear,
the sleeping breath of her girls
inside. She gathers more mint

than she'll ever need, scrubs
her harvest at the kitchen sink,
floats the choicest leaves with
two bags of tea in a gallon jar
which she carries to the garden
to brew. She washes the remaining mint

down the drain. Late in the afternoon
she fills a glass with ice and tea
and watches her girls from the kitchen

window, spinning on the grass
like dandelion seeds.
She bends herself to the faucet,
the water pulling her down
until the muscles in her neck strain
and her arms ache with the weight
of clean, wet hair and the smell
of mint rises up to meet her.

We begin this section on Wesley R. with one of his poems, because it illustrates so well what we learned about him and his practical approach to poetry and language. Now twenty-nine, Wes has lived in the same Western state his whole life. Currently, he is an English composition teacher and a graduate student who writes articles in his field as well as imaginative nonfiction essays, fiction, and poetry. As a practicing poet, he has published in small magazines like *Brushfire* and *Aethlon*.

Because he was the oldest child in a family of four sons, Wes "always felt motivated to achieve." "I don't know where that came from," he said, "possibly because I'm the oldest." His father was a high school English teacher; therefore, when Wes was growing up, there were always a lot of books around. As a child, he loved to read.

It is possible that some sort of comparison could be drawn between Wes's motivations for becoming an English teacher and poet and those of the two English teachers, Ellen and Jeanie, discussed in a previous chapter; however, such a comparison would not be accurate. Wes took a rather unusual route in his journey to become a teacher and poet. He always did well in school, like Ellen and Jeanie, and he has fond memories of a twelfth-grade English teacher: "A small woman, very conservative in many ways, but she was real interested in free expression and literature." This is similar to the literacy stories told by the two women, but Wes had another high school teacher, an accounting teacher, who had a profound effect on Wes's academic decisions right out of high school. According to Wes, "He was sort of a gruff old football coach who was on my side. And bookkeeping was something I could do; it was easy. He and I connected somehow." This teacher encouraged Wes to go to college and major in accounting.

Wes eventually got a bachelor's degree in business and marketing. But at twenty-two, he was not interested in working in business: "A lot of it [business and marketing] seems fraudulent and false to me now. It seems contrived. I don't regret the courses I took, but with different models and possibilities, I would have seen different options for myself at that point."

Two years later, Wes returned to school. He took some accounting courses, but his heart was not in it, so he signed up for two other courses. One was in library science: "I was thinking in terms of my love of books, that maybe I could turn it into a library job." His other course choice, sports literature, combined his love of both sports and literature. "I went dutifully to the accounting class until the first test, and I got a hundred on the test and lost interest. After that, the only time I went to class was for the tests, and I got an A in that course. The library class was pretty much figuring what's in the library. But the class I took for fun, the sports literature class, turned out to be an eye-opening experience, especially in terms of my writing."

The sports literature class helped rekindle Wes's old interest in language: "The instructor was a writer and poet, so all of a sudden, I had my desire for writing, which had been sublimated, brought to the surface." Wes credits this college instructor not only for encouraging his desire to write but also for the texts she chose for the class. One book in particular, he remembers, changed the way he thought about poetry. "I'm not sure what I thought poetry was," Wes said, "but it wasn't what I found in this text. We spent some time on these poems, the imagery and how it worked and what they were doing. And I decided I liked what I saw—the stories that they told in such a few words—and it impressed me. That changed what I thought about poetry."

Up to this point, Wes had always believed that poetry "wasn't something you worked at." Instead, it was "like a gift," something "divinely inspired," and "different than other writing." He said, "It was about trees and flowers and love and Shakespeare or whatever."

Wes's conception of poetry as an inspired, elite form of writing probably grew out of well-intentioned but misguided literary theories still in use in many schools today. Australian teacher-researcher Jack Thomson (1987) says that the literary theory promulgated by the New Critics and transported into the schools ignores "the reciprocity between text and reader and the relevance of a reader's individuality and extra-textual experience" (p. 100). It overemphasizes "objective" interpretation of a text. According to Thomson, "It is easy for young readers to draw the conclusion that technical skill is more important than felt literary experience" (p. 100). In other words, many students end up like Wes, believing that poetry is an enlightened and difficult form of writing, decipherable only through some vague and difficult method of analysis.

This view of poetry also distances it from the powerful, humanistic, and imaginative writing of the workaday world. The emphasis on poetry as form has probably turned millions of people away from the fact that it is merely the expression of human feelings and experiences. Many people have been educated to believe, as Wes once did, that since they cannot write in rhyme, they cannot write poetry. Worse yet, they think poetic inspiration comes from God or a muse and not from hard work like all writing. We believe most people are capable of writing poetry (though, of course, some will be better than others). Stephen Tchudi, for example, has discovered through his own teaching that all students, even those who are afraid of attempting poetry, have a natural ability for haiku. Imagine how these students feel when, as Wes did, they discover that they can write poetry.

After his own discovery of poetry as storytelling, Wes wrote a poem of his own. Although he had written poetry before this, mostly what he calls "drivel poetry," this new story poem was different, and its theme developed from fairly common human experience: "It was about baseball and not the stuff I usually wrote about. It wasn't about how some girl made me feel. It was about a new subject, and it didn't rhyme. I was trying to capture something, so I showed it to my teacher. She liked some of it, but she kind of tore it apart—how I should change this and stop moralizing here and end it there. And then I just didn't write any more poetry for a long time."

Wes did not want to make too much of the fact that his teacher was critical of his poem. This was, after all, the teacher who initially inspired him to write more poetry. His interest in poetry was piqued once again after he showed some of it to a friend and was invited to join a poetry group made up of graduate students. It was in this group that Wes was able to develop the unique combination of imagery, experience, and storytelling so evident in "Recipe for Tea."

Toward the end of our interview, it occurred to us that Wes was still struggling with the question of whether poetry is divinely inspired and dependent on some sort of unique "creative gene" or whether that creative spark is innate in all of us. In fact, the day after the interview, Paul Morris received a note from Wes. In it, Wes said he felt that "more people can write, and write poetry, than is generally assumed." Referring to his own teenage feelings of creative inadequacy, Wes said that whether we are born into artistic endeavors or not, "creativity is often not nurtured or acknowledged." As a writing teacher, Wes now attempts to remedy this by "teaching writing as if people can write." He said this allows him "to be receptive and better able to encourage" his students' efforts. "If I can open possibilities, like my teacher did for me," he wrote, "then that's great."

The rest of Wes's note dealt with his feelings about life experience and poetry, and it seemed to reinforce what we could readily see as his ability to make his poetry into storytelling. Wes brings the practicality of language to poetry—a technique drawn, no doubt, from the pragmatic view of life that first led him to consider a career in accounting or marketing. Poetry, he told us during the interview, should tell a story: "I like there to be a story in the poem. I'm not a poetry scholar or anything. I've read a little Emily Dickinson and a little Walt Whitman. I don't know the history of poetry. My poems are kind of a journal, capturing what's going on in my life."

Although originally intimidated by the elitism of poetry passed on through the New Critics and the traditional literary canon, Wes was able to adapt it to the pragmatic side of his personality:

> I think that working with and thinking about words and ideas so closely does transfer to the rest of life, even to jobs which may not seem to connect. But that's not addressing poetry directly. I don't want to assume a huge gulf between poetry and other sorts of writing, certainly not a hierarchical one. But poetry is definitely what I'm drawn to, what seems to fit my temperament and personality and attention span. And I think that writing—and poetry writing—do not exclude other life experiences and careers. Writing and poetry are ways for me to make sense of, record, resee, and revise what I experience and imagine.

For us, this makes Wes a very practical poet indeed. Wes's highly personal adaptation of poetry allows him to express through language his own particular style. And as we discovered in other interviews as well, poetry and creative energy flow from unique life experiences (Wesley R., interview with authors, Sept. 1994).

Jeff: Marching to the Beat of His Own Drum

For Jeff W., a thirty-eight-year-old professional drummer, the desire to express himself musically showed up early in his childhood: "When I was five years old, I was always beating on things—coffee cans, desks in school. It was kind of a natural thing." Jeff remembers that he was always attracted "to music and all instruments." The first instrument he wanted to play was the saxophone, and although his parents never got him one, they did buy him an acoustic guitar: "They didn't really want me to have drums because of the noise. So they bought me a guitar." Later, after Jeff's father went to Vietnam, his mother bought him a drum set: "I was in the eighth grade. She picked me up from school one day and took me to this music company for music lessons, which was very good. Instead of just buying drums and going for it, I got kind of a focus on how to approach bringing out technique that was already innate. I think this is already there inside of people. There's something inside that's already there, but there are avenues that can be taught to bring out what's already there."

In our interview with Jeff, we encouraged him to focus on the connection between his need to express himself creatively and the musical theories or techniques involved in playing his instrument. Jeff told us that it is only recently that he has become more interested in "technique" in his playing: "I guess I come more from the emotional side. But at the same time, I'm starting to put a lot more emphasis on studying technique."

"Why," we wondered, "after all these years, do you want to know about technique?"

"Learning technique," Jeff replied, "has helped me to release what's in my head to my hands." Jeff also told us that it allowed "something to click inside" of him, helping him to better "understand how to convey emotions and things that [I] already knew were there but didn't know how to express."

Despite Jeff's current interest in the technical aspects of playing an instrument, it is obvious from other statements that he began expressing himself through music with little or no knowledge of musical theory. For Jeff, this lack of theory and technique was never a handicap, probably because he always relied on that creative urge to "beat on things" that originally influenced his music: "This is going to sound real arrogant, but I'm in musical situations today with fairly good musicians who are technically more competent than me but don't understand the group dynamics of playing in a band. There's something missing in them which I think is innate. They don't understand the emotional aspect of a song, that simplicity which exists even when you're just accompanying yourself on a song."

We would not argue with Jeff's analysis of himself here; however, we might disagree with his implied assumption that only certain people are talented enough to grasp what has come to him so easily. In fact, it is quite possible that the emphasis by these "good" musicians on technique rather than on "group dynamics" or on music as an expression of experience grew out of their educational experiences, which stressed the skill of playing an instrument over the creative potential of the individual.

Many people feel a certain amount of insecurity about their abilities to express themselves, whether through art or language. Jeff's self-doubt as a musician reveals how tenuous a hold he had on the creative impulse to joyful noise: "I remember being attracted to music from way back when. Still, there was always this gut-level dichotomy inside of me that said: I really like this; I want to do this; this is great, and I have a natural affinity for it. But the other thought that went with that one said: you're really not very good; you're not going to make it because you can't do this."

In Jeff's case, his self-doubt at times led him to leave music to pursue other careers, but he "always had one foot in music." It is because of his perseverance that Jeff has become the musician he is today, but we wondered how many potential musicians become discouraged simply because playing an instrument "is too hard." We asked him if he thought the introduction of technique before someone is ready for it might thwart a person's interest in music.

Jeff answered yes to our loaded question and went on to volunteer how, through his own recent study of technique, he now sees how much he already knew about music: "By studying music more now, I'm starting to see that I already have a whole lot of basic knowledge that I was unaware of musically. And I'm starting to see how certain scales and modes I'm learning connect with patterns I already know. This stuff used to be just meaningless jargon to me, but the practical application of playing has helped me to understand it better. The theory doesn't make any sense in my head unless I can see it displayed on the instrument."

We want to be careful not to make any generalized connections between music and any of the other arts (or language, for that matter). Philosopher Susanne K. Langer ([1942] 1957) writes that "we should take warning against the fallacy of . . . assuming that through music we are studying all the arts, so that every insight into the nature of music is immediately applicable to painting, architecture, poetry, dance, and drama" (p. 209). Instead, we would use Jeff's analysis as a caution against the overemphasis of technique (or form or style) in any artistic medium, particularly in the early stages of a child's education.

We have discovered through our interviews that literacy develops as much, if not more, from doing as it does from being taught how to do. This is not to say that the two—doing and being taught—cannot reinforce each other; however, motivation and firsthand experience play a much larger role in the development of basic, critical, and dynamic literacy. Literacy is not something that results from prescribed teaching techniques. Instead, it seems to grow from a need or a desire to be an individual within a society of individuals and to relate to oneself and the rest of humanity as that unique person.

Jeff's interest in both the expressive and the technical aspects of music has grown out of these impulses. We were interested in Jeff's high regard for what he calls "the emotional" or expressive side of playing a musical instrument. Jeff continually emphasized the importance of "feeling the music" over what he usually referred to simply as "technique." He reiterated this experiential aspect of his involvement in art:

> Through good and bad times, I've been able to relate songs and music to my own experience. If I was angry, the music would get louder, and if I was happy, it got mellower. There were periods where relationship breakups became songs. A lot of my songs are

wishful-thinking songs—a made-up scenario that I wish would happen in my life. This can also reflect the tone of the music, but I don't know how conscious any of this is. I don't say, I think I'm depressed, so I'll write a song. It's just something that happens.

Jeff's concern for technique has evolved naturally, a little bit at a time. He uses music in much the same way Wes uses poetry—to express how he feels inside, and because technique or music theory has never been forced on him, he has been able to use what he learns through books (Jeff likes biographies and autobiographies of musicians), magazines, and other people to supplement what he already has learned through firsthand experience:

> By learning technique, something clicks inside of me, and this has helped me to understand how to convey emotions and feelings, which I already knew were there but didn't know how to express. There's something that goes on between what you hear in your head and how it actually comes out of your fingertips. There's a process there. I can play great in my head, but until you know how to take that thought and turn it into music, there's the dilemma for the musician. That's the whole struggle for a musician—what's in your head and how to bring it out.

Somewhere near the end of our interview, Jeff told us how happy he is now to be working full-time as a musician and not in some "greasy restaurant": "Now I have all this free time because I'm doing what I want to do—play music. And I'm trying to have fun with it."

Finally, we asked Jeff, who has lots of experience but has never taught music, how he would go about teaching a music class that allowed freedom of expression and technique to complement each other. "I know what I don't know," he told us. "So I'd use that to my advantage. There's different ways to teach music. You can teach them finger chords and songs to play. Or you can try somehow to incorporate teaching technique and theory with having fun and playing music so they can understand what's going on."

By far, most important in Jeff's music class would be "letting people get their hands on the instrument . . . even if they're just making noise." Jeff concluded, "If there is no interest there [in music], I can't make them enjoy it. But show them some easy chords, and then let them touch the instrument and play it. Just let them do that, and if there's an interest, they'll be back." Jeff's final advice to teachers supports the student-centered pedagogy we have explored throughout this book (Jeff W., interview with authors, Oct. 1994).

Diane: A Painterly Storyteller

Diane D. is forty-two years old. She grew up in Washington, D.C., where her father was an international businessman, and her mother was a librarian. Although they were not particularly supportive of her art when she was younger, they did not actually disapprove of it: "The rule from my parents was I had to choose college over art school because I might actually come to my senses." Fortunately, Diane never did come to her senses, and she is now a well-known painter with several shows to her credit. These days, she told us, her father even has a few of her paintings in his house.

To support herself as an artist, Diane also teaches art at a city high school. She remembers her own high school days as a time when she doubted her abilities and wondered whether she was "worthy enough to be an artist." She told us, "I thought about it today, when a high school girl said to me while we were sitting on the floor of a museum, 'Whoever told you you were an artist?' I told her that I didn't think anybody ever told me; I just did it. It was an interesting question though."

For a time, Diane worked as an artist-in-residence in a large, mostly rural Western state. Like the ancient Greek Sophists, Diane was a traveling teacher, and much of her teaching now is based on what she learned roaming from city to city teaching painting. Diane thinks of her paintings as narratives, stories. She developed this style from early childhood memories of the "story paintings" she did of "elephants, pilgrims, and Indians." She told us, "Instead of planning the whole thing ahead of time, I like to draw the way children draw, where you draw and tell a story at the same time—there's the mother and here's the father and here's this and here's that. I like to use storytelling in my art."

Diane remembered receiving some support from her teachers in school, but the only teacher she was able to recall vividly was a woman from middle school who emphasized design and form over storytelling: "You got one piece of paper from her for a whole week, and you got to design wallpaper on it." But Diane told us she paid little attention to teachers like this when she was in school.

We asked her how she was able to do this. "It didn't make any difference," she said. "You make art anyway. And as a teacher, I don't really think it's possible to squelch somebody's artistic talent or drive. If they're an artist, they're going to make art anyway." Since school is only a few hours out of the day, Diane does not believe that a bad teacher can inhibit an artist. (We disagree and wonder how many "bad" teachers have discouraged young writers and artists.) "What matters," she said, "is the three hours you spend in your attic or wherever after school's out. On the other hand, finding a good teacher is like finding a space capsule. They zoom you light-years ahead."

Diane told us a story about some dancers she traveled with in her artist-in-residence days: "I was watching these young boys in a small farming community doing modern dance, and suddenly I realized that the gift these artists were bringing was that we all have a right to movement, a right to music, a right to art. We not only have a right, but a need for it. But there are some people who are more gifted and are going to be the artists and writers. Others need a lot of encouragement because they're too afraid, so you have to help them along more."

Because of this and other experiences from her own childhood, Diane believes that art should be "individually tailored" to the different needs of each student. By way of example, she said, "When I started kindergarten, I wanted to play the flute with my friend Barbara. The music teacher told me I couldn't hear well enough to play any instrument. My friend was told she should play the cello because she had good hearing. Since there was only one class offered to play an instrument, I couldn't get in." We asked Diane if she thought this was right. "No," she told us, "it's wrong. There should have been a second class for people like me who like music and want to know a little bit about it but who may not want to try to be great musicians."

The idea that schools should have separate classes for different levels of enthusiasm rather than levels of supposed intellectual development, as now exists in most schools, is an interesting one. Imagine an elementary school that allows children to pick and choose certain subjects and classes, much like college students are allowed to do. This would truly be an educational process that empowers students to make decisions about the type of knowledge they believe is important.

Recently, Diane has gone back to college. She is taking a course in "descriptive grammar," and she told us that she is "really struggling" with this class, because it brings up problems she had in school as a child. "I thought I was a good writer until many people told me that I couldn't spell and my grammar was wrong. So I quit writing for a while." A college-sponsored writing project helped Diane gain more confidence in her writing. It was in this writing project that she "got back into the stories and the language and rhythm." "Then," she said, "I was tremendously happy again."

Diane believes her distress over the descriptive-grammar class is indicative of a larger problem that she associates with "right brain–left brain stuff": "When I'm in the left brain, analytical stuff, like analyzing words in this grammar class, I'm real uncomfortable." Diane found it very helpful to describe her own cognitive abilities in terms of what she sees as the compartmentalized aspect of the brain. For Diane, the left brain performs all the analytical, unpleasant functions like "grammar, driving cars, balancing the checkbook," and so forth. The right brain, however, is more emotional and experiential; it "likes pictures and stories and colors and music." Diane places a lot of emphasis on this right brain–left brain cognitive scheme, especially as it relates to her art. "I work lyrically and narratively," she said, "and I work with my emotions. When I get too analytical, my paintings lose their soul."

While we may not agree with this cognitive model, we respect and acknowledge her use of it to analyze not only her art but also her intellectual preferences. Diane told us, "When I'm asked to take a literature class and I read books and write stories and things about the stories, I love it. It's so easy and so much fun. When I'm asked to read texts, like in these education classes, I do very poorly. I'm lost and out of my element." She clearly distinguishes between what she refers to as "literature"—stories, narratives—and "texts"— textbooks. We see something more basic at fault here, and it has nothing whatsoever to do with Diane's cognitive abilities. Most textbook writers seem to have little regard for their audience, perhaps because the authors seem to have little purpose beyond disseminating information. There are, of course, many textbooks circulating that are much more entertaining (a ghastly term to use about education, but apt nonetheless). Rather than dispense dry facts, these books encourage students to connect their own knowledge and experience to what they find in the text.

In spite of the unpleasant education classes Diane is taking now, she tries hard to make her own students' introduction into the world of art as painless as possible:

> I always start with a safe project. Sometimes I'm not sure if that's a good way to start. I'm afraid the next thing might be too hard and discourage them. I think of it as building in complication. It comes from being an artist-in-residence for ten years where I only had at most two weeks with people. So I had a lot of projects that needed to be completed quickly, and the purpose was to build self-esteem and confidence in a short period of time. Now I'm learning how to make those projects deeper.

In the teaching of art, painting and drawing in particular, Diane is very careful to draw out her students, but she is never quick to point out mistakes in students' work. "Most of my students," she said, "are convinced before you even meet them that they can't do anything. They often walk in with an intensely defeated attitude. So I try to pull them out of that."

When we asked Diane what she found most difficult in teaching art to teenagers in a tough high school, she explained: "It's hard and frustrating to teach something that you love and find out they may not love it as much as you. But at the same time, high school kids are in many ways more passionate."

We found this answer intriguing and asked her to elaborate. "If you hook 'em," Diane said, "they'll work forever. They'll work on Saturdays; they'll work all night. I think you need to give them opportunities. The mural project we did for the Asian Pacific Art Festival was a wonderful opportunity. I was able to say to the kids, 'Here, go for it.'" Diane's comments here are remarkably similar to what Jeff said about letting music students get their hands on the instruments. "Just let them do that," he said, "and if there's an interest, they'll be back."

During the mural project, according to Diane, the kids did "go for it," especially one African American girl. "But," Diane complained, "the system made me fail her because she never goes to school." In spite of this girl's absenteeism, Diane sees the girl's enthusiasm and ability to express herself artistically as something extraordinary. "She just likes to paint. This girl is an incredible artist, in the true sense. She's so into this process, and so in love with it, that the fact that she's not passing school doesn't matter to her."

"Don't you think," we wondered aloud, "that we, as teachers, are missing a tremendous opportunity with this girl?"

"I can't make her go to her other classes," Diane replied. "But she's something special, and she knows it, and that's really nice." With teachers like Diane around to inspire and encourage her, we think it may be possible for this young lady to become an artist. And it's people like the next artist who encourage our optimism (Diane D., interview with authors, Sept. 1994).

Michael: The Common Bonds of Human Experience

When we spoke with Michael S., he was participating in a street exhibition similar to Diane's artist-in-residence program. The university where he taught was encouraging him and the other instructors in the art department actually to work on the street. It was kind of a public relations project that allowed the public to rub elbows with the artists and see how they worked. He was running a little late for our interview, so he asked us to join him at a little sandwich shop across from the university for lunch.

Michael is a painter who also teaches at a university in the West. He has had several showings of his work in places like Sacramento, Seattle, Clarksville, and Las Vegas. Although Michael mostly paints, he also has sculpted and even has worked with writers to combine their texts with his paintings. He believes it is important for all kinds of artists—writers, musicians, painters—to support one another.

Born in the early fifties, Michael grew up in Chicago in a tough Irish neighborhood, where he went to Catholic school: "Basically, when we were in school, there were poverty-level kids and upper-level kids. They didn't really treat the kids who didn't have money all that well." There was a lot of corporal punishment in the school Michael attended, and he, like Harold and Stanley in our chapter on motivation, remembered being punished often for acting out in school. "It was a weird thing," he said, "that this all-forgiving Catholicism was based on beating the shit out of you." Michael told us he was in trouble all the time for "being a constant asshole." Because of this, he was kicked out of his first high school.

In his second high school, things began to change for him. "I went to the second high school, and I got involved with the art department. I just started making things, and I never stopped." Michael virtually lived and slept art when he was in high school. Although Michael was often in trouble with school authorities, his art teachers usually interceded on his behalf, allowing him to do in-school suspension in the art room. Because of this, Michael credits art with saving his life:

> The thing about art is it just gave me a visual language to deal with. It was also something that I became obsessed with at a very young age. By the time I was sixteen, I was working seven days a week at the school. My teachers were also working as professional artists, and they were using the school facilities as their studio at night. They'd let me stay there at night, and I'd come in on weekends and work, too. So it was like I had these role models that I could identify with.

As in the case of Camus and many of the literate people we interviewed, Michael discovered himself through teachers who allowed him to develop his own style and worldview. His high school art teachers took him to art shows and introduced him to the work of pop artists like Claes Oldenburg and Andy Warhol. It was these teachers who helped Michael to open his eyes. He believes most of us "run around with blinders on," and he thinks this is true not just of artists, but of people in every field. "It's just being aware of the things around you," he told us, "not just spiritually, but visually." We asked him to elaborate. "It's subtle, but basic," he said. "It's the way a floor goes into a wall or a tree breaks the horizon or even the way a piece of garbage lays across the green grass. There's language in all of this; there's stories in all of this."

Whether teaching or creating, Michael is a storyteller. Since he had problems with reading and writing when he was young, his discovery of this "picture-oriented language" allowed him to create in a voice and a style all his own. Like Diane and many of the other artists in this chapter, Michael has always discovered his art in life experience. "A lot of image making and writing are stories of life," he told us.

As a storyteller, Michael believes there are things that "link us together." These, he says, are the things that are important to his art now: "A lot's being said about how different we are, but not much is said about our common bonds. There's threads of love, hate, and survival which have existed for everybody." When he is teaching, Michael likes to help his students discover those common bonds. He begins by getting his students to talk about their experiences: "It's too abstract sometimes to get them to think about the past or future. Just think about you existing right now in this time period. What's happened in the last year that's affected your life and made you perceive things differently? That's a place to start. Now, tell me the story. Okay, now visually narrate the story. Then you break it down to formal content. It's a way of getting things to move."

Experience, as we, too, have found during our years of writing instruction, often provides the easiest access to a student's critical literacy. Before children ever begin analyzing texts, they are constantly scrutinizing the world and the way it relates to the self. The much-maligned personal-narrative essay, often the first essay students are asked to write in high school and college, can be used to teach critical skills as effectively as any term or research paper can. In our experience, when the personal essay is an assignment that emphasizes what William A. Covino (1988) calls the "thoughtful uncertainty" of writing, "the attitude that necessarily informs full exploration and motivates wonder" (p. 130), students' personal narratives turn into powerful, self-searching stories that further not only their understanding of themselves but also their critical literacy.

Michael may criticize his students and others for having blinders on when it comes to "seeing" the world, but he reserves the harshest criticism for himself. He related a story about a writers' conference he attended in Montana. "It was the first time I was ever around a bunch of writers in one place. We sat up for three days talking and drinking and shootin' the shit. These writers called me an idiot, and every day they would give me a stack of books, people like Thomas McGuane, William Kittredge, and Richard Ford." We asked Michael why they called him "an idiot." "Basically for the same reason I get mad at my students when they say they haven't been reading anything for a while. 'You're making all this work,' these writers told me, 'and it's telling us stories, but you should at least read some of ours.' And they were right."

Michael says he has been reading ever since, no doubt trying to discover, through other's storytelling, some more of those "common bonds" he believes are so important to his own art and his students' education. Near the end of our interview, we began to reminisce with him about growing up in "the turbulent sixties." Michael was still deeply disturbed by the race riots he had witnessed in Chicago during those times.

As we were leaving, Michael gave us his assessment of what needs to be done in education to help make society a better place. "We have to remap the language, the educational structure, and everything else," he said. "We've got to start teaching people to get along when they're four years old, not when they have all this baggage in their thirties." It is obvious that Michael, as a teacher and an artist, is trying his damnedest to accomplish this (Michael S., interview with authors, Sept. 1994).

Eileen: A Touching Novelist

Eileen W. has been writing since she was ten years old and read John Steinbeck's *Grapes of Wrath* for the first time. "I didn't understand half of what was going on," she told us, "but it was sad. One thing I did know: this was about real people; this wasn't bullshit." One of the main reasons the book "touched" her was because her own childhood was so difficult. To escape from the pain of growing up in an unhappy home, Eileen turned to reading and writing as an escape:

> I wrote for myself—drawers of things that nobody ever saw. I wrote about life the way I wished it would be because it was very bad at home. I wrote myself into a nice world. This was in the fifties when

there was this ideal about how families were supposed to be, and our family didn't know at the time that all the other families weren't that way either. My mother wanted us to be like that, but we weren't. And I wasn't holding up my end, so I wrote about cozy, warm things.

In those early years, Eileen received no support for either her reading or her writing. She told us that her mother regularly went through her room, read what she had written, and then tore it up. "My mother," Eileen said, "told me I was insane and asked me why I wrote this kind of stuff."

Despite her mother's attempts to thwart her, Eileen continued to escape into books and her own writing. She simply learned to hide her work in safer places. In fact, for years she hid it so well that "nobody ever saw it—not family, husbands, nobody."

Then one day Eileen showed a friend something she had written, and without her knowledge, the friend gave it to a local newspaper editor. "I got a call from a weekly newspaper editor," she said, "and he gave me a job writing a column. Later, I was hired by a daily paper and wrote hard news, society stuff, everything there was to write."

Eileen worked for eight years in the newspaper business. She told us she often felt ashamed because she was the only one working for the paper who did not have a college degree. This did not, however, seem to bother her editor, who eventually gave her her own column. It was while writing for the paper that Eileen was finally able to see how her writing affected others: "All of a sudden people knew who I was, and I couldn't even go to the supermarket because people used to tap me on the shoulder. I didn't care too much for that, but I was touching these people. They'd tell me how they read my stuff and say, 'My God, I read your piece and just cried,' or 'I read your piece and just howled.' It was great to know that there were people somewhere who felt like I did." We asked her how "touching these people" made her feel as a writer. "It made me realize that I was making word pictures that would come off the page so that other people who hadn't lived in my shoes could see it and understand it. To me that's a gift. Nobody taught me that."

The phrase "touching people" came up time and time again in our conversation with Eileen. In her writing, she has always tried to make a connection with people. We recognize it as that "common bond," which Michael spoke about trying to realize in his work as both a painter and a teacher. Books like Truman Capote's *In Cold Blood,* which Eileen read when she was barely a teenager, inspired her to use words to paint her own pictures. "Capote," she told us, "touched me in a way no other author had, and I wanted to touch people. I remember writing one time, 'What do you want to do with your writing?' Then I wrote down, 'I want to touch people.'"

Eileen believes she taught herself how to write. As with the rhetorical entrepreneurs, her desire to write coupled with her desire to bring a wholeness to her life provided the motivation for her to discover the rhetorical skills that she needed. Even though she has published many times in newspapers and magazines, it was not until somebody told her that her "stuff" was good that she actually thought of herself as a writer. For years, Eileen received no support for her work. Most of her early attempts at fiction were hidden in drawers, away from the prying eyes of first her mother and father and later her first husband. Finally, she was encouraged to go public with her work by reassuring friends and readers. Because of this support, Eileen recently has felt strong enough to return to school for her undergraduate degree.

She has always wanted to go back to school, but her parents, grandparents, and everybody else told her she was not college material. "Then, I finally came back," she said, "and found out that I'm not only college material, but I'm doing pretty damn good." She has done so well, in fact, that she now works as a tutor in the campus writing center.

Eileen's enthusiasm at this point in the interview was positively inspiring. At forty-five, Eileen has been in college for two years now, and she already has begun to see an improvement in her writing. She is infatuated with knowledge and books, and we wondered how we could capture and bottle her excitement.

One could easily compare her experiences with college to those of Wes. Both were not sure they could write, but both found people willing to encourage their efforts in an academic setting.

Wes found his friendly poetry group, and Eileen found "one or two" good professors, new literary models, and an intellectual atmosphere conducive to her work. "I've never been in this kind of atmosphere," she said. "People are so smart and reading all these wonderful books. I go out there every day and wonder how much I can haul in."

It is possible that the vacuum in which Eileen wrote for so many years, although useful for the practice it gave her, was actually harmful to her writing. The idea of the lone-wolf writer busily typing away in a loft somewhere perpetuates the American stereotype of the rugged individualist making it alone, but it often denies a reading and writing self within a social context.

Eileen asked us to imagine how hard it was for her all those years when she had no one to show her writing to. "There wasn't anybody I could talk to about it until the paper," she said, "and then I had people calling me on the phone and stopping me on the street about my column." It was only after she went public with her writing, through her work at the paper and later in college, that Eileen was able to see that the things she had to say had value.

Eileen has written over thirty novels but has only recently felt confident enough to start letting people read them. She wants to be published as a novelist "more than anything in my whole life." "I live to write," she told us. Yes, and like the rest of these writers and artists, she creates in her art what she lives in her life. "Practice, practice, practice," is what she tells her students in the writing center where she works. This advice is as good for living as it is for creating art (Eileen W., interview with authors, Oct. 1994).

The Creative Synthesis of the Personal and the Public

There is a connection in these interviews between private and public writing, which we would like to emphasize. Eileen and many of these artists have been able to use their own experiences to help shape not only their style but also their work. In the beginning, Eileen used her writing as a kind of therapy to escape painful situations at home. Later, she gained confidence in herself as a writer but only after going public and receiving validation for her work. In some of his freshman writing classes, one of the authors, Paul, has researched what he calls self-revelatory writing and its relationship with public writing. Many students, he has discovered, fail to see the connection between their private writing and what they believe to be public. They are convinced that the writing they do for (and often about) themselves in a letter or a diary or even a short story is inappropriate for the essays they write even for their English classes. They feel they must somehow adopt a more academic and less personal voice.

While researching this schism in public and private writing, Paul found a textbook (*Elements of Rhetoric,* [1846] 1963) over one hundred years old that worriedly made mention of it. In the middle of the nineteenth century, its author, rhetorician Richard Whately (1787–1863), talked about the importance of "a most scrupulous care in the selection of such subjects for [composition] exercises as are likely to be interesting to the student, and on which he has (or may, with pleasure, and without much toil, acquire) sufficient information." Whately goes on to give an excellent example of this by comparing a boy's private letter to a boring class theme on "virtue" as a gift from "nature" to make all men happy. The private writing he calls "lively, unfettered, natural" and the class theme, with its emphasis on public, adultlike themes and imitation, he compares to the absurdity of dressing up a child in grown-up clothes (pp. 23–24).

We believe the distinctions, often encouraged in classrooms, between private and public writing do more to confine language and the development of individual style than they do to liberate it. Further, we think there may be a relationship between the school-induced secretiveness of private writing and the kind of double-speak that turns up in some public discourse, such as that of the admiral mentioned in Chapter One who seemed compelled to clean up or change his language for public consumption. We are not saying, of course, that different types of writing situations do not require different voices or styles. Certainly, you would not write the same type of letter to your mother as you would to the Internal Revenue Service. But if, as we suspect, the admiral's rhetoric is an example of what can happen when the private voice is completely severed from the public voice, then perhaps we should reassess the importance of this connection.

Along with their successful syntheses of the private with the public, the creative people interviewed for this chapter demonstrate a reliance on and a confidence in hands-on learning-by-doing. Whether mastering drums or a newspaper column or poetic structure, they follow a pattern we first saw with the rhetorical entrepreneurs.

This use of learning-by-doing should not be seen as implying the death of schooling. Although these writers have successfully discovered literacy on their own, Eileen's view of her present college education is encouraging: she is learning faster and more now than she ever did on her own. The schools do not, as Richard Whately saw, need to place themselves in opposition to natural learning. Indeed, common sense suggests that by aligning themselves with people's natural rhetorical powers, schools and teachers can make strong gains in developing students' reading and writing skills.

Perhaps in no other ways can this alliance be better forged than in two other areas about which our writers and artists offer suggestions—the need for community support and the need for literacy to play a role in integration and synthesis in one's life. What we are seeing is quite Hegelian, actually. It is a breaking down of traditionally perceived dichotomies, not through a quest for a simplistic happy medium or a golden mean but through a recognition that the so-called opposites influence each other in significant ways: who we are as private people inevitably shapes even the most voiceless or abstract of our writings. The need to gain support from an audience or a community invariably shapes who we are as individuals. Our work literacy is not disconnected from our private literacy. Reading and writing for aesthetic purposes helps integrate the person who reads and writes for social, political, academic, or economic purposes.

Chapter Six

The Media Literate

*If you can't physically be center stage in an auditorium
addressing a huge audience, you can most certainly be
center stage as the creator of a particular piece of work. . . .
It gives you the chance to play God in the universe of your
own choosing.*
—STEPHEN P.

*Our government could become a true democracy through
the Internet. Everybody could vote on everything.*
—MELODI R.

*If the broadcasters had any standards and would apply
them to their employees, then I think you would see not
just the Columbia School of Broadcasting but a real good
graduate program here and there.*
—WARREN O.

Back in Chapter One, we talked about the concern some people
have regarding the effects of mass communication on the public.
From Plato to Paglia, folks have both venerated and vilified the
techniques and tools used to spread the word. Our own stance is
one of cautious optimism. We realize any communication tool has
the potential to be used for ugly purposes, but we applaud the
development of any new communication device that extends the
range of the human voice and allows language to be used in new
and creative ways.

The speed at which these devices are developing may be overwhelming and intimidating to some, but the successes of television and the computer suggest that an enormous number of people are pretty excited about the future of human communication. During the month that we drafted this chapter, three innovative advances in communication were announced: Microsoft chairman Bill Gates and NBC president Robert Wright introduced a news service that will combine Internet on-line services with a cable news channel; several rock musicians, including Bush, Primus, the Residents, David Bowie, and Brian Eno, are producing a new CD format called CD Plus, which mixes audio with multimedia and can be used on your sound system or as a program on your computer; and although it is not completely user-friendly or cost-efficient enough for everybody, CD-recordable drives are now capable of doing everything from backing up entire hard drives to recording multimedia presentations or even your vacation video of Disneyland. Whether you embrace or abhor or do not care about these changes, it is clear that literate expression continues to evolve in ways our distant ancestors never could have imagined. We believe the evolution of human communication requires a reciprocal evolution in the way we school for literacy.

Just nine short years ago, Paul Morris remembers buying his first XT Turbo computer. With this machine, he could push a button and go from six megahertz to the then lightning speed of twelve megahertz. (Machines today can run at speeds of over one hundred megahertz.) At the time he bought his XT, Paul was a broadcast engineer for a major television station in San Francisco. All his friends were buying computers; in fact, many had already purchased them, and he did not want to be left behind. He bought the XT at a computer show, consulting a grocery list of components that a co-worker had helped him put together. He knew next to nothing about computers, but he wandered from one exhibit to another with his list until he finally found the machine he wanted for a little under a thousand dollars.

At home, sitting in front of the little monochrome monitor, he poked tentatively at the keyboard. Like most computer novices, he believed a finger on the wrong key could destroy his new and expensive toy. Several days of key depressing helped dispel this myth, but he still could not get the damn machine to do exactly what he wanted it to do. Finally, after making many phone calls to experienced co-workers and perusing a few badly written technical manuals, he was up and running.

Paul, for the most part, taught himself how to use computers. We say "for the most part" because the process was both experiential and collaborative. He learned about computers by reading about them, by picking the brains of every computer user and expert he had ever met, and by sitting for hours in front of a flickering monitor pressing the right and the wrong keys. Since the time that he purchased that XT, Paul has learned enough about computers to start a part-time consulting business.

His experience is not unique. Most of this generation of computer users became computer literate not by going to school but by reading books, talking with friends, and playing around with the machine. Of course, many schools now have computers and try to teach their students the basics of how to operate them. Teachers and students in such courses are quick to acknowledge that they merely explore the fundamentals, so that many, if not most, people today, young and old, are still teaching themselves how to use computers, as well as a host of other communication devices generated by the invention of the PC.

The people we interviewed for this chapter, most of whom work with computers in one way or another, are employed in some segment of the communication industry. The specialized and complex communication techniques that they have had to learn to become experts in their fields are further evidence of what we have been saying about the need for schools to move beyond the narrow notion of literacy as a simple skill that can be taught, tested, and standardized.

Ludy: Writing for Speakability

Ludy T. is a Hispanic American who works as a newswriter for a network owned-and-operated television station in Northern California. She started out writing stories for a small community paper while living in Berkeley.

"This friend of mine and I," she told us, "used to hang around a lot together during the sixties. He started putting out this community paper, and I helped him. He was a good writer, and he motivated me by telling me I could write. This is the guy that inspired me, and I probably learned what I know from him."

We noted with interest her reference to motivation for print literacy. As with most people, though, there were other influences on Ludy's literacy. She did not remember a lot about her early school years, except that she liked to read a good deal when she was growing up: "Even before puberty, I remember reading a lot of love stories and true confession magazines. That really gives you a distorted view of life and relationships, but things got mentioned in these magazines—books and titles and stories. This is what led me on to a wider range of literature."

Ludy also remembers a high school English teacher who motivated her. She told us he was "real strict" and had "high standards." "We read Dickens and that kind of stuff," she said. "That was really new to me, although I don't think I was ever very good at writing, or English for that matter." Ludy liked the class mainly because of the literature they were reading, but she never really believed that she could write.

It was around this time that Ludy began to read books about politics. "Not so much nonfiction," she said, "but novels (sorry, can't remember any titles) about high-powered politics in Washington." These books, as well as certain circumstances in her family life, helped to shape her ideas about the world. She told us, "I suppose that I always had a social conscience very early on. I had an interest in the human condition and government and human affairs. My grandparents and parents were migrant workers from Mexico, and I can remember my grandmother telling stories about some of the experiences they had with discrimination."

In college, Ludy majored in social science with a core in political science. After graduating from college with a bachelor's degree, she went to University of California, Berkeley, and met her friend who started the community newspaper for the Hispanic community. "*La Voz del Pueblo*, we called it," Ludy said. "The voice of the people. It was a Spanish-American newspaper, but it was written in English. It was about things going on in the community. It only lasted for about a year. I learned a lot about writing with it. At least it gave me more self-confidence in my writing."

After Berkeley, Ludy tried to go back to school to get a master's degree in mass communication: "My graduate adviser was an exbroadcaster, and the graduate emphasis was on TV broadcasting and very theoretical." She admits she was not a very good student, and she eventually dropped out of her graduate classes and began taking journalism classes, which she enjoyed. Ludy realized that she preferred actually writing articles to studying theories about mass communication. Finally, she dropped out altogether because she could not afford to go to school any longer.

Soon after this, thanks to her "contacts in the Hispanic community" and affirmative action, Ludy landed her first job in broadcasting. She explained to us that the lack of Hispanic journalists and broadcasters ("due to language and social problems") was the main reason she got hired at a top-forty radio station in the late 1970s. She said, "I was in the right place at the right time. I was a woman and I was Hispanic and I could write."

It is obvious to us that Ludy had a lot more going for her than affirmative action—for example, her background and her interest in social and political affairs. Here is a good place to emphasize the importance of affirmative action, however, as a tool for helping create literate citizens like Ludy, who can be role models for young people of color. While we were writing this book, the California university system eliminated its affirmative action policy. We believe that actions like this, especially in an institution of higher learning, are detrimental to the kind of human communication necessary for *all* citizens to participate effectively in this democracy.

Ludy was more than qualified for her new job at the radio station, but she had to learn the difference between writing for the print media and writing for broadcasting. Her teacher was a young news director at the station: "He was really the guy who taught me how to write for broadcasting. Basically, he simplified it for me. He'd say, 'Just pretend you're having a conversation with your mother, telling her the news.' He'd make me do these exercises, like reading newspaper stories and then condensing what I could remember of it in writing to a minute of copy. He created all these little drills for me, and he was a great teacher."

From that top-forty station, Ludy went to a larger station in San Jose. She worked there for six months, and then her Hispanic friends entered the picture again. "They told me to apply for this television job at ABC in San Francisco," Ludy said. "I was hired on full-time about a week after I started."

Ludy has been at ABC for fifteen years now, and she sees a big difference between the experiences of the young interns coming in right out of school and her own introduction to the business. She got into the business by practicing her trade in the real world. Many of the people Ludy's age, fifty or so, who have been in broadcasting for some time, started in print journalism, received degrees in the liberal arts or humanities, and became more or less self-educated in broadcasting. She described them as curious people who like to dabble in a wide variety of things. "Now," Ludy told us, "most people major in broadcasting in school. The kids coming to work for us don't seem very well informed and are kind of single-minded about what broadcasting is."

Some of Ludy's criticism of her new colleagues can be blamed on generational differences. We can envision these same interns making similar comments about the newcomers they will someday train for the station. However, we see something else at work here, too. The emphasis on specialization in many schools and universities often helps foster the misconception that schools can somehow teach the specific skills needed to, say, be a newscaster, a newswriter like Ludy, or any of a hundred other professions. Ludy, like Dennis B. in Chapter Four, lost interest in her graduate studies because she wanted the firsthand experience of writing and being a journalist. For whatever reasons, the graduate program she enrolled in was unable to fulfill these literacy needs for her. It was a combination of influences—social (family heritage), experiential (internship on the community paper), and academic (writing practice in journalism and other classes)—that convinced Ludy she was, as Dennis so aptly put it, "ready to do it."

Ludy later admitted that since she did not know all of the interns personally, she probably should not generalize about what they had or had not learned about broadcasting in school. She did say, however, that the new recruits almost always required training in the techniques of writing for a real television news show. We were curious about what she did to bring the new people up to speed:

> Essentially, it's like teaching people how to manipulate things and make them more palatable for other people. You emphasize the most sensational aspects of any story, what we call "punching up" the story. And then there's the actual writing. Besides being conver-

sational, the style is very action oriented. Time, too, is important, since no story is longer than three minutes and most are only thirty seconds.

Finally, I usually give them the same advice that that news director gave me. Just pretend you're having that conversation with your mother. Don't go into depth. Cover the basics. Make it a conversational style because it's not print. Broadcasting is scripted, like you're talking with somebody. There's somebody speaking the text, so it has to sound natural. It's the speakability of the written word that we're striving for.

Along with all this, Ludy told us about the collaborative aspects of working on the news. The "show," as camera operators, videotape editors, writers, producers, reporters, anchor people, and everybody else refers to the newscast, is a collaborative effort. Unless you are someone like Ted Koppel, Ludy said, you do not have much power over what goes on the air:

In a major market station, it's not just up to you. It's a collaboration between a lot of different people. What you do is just one small part. You can work on the assignment desk and assign the reporters, but you won't get to do the reporting. You also have to get permission from the different executives, all these different levels of power. Even then, when you send out the reporter, that person's going to give their perspective, and the camera person is going to shoot what they want. By the time it comes back, it gets edited by different people, so it's watered down, and not any one single vision is apparent.

Schools can prepare students to be creative, rhetorical, and multifaceted enough to gain positions as broadcast journalists, in part by promoting the kinds of things that Ludy emphasized—curiosity, an interest in all affairs human, and a good background in the liberal arts. But it will take more than just inquisitiveness and an education in English, history, or political science to turn students into professional journalists; nor can tips and pointers on writing for television turn them into TV newswriters.

We hesitate to recommend that schools teach the techniques for writing in a specific field, since these are more successfully learned on the job. We suggest more emphasis on firsthand experience in the classroom, the kinds of collaborative activities that gave Dennis and Ludy the writing practice and rhetorical skills they needed to get jobs in journalism in the first place. These activities should grow out of community-based collaboration, so that students make contact with experts in their fields and get a real feel for how the print and television media work in their communities. The teachers supervising these activities should have firsthand experience in print or broadcast journalism, preferably in both. We believe any school that takes advantage of these mechanisms for literacy has an excellent chance of producing a newswriter as good as Ludy (Ludy T., interview with authors, Nov. 1995).

Warren: A Writer Who Likes to Perform

Warren O. has been a broadcaster since 1965. Most of his work has been in commercial television, but three years ago, he quit TV and went to work for a public radio station in Los Angeles. "I should tell you," he said, "that I grew up on radio, and I believe that radio and the spoken word is a much more intellectual medium than television because of the absence of the picture and the distractions."

Warren says that he was not an early convert to television. He remembers sitting around the radio with his family, listening to the different shows. When the TV arrived in their home, he did not really watch it that much. "Oh, I watched it," he said, "but I didn't have the passion for it that others of my generation did, perhaps because we didn't get it as early as others did."

Warren recalls being encouraged to read at a very early age, even before he started school. He also recollects being read to and then being able to remember the words: "So when my mother tried to trick me by moving things around in a story, I could tell her she was reading the story wrong."

Warren's mother was a singer when she met his father. His father was a lawyer who worked for Earl Warren before and during his rise to the Supreme Court. Warren's grandfather was also a lawyer of some repute, who helped to establish the Federal Communications Commission and set up broadcast regulation in the

1930s. His great-grandfather was a lawyer, too, who at the turn of the century became mayor of Oakland, California. During the Civil War, he was an officer in charge of black troops for the North in Iowa. Later, as a friend of naturalist John Muir, Warren's great-grandfather was instrumental in starting the Sierra Club.

Warren attributes much of his interest in oratory, performance, and writing to what he calls the "performance gene" in his family background. When we reminded him that as lawyers, most of his father's ancestors were orators, Warren said, "It just seems more genetic than anything else. I think they did a lot of talking. They were all speakers in court or on the stump at one time or another. I've had that sort of public service, public involvement all my life. And as I say, I think I probably inherited that inclination."

We see good evidence of social construction rather than genetic inheritance in Warren's behavior, but inherited or not, Warren's desire to perform was never discouraged. He says that even in elementary school, he liked performing in plays. "I didn't have any particular training or push in that direction," he told us, "but I'm sure I experienced a lot of approval. I liked to do it, and once I got the approval, I continued to do it. I was probably in the third or fourth grade when I became interested in being in and writing little plays."

Here one can see what was probably the principal motivation for Warren's desire to perform—the approval of his peers. We have seen this mechanism at work over and over again in our interviews with literate citizens. Warren was not dissuaded from pursuing what comes naturally to all children—the desire to create, explore, and verbalize, to express themselves and make themselves known. Eventually, Warren would parlay this interest in oratory, writing, and performing into a job in broadcasting.

After graduating from Amherst in 1959 with a bachelor's degree in English, Warren tried graduate school at Cornell but found himself "bored with the academic life." "I felt I needed to get into the world," he said.

Around the same time, Warren's father pressured him into trying law school. Since he did well on the admissions test, he decided to give it a chance. Going to law school also meant receiving some financial help from his parents. But law school did not last even as long as graduate school. "I tried it for my father," he told us, "but I didn't like it. More than anything, I wanted to get out and do something. I didn't want to be in school anymore."

Like Ludy and Dennis, Warren had reached a point in his life when real-world experience was more important than whatever the schools had to offer. He kicked around for a while, doing everything from grave digging to working in the mail room for the office of the Secretary of Defense to working for the Library of Congress. Warren, again like Ludy and Dennis, had an active interest in the politics of his time. When Richard Nixon ran against Edmund Brown for governor of California, Warren headed west for a writing job "working indirectly with the Brown campaign."

In 1963, he was drafted into the Army and stationed at Fort Monroe (where, he informed us, Edgar Allan Poe had been a sergeant major and Jefferson Davis had been a prisoner) in the information office. "I had done a lot of writing before the Army," Warren said. "None professionally, but I had written a lot for the Library of Congress. In the Army, I ended up writing speeches for generals along with newspaper articles. I also moonlighted as a reporter for a local paper."

By the time he left the Army, he knew he wanted to write, but he was unsure how to make a living at it except in the newspaper business. "So I got a job at the *Sacramento Bee*," he said. "I worked there for eight months. I wrote low-level stories. At the time, the *Bee* also owned a television station. Eventually they came to me and asked—since I knew something about politics—if I wanted to be a reporter for their television station and cover the state capitol. I did that from 1965 to 1966."

From Sacramento, he went on to work for all the major networks, once as a news bureau chief in Washington, D.C., and ending up as an anchorperson in Los Angeles. It was while anchoring the news that he finally lost interest in television. According to Warren, he could not convey any of his political ideas in either his political stories or his investigative pieces because of the short segments he was given to present his views. Warren, like Ludy, is a bit cynical about television:

> The people who run the business just want you to fill the time with images that will hold the audience's attention. On television and

the news, they've devoted themselves to a format that almost defies comprehension of any sort of intellectual content. What you get is a series of images that go by so fast, and are intended to be so laden with meaning, that they don't last long enough for one to do anything beyond the subliminal. You see shocking pictures, happy pictures, advertising pictures, all mixed in together without any real distinction being made for the viewer. Now you even have commercials that try to look like the news.

In his current radio job, Warren can spend a whole hour on a single topic. To prepare for his show, he does considerable reading. "I also have research assistants who help me," Warren said. He especially enjoys the spontaneity of the radio format. Often the shows go off in directions he could not possibly anticipate. He compares preparing for each show to cramming for an exam: "I do these programs, get to be somewhat of an expert on something, then have to do another one the next day." The list of topics he covered in just one week was impressive—gridlock in Washington, hunger in America, and the tobacco industry. We wondered what differences Warren, as a polished orator, saw between writing and oration:

> With writing, all you have is the language, but I believe writing allows one the luxury of a certain detachment. With oratory and speaking, you have nuance and emphasis and verbal games and tricks you can play with your voice. In writing, you can anticipate the problems your audience might have with a part of your text. You can organize your thoughts and see where they go without being stuck with them. Then, if you don't like where they're going, you can always revise.

> When speaking and interviewing and talking to people live, you can't do that as easily; however, I must say that I've now gotten to where I will change directions during a show. I'll say, 'Wait a minute, we're not getting any place with this. Let's try something else,' and I'll often stop and make people clarify themselves. But it's all spontaneous and in real time, and that's a very different process from writing.

Warren thinks that his writing helps his speaking, and he was quick to suggest that anybody interested in pursuing a career in broadcasting should study English, history, and government. He contends that if reporters knew more about what they were talking about, the public would find their stories more interesting. "I think," he added, "that you ought to be required to take a test about how the government operates before you're allowed into the broadcasting business."

"But," we reminded him, "didn't you learn most of that yourself through experience?" Warren paused before he answered this question, then finally he said:

> I did learn much of it through experience. Sure. Until I learned it, I was an incompetent reporter. I hope you won't write a book that will take college administrators and others off the hook as far as their responsibility for preparing for certain kinds of jobs. If the broadcasters had any standards and would apply them to their employees, then I think you would see not just the Columbia School of Broadcasting [a technical school] but a real good graduate program here and there. You see more of them, but they sort of wax and wane according to how important it is to the people who do the hiring. And if all they're hiring for is blond hair and blue eyes and what looks good on TV, then it won't happen.

Although we address the connections between schools and the business community in another chapter, we think Warren's reference to the television industry's standards for hiring (or lack of them) says volumes about that industry's commitment to a literate society. Warren suggests that television executives may be more concerned with appearances than they are with how critically or dynamically literate their new employees are. If this is true, then they, not the schools, must take primary responsibility for the quality of their product. We assured Warren at the end of the interview that we were not trying to let public school or college administrators "off the hook," but that neither did we believe schools should become so technical and specialized that they neglected the very processes that nurtured his "performance gene" and helped him become the literate and accomplished broadcaster he is today (Warren O., interview with authors, Nov. 1995).

Stephen: A Communications Futurist

Stephen P. is a tall man in his late fifties, who wore Levi's, cowboy boots, and a Celtic earring to our meeting. "I have a huge interest in Viking lore and Egyptology," he told us, touching the earring. He has a deep and resonant voice, and during the interview, he often gestured with his arms and interlaced his fingers to convey to us the fluidity and meshing of diverse realms of what he calls the field of "human communication."

If you ask Stephen when and how he first decided to become a "human communicator," he will tell you that as far back as he can remember, he wanted to be one. The very first story he related hints at his motivational sources. Stephen was in the first grade, and his teacher asked the students to write something, anything, on the blackboard. When he was called on, Stephen went to the board and started writing. He penned, or chalked, a rather long sentence, but as he was writing it, his classmates began laughing at him. "When I sat down," he told us, "I saw that my sentence started off horizontal, then made a curve toward the bottom of the board. I was completely oblivious to it and did not know my writing made almost a ninety-degree turn toward the floor. The teacher made a comment that I'd be a great writer someday. I hope that she was prophetic."

Stephen said this story emphasizes his ability literally to block out the world's distractions when he is working. This ability to focus on his craft has enabled him to write five books and over two hundred scripts for film and video; to produce and edit numerous films and videos; and to be a technical writer, a speechwriter, an orator, and a guest speaker in many classrooms. Because of his versatility as a communicator, Stephen has a special title for himself: "I have always been fascinated with human communication, and for the last twenty-five years, I've been a member of the World Future Society. I think of myself not so much as a writer or even a human communicator but as a 'communications futurist.' In almost every project I've worked on, I've always been ten, twenty, or fifty years out in the future."

These days, Stephen is working on a nonfiction book about the *Star Trek: Voyager* television series. Although this particular project has a strong behind-the-scenes component, it allows him to draw on other interests he has in computers, art, and human psychology:

> The book has twin themes. One is that it's generally about
> *Voyager*—how it got started, why, and where it's going. Wrapped

around that is the exploration of the much larger cultural issue of what's going on with *Star Trek* in general. Why has this particular entertainment series—in all its various iterations—become such an enduring phenomenon and so generationally popular for thirty years? Few things have ever crept into every aspect of our society the way this has. I've spent hours, for example, with people at the Carl Jung Institute exploring archetypal characters and situations in the *Star Trek* TV series and films.

Since Stephen prefers to shift around to different areas of human communication, like speech, writing, audiovisuals, and computers, Paramount Pictures is setting up a page for him on their new Internet Web site. "They asked me to be one of the hosts for the site," he told us, "so that anybody worldwide can ask me questions about *Star Trek* or *Voyager* specifically. And I can do it right from home."

Like Warren's, Stephen's literacy development was driven by his desire to be center stage, but unlike Warren, Stephen never attended college. In spite of his lack of a college education, the breadth of his knowledge is astonishing, but according to him, his pursuit of knowledge has been very calculated:

> I look at areas of human communication and search for gaps or holes. Then I try to figure out how I can fill in those gaps and holes with new knowledge. I've freelanced for different magazines because I wanted that experience. I worked in-house for an ad agency because I wanted to know what that was like. In effect, there I wanted to sharpen my skills on how to present things visually in a more impactful way, a more influential way. I wanted to know how text was placed on a page, how fonts were used with pictures, etc. After I learned what I wanted to learn, I moved on to something else.

Since Stephen is self-educated, we gave him several chances to criticize schooling in the academic sphere, but he was reluctant to do so. He sees school learning as more structured and refers to his own education as deliberate but "roundabout." Still, it may have been the highly structured aspect of formal education that turned Stephen away from school. Although he loved the reading in his English classes, even *Beowulf* and Chaucer, he "detested" defining the principal parts of a sentence. "I can't tell you to this day," he said, "an adequate definition of a dangling participle or a gerund. What I have said to people in this area is that I write by feel, and that's not acceptable to a teacher."

Although we would not agree with Stephen's generalization about teachers, we continue to criticize any emphasis in the class-room on teaching literacy as a group of bookish skills that can be tested and categorized. Fortunately, Stephen did have one or two teachers who encouraged his desire to be a great communicator. He credits a forensics teacher in high school for giving him a solid foundation in oral communication—debate and public speaking.

Stephen places a great deal of importance on orality, which is not surprising given his sonorous voice and what he refers to as his "flair for the dramatic in wanting to be center stage in one way or another." "There's a psychological or emotional element attached to that which has to do with being center stage," he said. "If you can't physically be center stage in an auditorium addressing a huge audience, you can most certainly be center stage as the creator of a particular piece of work. That's kind of fun. It gives you the chance to play God in the universe of your own choosing."

Although Stephen believes words are very important, he also emphasizes communication without words, a combination of images and sound and music. Stephen, who has written or pro-duced everything from speeches to promotional films for industry, is truly a self-taught rhetorician. Whether he is working in front of an audience of Fortune 500 businesspeople talking about the future of laser discs or talking to a group of elementary school stu-dents about his new *Voyager* project, he is acutely aware of what is going on in the audience, and he adjusts his speech accordingly. "I always involve the audience in my process," he said, "so that they are drawn in and it's not just me talking to them. That, too, is important in human communication, to absolutely involve your reader and audience so that in a real sense, you own them. You have them in your grasp, and they enjoy being owned. They enjoy that part of the process that allows them to come and play in your world."

We got the impression that Stephen, as a communications futurist, was on a kind of mission to dispel the fears that many peo-ple have about using technology to facilitate and expand the range of human communication. He spoke often about viewing technological advances—from the Pentel pen to the most advanced computer—as merely tools that allow the user to communicate to the audience in a variety of different ways. Stephen believes the message is what is important and not what you are using to deliver it. "I am fascinated with what we're doing now," he said, "and where we are going in the future. By the same token, I want to know how *what* we're doing now is going to affect *where* we are in the future, and how we get there."

Five or six times a year, Stephen goes to different parts of the world, talking with research-lab people from Sony and Fuji and RCA and Philips and checking out what they are working on for the future. He feels that if he does not know what is coming out before the year, say, 2002, it will be too late for him to take advantage of it.

What, we wondered, does this mean for schools? How can schools be a part of the message that Stephen is so passionately and articulately trying to convey through his work? He told us:

> Educators need to involve more real-world influences in the classroom rather than try to do it all themselves. I don't know if that's the case at present or not. Periodically, I get asked to speak in classrooms, and I very much enjoy involving the kids in the process. It's going to take some astute and willing educators to bring them along and then hand them off to the next teacher. I don't know if there's any organized process for that in the public school system. Perhaps there needs to be.

"It's true," we said, "that you can show teachers how to take advantage of a child's natural creative curiosity, but you can't actually teach people how to be Stephen P."

"Like it or not, we are all products of our own experiences," Stephen agreed. "Some of those experiences take place in academia, and some take place on the street." Even more important, Stephen thinks all people in a literate society need to be more than just computer literate:

> Nowadays, it's not just enough to be computer literate. I think you have to be technologically literate. You need to know some basic things about all kinds of technology. There is a trend today for

more and more of these technologies to combine. Your fax machine is now a part of the computer. The printer is a scanner. People need to know just enough about them so that they don't allow them to get in the way of delivering the message. If you can read and write and are computer literate, you have a greater voice in your own destiny.

Obviously, for Stephen, it is important to gain experience in as broad an area of study as possible in order to be an adept human communicator in our society. This means throwing out traditional notions that education in literacy (or science or math) is simply imparting a group of technical skills and replacing them with a process of knowledge making that takes advantage of the student's creative interactions with and through diverse areas of human communication and knowledge.

"If I were talking to a student," Stephen told us, "I'd say: Learn as much as you can about every aspect of communication, because you will synthesize all of them. What will come out of that is a kind of a communication gestalt that will be unique to you." We could not have said it any better ourselves (Stephen P., interview with authors, Dec. 1995).

Melodi: Asking Questions About the Unimaginable

Melodi R. has a very small voice but giant ambitions. She was one of the more optimistic and inspiring people we interviewed, partly because of her refreshing worldview and partly because of her unshakable determination to become an astronomer. At age thirty, Melodi is close to reaching her goal. Currently, she is finishing up her graduate work in physics, writing her dissertation on interacting galaxies (the positions of galaxies millions of years ago), teaching classes in computers and astronomy, and working for Powernet, an Internet service provider that her friend started.

Although she probably would not refer to herself as a Trekkie, Melodi grew up watching the original *Star Trek* series, and she once listened to Gene Roddenberry give a talk about space. As a child, she was fascinated with astronomy. "I always read a lot," she told us. "I suppose that's what got me into my field, because I read every book about astronomy that I could get my hands on."

Melodi was the youngest of five children. Her two oldest sisters were grown up and out of the house by the time she was born. When Melodi was five, her father died, leaving her mother, a brother, and another sister. Her mother supported them by working as a cashier in Nevada casinos. Melodi was actually the first in her working-class family to get a college degree.

Her brother, a science buff who "never thought he could do the math," was most instrumental in pushing her toward science as a career. "He always encouraged me, which really helped out," she said. "At the time I started in the university in 1982, it was rare for a woman to go into physics. It wasn't easy to be accepted, and I became kind of a mascot for the physics department, more than a real member of it. It probably didn't help that I was shy and not very talkative."

From a very early age, Melodi had to overcome obstacles in her education that many girls and women still face today. One of her clearest memories is of being in the first grade and wanting to answer every question that the teacher asked the class: "No matter what the question was, I put my hand up. After that, I got more and more shy and didn't interact so much."

Melodi does not remember if her sudden shyness was related to gender bias in the classroom or to a change in her personality. For over twenty years, researchers like Myra Sadker and David Sadker (1994) have observed and written about sexism in the classroom. According to them, "Each time a girl opens a book and reads a womanless history, she learns she is worthless. Each time the teacher passes over a girl to elicit the ideas and opinions of boys, that girl is conditioned to be silent and to defer" (p. 44). The Sadkers blame our patriarchal culture and two centuries of American education in which, in the European tradition, girls were not allowed to attend school: "Education was the path to professions and careers open only to men" (p. 44).

Around the same time Melodi was trying to assert herself in school, she remembers being rebuffed for asking questions about God in a Bible-study class at church: "I remember in a Bible-study class, at about six or seven years old, I asked, 'Well, what does God look like?' And I was told that I wasn't supposed to ask questions like that. I thought about that a lot. If I *can* ask the question, if I'm able to ask it, then it must be okay."

We suspect that Melodi, even at a young age, had keen instincts about how to use language, and despite the obstacles put in her path by some, she managed to find a teacher who supported her desire to become an astronomer: "My sixth-grade science teacher, a woman, asked us to pick a field of science and do a project. I picked astronomy, because I'd always been interested in it. I did several things, but what I most remember is a picture I drew of what the sun would look like from Pluto."

In this project, Melodi was able to ask and even answer the kinds of questions about the unimaginable that once had prompted her to ask about God. By assigning this project and giving her students the freedom to follow their own interests, this teacher renewed a young girl's faith in herself and her ability to make knowledge. "I think," Melodi recalled, "we did several things in the one field that we picked. And that was when I realized I wanted to be an astronomer. When I realized that I would have to take physics to get to astronomy, that was a little more intimidating. I took physics in high school and thought, Well, this is okay; I can do this, and just trudged forward into college. I've never turned back."

Marching forward was not always easy for her, especially in college. In the beginning, she was afraid that someone might try to talk her out of pursuing a degree in a traditionally male-dominated field, so she avoided going to an academic adviser:

When I was eighteen years old and had just come to the university, I was afraid to see my adviser. I was afraid he'd tell me not to go into astronomy. So I picked my own classes and did my own thing and had a wonderful time the first semester. And when I finally did go see my adviser, he asked, "Why did you take all these classes?" or, "Why did you do it this way?" I told him it was my education and I felt this was the way it worked best for me.

For example, I took the lowest level of algebra over again, even though I'd taken it in high school. But that's just the way I wanted things. If I could get that foundation firmly in place, then I knew I'd be much better off when I got to another level of school. I knew this about myself, but the counselor didn't understand. So I didn't go back to him the next semester and continued on my merry path.

Melodi has enjoyed her years in college, especially now as a graduate student. "College," she says, "is a great place to experience different things, to feel out what you're best at."

Another place where people can experience different things is on the Internet, with which Melodi has become closely involved. She sees the Internet as an "exciting new tool" with much potential. "For example," she said, "our government could become a true democracy through the Internet. Everybody could vote on everything."

We informed Melodi that Ralph Nader had said something similarly optimistic in *PC World* (Crawford, 1996). He said, "The Internet is more than just a collection of databases. It's the interaction of a large community of people who see themselves as citizens rather than customers. The political activity on the Internet is a positive resurgence of democracy" (p. 193).

In response, Melodi told us, "It's getting to the point where it's so easy to use. My little boy asked me the other day about hummingbirds, so we went into the Internet. I typed in hummingbirds and it brought back pictures, what they like to eat, where you find them, and what they do. Everything like that is out there, and that's why it's so neat."

We interviewed Melodi for this chapter because of her job at Powernet, a small service that hooks several hundred users into the Internet, and because of the ten-plus years of experience she has had with computers, but during the interview, it became obvious that her connection to media literacy and the myriad forms of communication goes beyond computers into outer space. Melodi is involved with the International Ultra Violet Explorers Satellite Telescope, which has been operating since 1978. It is a device similar to a radio telescope, only it detects light waves rather than radio waves. We wondered if this was just another kind of communication tool, since this and other space telescopes and probes are now so dependent on computers for gathering data and interpreting it. Melodi thought for a moment, then said, "It's a communication tool because we're getting information from distant objects."

Not too long before we interviewed Melodi, astronomers were excited about a small probe that for forty minutes had sent data back to earth about Jupiter before burning up in its atmosphere.

"What's really interesting about those probes," she told us, "is that the computers are old by today's standards. The Jupiter probe was launched in the eighties, but the Voyager probe was launched in the late seventies, and it's still sending back data."

According to Melodi, NASA had a lot better funding when those probes were made. She blames NASA's current lack of funding on "the bad image of science" and a growing bureaucracy that hinders new and progressive research in the scientific community. Because of these problems, she thinks science is in a lot of trouble today. "Albert Einstein and Kepler," she told us, "wouldn't have survived in our scientific world because they were focused on doing their science. They wouldn't be interested in writing grant proposals, finding money, and dealing with the bureaucracy the way we have to today. I don't think they could've survived in this kind of environment."

In other words, we mused, the nature of today's scientific establishment might have prevented these acknowledged geniuses from most fully developing their critical and dynamic science literacy. Melodi credits people like Carl Sagan and Isaac Asimov, both of whom inspired her own participation in the science community, with trying to reverse this trend by popularizing science and making it more accessible to laypeople. In her own teaching, Melodi tries to demystify science, as Sagan and Asimov have done, to make the subject more approachable for her students.

"However," she said, "scientists, in general, are very conservative. They hang on very tightly to their own beliefs, even going so far as to kick people out of their groups. You can't be a part of the club if your ideas are too way out there. They've done that often throughout the ages." After saying this, Melodi paused and smiled. "It's scary to let your ideas go and be open-minded," she continued. "It's scary to believe that anything's possible."

Melodi is certainly not one of those stuffy, conservative scientists; nor did she seem to be particularly frightened of anything. Indeed, Melodi seemed to take pride in the fact that she does not have all the answers, at least not when it comes to questions about the universe. "Scientists," she said, "keep getting to that point where they think they know so much, but we don't. Astronomers think today that we only really see about 4 percent of the universe. We can detect it with our telescopes. The rest of it we can't see and have no idea what it is. When you think about that, you think, Gosh, how can we really say we know anything about any of it?"

"Do you think," we asked Melodi, "that schools are teaching that aspect of science to students?"

"We need to," she said. "The mistake we're making in school is that we're not teaching kids how to think." Melodi certainly doesn't believe that the public schools can teach her child to think. Her son goes to a Montessori school, where "the kids are encouraged to decide what they're going to work on and how they want to work on it. They have routines, but they are encouraged to make choices."

Like Stephen P., Melodi believes that experience decides who you are and how you interact with the world: "It affects the decisions that you make and the path that you take." When we asked her for a final comment on schools and literacy and learning, Melodi said:

> I think of myself as a student. Even when I finish my dissertation, I'll think of myself as a student. But I also consider myself a teacher. I think the best teachers are also students. Even when I'm working with the Internet stuff, I'm teaching people and I'm opening this wonderful world up to them. There's all this information on the Internet. As a teacher, I think you have to teach them how to fish and not feed them. That's what the most effective teaching is. It's teaching them how to think, teaching them how to find the resources they need, and teaching them how to go with their curiosities, so they can find the answers to their questions.

When we turned off our tape recorder, Melodi stayed around for a while chatting about the community work she does in the public schools. She has become something of a role model for young female would-be scientists. She often goes into the high schools to talk with teenage girls about her field and to try to convince them to become part of the scientific community. We believe that Melodi's work in her field, in teaching, and in the community is proof of the advantages to be gained from schooling for literacy in as wide a range of subjects and media as possible (Melodi R., interview with authors, Dec. 1995).

The Rhetoric and Politics of Media Literacy

In the essay "Hidden Impediments" (1985), James Moffett says that most American parents only want their children to learn enough about reading and writing to get good jobs. Moffett calls for a much more extended approach to literacy, even as he admits that critical and dynamic reading and writing are often perceived as dangerous, since they are "at least as likely to transform as to transmit culture" (p. 92). Give students too much knowledge about communication, and they may grow up to threaten the status quo. "Such an attitude," Moffett warns us, "steering ambivalently between the necessity of literacy and the threat it poses, ultimately delivers to schools the message that they should teach youngsters to read just well enough to follow orders and to write just well enough to take dictation" (p. 93). If reading and writing are dangerous, then it is easy to imagine how threatening some people must perceive television, the computer, or the Internet to be.

In fact, as we learned from our media-literate folk, it is not merely these means of communication that people fear but the ideas that can be spread by them and through them. Melodi perceives the scientific community that she belongs to as being more concerned with its own Truth(s) than in open debate or dialogue with the public. Stephen P. saw the same kind of thing in the business community when he once tried to give a speech about the technical limitations of laser discs, and half of the audience (Fortune 500 business leaders), refusing to believe him, got up and walked out. Warren criticized television executives for their myopic perceptions about what the public needs or wants to know. Ludy and he chided both the broadcasting schools for turning out ill-prepared broadcasters and the broadcasting corporations for hiring them based on their appearances and not on their knowledge or abilities. These complaints are all related to the larger concerns of schooling for literacy that we have been addressing.

There are, of course, plenty of scary ideas being spread by, say, the Internet, including things like violent right- or left-wing politics and child pornography; however, the tendency to want to damn the whole medium, rather than those delivering the scary message, creates the sort of societal dilemma that Moffett sees happening in the schools. Recently, the German government buffaloed CompuServe into cutting off access to explicit sexual material on the Internet for its four million customers. The desire to control and censor the Internet is based on the fear that consumers either are not literate enough or perhaps will become *too* literate. Either way, it implies an outside authority is needed to control the moral, intellectual, and aesthetic content of the Internet. Right or wrong, in a free society, with unlimited access to most information, some of the ideas available are not going to be as truthful or as beneficial to society as others. We believe the answer to this problem is not censorship of the medium but rather an education that teaches people to understand the political and ethical consequences of a diverse range of issues and themes. This, we submit, is why it is so important to school our literate citizens to be prepared to make the rhetorical choices necessary to distinguish between what is true and practical for them and what is not.

Along these same lines, we would like to reiterate the importance of role models like Melodi or Ludy for future media-literate citizens. Many of American parents' fears, as described by Moffett, about certain progressive ideas for communication and literacy are irrational and, in too many cases, are based on ethnocentric theories and centuries of male-dominated culture. In any true democracy it is important, no, imperative that all citizens be given equal opportunities to literacy, education, and work. Melodi and Ludy would not be where they are today without the help of government affirmative action programs and the legions of women and minorities who paved the way for these programs. While Melodi works to make it easier for young high school women to join the scientific community as equal members, Myra Sadker and David Sadker (1990) are working with groups of college teachers to eliminate sexism from college classrooms. Through successful intervention techniques, the Sadkers have helped postsecondary faculty learn to conduct classes that meet the needs of both their male and their female students.

Near the end of our interview with Stephen P., he said, "It all starts with the word. If you're not able to use the word, you're going to be in trouble as a communicator. But you can build on that foundation and then bring in a lot of other elements." We agree with him. These media-literate citizens have demonstrated the various connections the word has to areas of human communication other than print. The insights they have offered about these connections and about their various professions support our contention that schooling for critical and dynamic literacy is essential for preparation in a society as media conscious as our own.

In the last five chapters, we have shown how literacy functions holistically for adults. But lest we imply that what is good for the grown-ups is ipso facto good for the children, we need to talk with some kids.

Chapter Seven

Kids in School

I want to learn whatever I can until I figure out what I want to be. I want to know how to do what I want to do.
—GRACE J.

When you're a kid, I think every teacher's your enemy.
—JENNIFER P.

Paul Morris has just finished interviewing a freshman in a high school English class and is standing in the hall talking with an English teacher, Bob, whom he once met at a party. The school is located in the western Nevada city of Sparks. It is not thought of as one of the best high schools in the area, but neither is it one of the worst. Like most high schools across America, it has some motivated, high-achieving students and teachers and some who do not rank so high.

Bob is talking about the classes he teaches. He is a big man, middle-aged with short white hair. He has been teaching at the high school for four years. "I teach two remedial classes and two advanced English classes," he tells Paul.

"What's the difference between the two?" Paul asks.

"Attitude."

"Attitude? What do you mean?"

Bob glances over at the students streaming past in the hall. "I've got kids in my remedial classes who are just as smart as the kids in my advanced," Bob says. "But the kids in my advanced classes are college motivated. The others just don't care anymore. We're baby-sitting them until they can get out of school."

166

A male student leans up against Bob. Bob looks down at the young man. "Hi, Larry," Bob says and shoves Larry playfully away. "Larry here is one of our successes," he tells Paul. "He'll be graduating this year. Right, Larry?" Larry smiles and moves back into the stream of students. Bob watches the boy disappear down the hall. "Most of the kids want to graduate, you know," he says when he turns back to Paul. "These days you can't get into the armed services with a GED. Gotta have a high school diploma."

Paul glances at the young men and women moving past them in the hallway. It is late winter in Nevada. Soon it will be spring, and a new batch of seniors will leave the public schools for college or a job. Paul remembers his own high school days as not being a very pleasant time in his life. But there was one teacher, an English teacher who had let him read the part of Pip in Dickens's *Great Expectations*. After all these years, he can still recall how that teacher changed the way he felt about books. Watching the kids in the hall, he wonders how they will one day feel about their high school years.

"I also teach a career-training class," Bob says. "Big emphasis in this school on career training. You know what I do in my class? I show them *Endless Summer II*."

"I don't think I've seen it," Paul says.

"Doesn't matter." Bob smiles. "*Endless Summer* was about a bunch of kids surfing and partying. In the sequel, *Endless Summer II,* the kids have grown up. They're all over thirty, have their own businesses and now make a living catering to surfers and people on vacation. When the film is over, I always ask my students to tell me what they've learned about career planning. They always tell me, 'Find something you like and do it.'"

"Do you believe we can train students in high school for careers or vocations in the real world?" Paul asks.

"I don't think so," Bob says. "If you don't have a passion for it, you aren't going to pursue it. It's the same for everybody, not just kids. I was a bartender once because I used to like to drink and socialize. Now I'm a high school teacher, and at this time in my life, I'm loving it. I once read somewhere that people change jobs on the average of seven times in their lifetime. How are we going to prepare students for that?"

The Conundrum of Preparation

How, indeed? It seems to us that Bob has hit on a problem that most schools (K–12 and college) perpetuate and most students accept: school should prepare you for a career. Unfortunately, there seems to be little conscious correlation between what is taught in school and what actually takes place on the job; nor should there necessarily be any. Most of the literate citizens we interviewed for this book confirmed this point when they told us that what they had learned in school was of little help to them in their current careers.

We do not mean to suggest that school should be merely a job-training pre-factory. Even advocates of general, liberal education are often quite vague about the connection between teaching global skills—literacy and critical thinking, for example—and preparing students for the demands of later life. Indeed, some general educationists seem to take perverse pride in the impracticality of what they do: "Read *Moby Dick* now; you may thank me for it later." Actually, this discontinuity between school and life does not seem to diminish the fact that a diploma from a high school or a degree from a college is still seen as important to career-minded citizens and employers. Just having the diploma and the degree can be helpful on a résumé or job application, even though, as illustrated in previous chapters, there often seems to be little correlation between the degree and the job. Paul has a friend who graduated from the San Francisco Art Institute and parlayed his bachelor of fine arts degree into a computer job with a utility company. "All they wanted me to have was a bachelor's degree," he told Paul. Clearly, this is not uncommon.

Still, we cannot help but wonder how effective schools could be if they concentrated not on training students for specific careers but on teaching them how to operate creatively, critically, and dynamically in society. In the long run, we believe, this would be a much more practical approach to preparing students for their future roles in society. With this in mind, we asked the future literate citizens of America to give us their opinions about schooling. Of course, let us recall that most of us had major and minor gripes about schools while we were in them. Students are not necessarily the best judges of what constitutes good schooling; nevertheless, please listen carefully to what these young people have to say about what is right and what is wrong with school.

Chris: Using Imagination to Kill Boredom

Chris J. thinks it is boring to talk about "reading and writing and school stuff." It is not that he actually believes reading and writing are bad; he just does not "like talking about things that are already gone," that is, in the past. Once he settled into the interview though, Chris had quite a lot to say about his past and present experiences with school.

Chris is ten years old and in the fifth grade. "Actually," he told us, "I'm in the fifth doing sixth-grade work." He is a blond, gap-toothed boy, who tolerated but made faces at most of our questions. Chris lives with his mother, stepfather, and stepsister. His real father was killed in a car accident when Chris was a baby.

The first experiences Chris remembers about learning to read and write were with his mother and grandparents who used to read to him. "I remember reading simple books when I was really young," he told us. "When my mom saw that I was reading, she let me get a library card. When I was four, I could write my name and some simple words. I think it was from reading. I'd see the words and I'd practice them. I'd still get my *s*'s and stuff mixed up, but I could basically write."

Chris used his new library card fairly often, but mostly when he was bored, which, he told us, was "every two or three days." Once he started school, Chris proved to be an above-average student, and in the second grade he ended up in his school's Gifted and Talented Education (GATE) program and was allowed to do third-grade work. Chris has been in GATE ever since. "How do you like school?" we asked him.

Chris made a face. "It's okay, sometimes," he said. "There are some bad parts about it, like when you have to do a lot of assignments in a limited time. And then there's the good stuff, and sometimes your teachers are nice and you make lots of friends there."

In our interview with him, Chris complained about teachers who gave writing assignments in class and expected them to be finished in class. About his current teacher he said, "She gives us so much stuff, and we have to finish it by the end of the day. We're always doing other stuff, too. The homework assignments are easier."

We should note here that Chris does not have a qualitative sense of the assignments. They could be engaging, difficult, good or bad, math or history assignments. Homework is "easier" because it allows Chris to finish the work in his own time. Giving writing assignments in class is convenient for the teacher, since they can be collected and graded quickly, especially if these assignments are driven by basal-style work sheets and predictable questions that focus on a summary of the plot. Chris did say that most of the assigned writing has to do with predictions, answering questions, and miniature paragraphs. He does not actually get to write about what he called "topics," by which we figured he meant his own topics rather than the teacher's. He does, however, do journal writing in his class, although he was actually more interested in talking about his own private journaling with a friend.

"Me and my friend on the bus used to draw things and then write a story about them," Chris told us. "We had a folder full of things." He showed us some of these drawings, and we were impressed. He said he had never shown them to any of his teachers. It is interesting that Chris is already very adept at making up his own stories. Story writing is common in young boys and girls when they are growing up. As Glenda Bissex (1980) observed in her own son, children enjoy building their own books. It appears to us that Chris's teacher is drawing on a mixed bag of pedagogical practices that range from the antiquated (practice paragraphs) to the contemporary (predictions, journaling). It may be the eclectic nature of her assignments that Chris rebels against.

We do not want to single out Chris's teacher for criticism. Chris told us that she began to give more in-class assignments after her class size was doubled. According to Chris, this is a "combo class" (fifth and sixth graders together), and his teacher is not used to teaching this many students. All the students' grades went down after the class size went up. "Her grades were way up there," Chris said, "and then she got more students and her grades went way down. We used to have fourteen students, but over vacation, we got up to twenty-eight. That's when she got harder." Obviously, in larger classes, drill-and-practice assignments can be very appealing for a teacher. The students, however, usually do not find them to be much fun.

Chris, like most children his age, still has a natural creative drive that drill-and-practice and basal readers have done little to diminish. He loves to draw and write in his notebooks. He no longer is able to do it with his friend who moved to another school, but he carries his cartoon notebook wherever he goes. In fact, he had it with him when we interviewed him. The writing and drawing he does in his notebooks, he told us, "makes me think and keeps me busy."

Boredom is a killer for children. Time literally crawls along when you are a kid. Children (and most parents) have long known that using imagination and creativity can help alleviate boredom and the tedium of passing time. Chris draws space monsters and adds text to them: "It's like my imagination expands it, and I get to think about more stuff. And it relaxes me, takes all my stress off." We wonder how often Chris's teachers, perhaps with all the best intentions, have discouraged his natural desire to bring his imagination to life in his notebooks. Writing and drawing, Chris told us, is even more important than television: "It keeps my imagination going just like TV does. But TV is something you stare at. You don't do anything with it. In drawing and writing, you use your mind."

Chris has liked most of his teachers so far, but his second-grade teacher stands out as his favorite. She was always "nice and friendly and helped everybody a lot." He told us, "She'd bring in special stuff to show us all the time, like a giant salmon. We dissected it. We got to come up and touch it, and then we'd write about it in journals." This teacher obviously knew the value of letting the kids get their hands dirty in a collaborative setting. Just as obviously, she knew the value of having the kids write about their experience afterwards.

Although Chris gets good grades in his classes now, we wonder how long teachers will be able to keep him from becoming bored if he is not allowed to be more creative in the classroom. Chris remembers that he and his former drawing companion "always were talking with each other about stuff": "We both gave ideas about what to draw and then we'd mix the monster up. We'd have different ideas, but we'd each have our thoughts in there. It's like we mixed our minds together so we could decide on the age or where the monster came from."

This space monster does a lot more than just kill boredom for Chris. It teaches him to value the collaborative aspects of language;

further, it shows him that reading and writing can be valid for its own sake. Like his favorite teacher's assignments, the creation of this imaginary monster supports the development of critical skills that Chris later will use as a literate citizen (Chris J., interview with authors, Jan. 1995).

Grace: Telling Stories for Fun

Grace J. is Chris's stepsister. Her father has been married to Chris's mother for almost nine years now, but Grace has only been living with them for about six years. Before that, she lived with her mother who "moved around all the time." Now, at age thirteen, Grace has a more stable home life.

Grace likes the junior high school she attends. She also likes to write "off-the-wall" stories and read Judy Blume novels. One of her favorites is about a boy her age who has a troublesome younger brother. "The younger brother is a brat," Grace told us. "The older brother knows this, but nobody else in the family believes the younger one could do anything wrong." Grace can relate to the older brother's despair. "Chris," she said, smiling, "is my brat."

Grace is in the eighth grade and on the verge of entering high school. She found elementary school a lot easier than junior high school: "It was a lot easier than it is in junior high. I did a lot of writing in sixth grade, too. We wrote stories about things that had to do with memories." One memory writing assignment involved an old jewelry box Grace's mother had given her. Grace also remembers rewriting fairy tales, "like writing about Jack and the Beanstalk and making the giant a good guy and Jack the bad guy."

"I like to write," Grace told us. "I like to create stories." Grace's latest story is about flying carpets. In it, one of her favorite teachers is flying around on a magic carpet. This teacher just happens to be her writing and reading teacher: "He lets us write about whatever we want to. He makes us work with creative words, words that make the story stand out, but he lets us have fun with it." On the one hand, although some critics worry that this sort of free-choice imaginative writing is precisely what is wrong with the schools, we see it as quite consistent with the exploratory rhetoric of our entrepreneurs, writers and artists, movers and shakers, and other literate adults. On the other hand, many of the kids we interviewed chose favorite teachers on the basis of whether the teachers or their assignments were "fun." While we see the value of giving students engaging assignments, we also recognize that given the choice, students would much rather be entertained than be required to revise an essay or study math. Still, if schools expect students to work hard, they must challenge their imaginations with creative assignments.

Grace likes her science class because it captures and tries to nurture her own creative curiosity. "We dissected a frog," she told us. "It was gross, but it was a lot of fun. We also got to make our own radios." When we asked Grace if school-sponsored field trips were as much fun as lab, she said, "No, I don't think so." Why? "I don't know. It should be, I suppose, since you get to leave school and everything. But I like to go to lab."

Grace's assignments for her other classes, like history, are not nearly as exciting: "Usually we have to take a couple of sentences from the history books and turn it into a paragraph, make it bigger." These classes could obviously benefit from more inspired writing assignments. We were thinking along these lines when we suggested to Grace that it might be interesting if kids could make up their own stories about history, or even put themselves back in history, a common practice in writing-across-the-curriculum programs. Grace was enthusiastic. "Yeah," she said, "be a soldier in a war or be Columbus sailing to America. That would really be neat." The lawyer-mover-shaker Margaret (in Chapter Four) had proposed the same idea, suggesting that it would teach powers of synthesis and analysis. Could writing make Grace's least-favorite class, math, more enjoyable? "I think so," Grace told us.

Writing may or may not make a class "more fun," but it can make it more effective as a learning experience for children and adults. In a study done in several San Francisco schools by the National Council of Teachers of English, Arthur Applebee and Judith Langer (1987) sought to challenge the traditional notion "(1) that writing is primarily the job of the English teacher . . . and (2) that writing within other subjects has no fundamental relationship to the teaching of those subjects" (p. 150). In their study, Langer and Applebee set out to discover whether writing could make a significant contribution to the learning strategies in subjects other than English, and they concluded: "Written language does indeed make a contribution to content learning and it can support the more complex kind of reasoning that is increasingly necessary for successful performance in our complex technological and information-based culture. It becomes essential, then, to make clear and effective writing in all school subjects a central objective of the school curriculum" (p. 151).

Obviously, the operative word here is "effective." Asking students to make a couple of sentences "bigger" is undoubtedly not as effective or as creative as allowing them to write stories about a particular historical incident as if they had actually been there when it was taking place. Is it possible that what is fun or intellectually pleasurable is also what teaches students the most? Again, we invite the readers to reflect on their own experiences.

Grace's other favorite teacher and class is her technology class. The way she described it to us, it sounded very much like a computer lab. "We have assignments from all our classes, and we do them on computers," Grace said. "Depending on how we do on those assignments, that's how we get our technology grade." Grace does not have a computer of her own, but she hopes someday she will. We wondered why, aside from the games she gets to play when she is through with her assignments, she liked computers so much: "It just seems easier. Easier than using a typewriter or writing by hand, and I have more fun with computers. It just seems real comfortable to me." We would have to agree with her.

When she was younger, Grace used to write in a diary. She no longer does, but on occasion, she writes letters to friends and relatives. Most of her writing is for her reading and writing teacher. About her lack of interest for out-of-school writing Grace told us, "I guess I'm kind of bored, you know. If something catches my interest, I'll make something up." We wonder how much more writing she would do if she had that computer of her own.

Throughout our interview, Grace reiterated how much she enjoyed relating to books and making up stories. Since eight or nine years of age, her family has encouraged her to write: "They bought me things to write with, and I could write in my diary about when I went to the circus and stuff." Grace has been using writing for a long time to record and invent her own history. This desire to record and reinvent ourselves is something all human beings do not only with writing but also with painting, music, photographs, films, and now, of course, video.

Grace is still excited about learning. She is getting excellent grades, but she worries about some of her friends: "They'd rather be doing anything else than homework. They don't care about grades, just as long as they can get by with C's." According to Grace, the only reason many of them have any interest at all in school is so they can graduate: "School is almost over now, and they're working harder now because they want to graduate."

Who can say what Grace will want to do when she grows up? Even she is not sure. She plans to go to college: "I want to learn whatever I can until I figure out what I want to be. I want to know how to do what I want to do." Grace has certain expectations about the schooling she is receiving and will continue to receive. Will schools be able to teach Grace what she needs so she can become an effective, literate member of society? Or will she someday say, like many of the adults we interviewed, that school was a waste of time?

At the end of our interview, we asked Grace how she would change school to make it more interesting for herself and her friends. Her response was an obvious one: "Make it more fun." It may or may not be possible to make pleasurable *all* the work that is required for students to become critically literate, but it is certain that keeping them interested requires innovation and hard work from teachers and schools (Grace J., interview with authors, Jan. 1994).

Bart: Spiderman, Stephen King, and School

Bart C., a small, shy young man with braces, is the oldest child of three. He is fourteen years old and a freshman in high school. His mother often read to him when he was a little boy, while his father never really cared much for reading. At his mother's request, Bart went to a speech therapy class after entering elementary school. "I couldn't say my *r*'s very well," he told us, "and people couldn't understand what I was saying sometimes." Bart spent only about a year in speech class. Around this same time, he also was sent to a special reading class. "I couldn't read that well," he said. During our interview with him, Bart enunciated every word perfectly, and it is hard to believe he ever could have had a problem with reading.

Bart likes school; in fact, he says he has always liked it. His favorite classes are math and ROTC. Someday Bart wants to be a marine or a football player or a biologist, preference not necessarily in that order. In his biology class, he is being taught both creationism and evolution theories. Bart said he is "kind of in-between" as far as creationism and evolution are concerned. Bart's indecision about something as important as the origins of man suggests to us that his biology teacher is merely dispensing information and not teaching his students how to scrutinize, analyze, or synthesize—skills essential to critical and dynamic literacy—disparate theories.

Bart reads a lot, especially the horror stories of Dean Koontz and Stephen King. His mother introduced him to these authors. Often Bart and his mom discuss the plots and characters of their favorite novels, like *The Stand* and *Pet Semetary*.

His English class has been reading Shakespeare lately, and we wondered—in a possibly loaded question—if Shakespeare was as good a read as a King or Koontz story. "It's okay. I'm more into horror or supernatural stuff," he told us. None of that in Shakespeare? "There is some supernatural," he responded, "but they should try to make it more modern." How would King or Koontz rewrite it? "Probably change how they died in it. He'd also change the characters a little."

In his spare time, Bart likes to play football and create comic books. His comic books are usually the result of collaborative work with friends; however, these days, when he does it, he works more by himself. His subject matter is usually "supernatural stuff," but sometimes he, like Chris, delves into the future, "laser weapons, aliens, and stuff like that." Before he ever became interested in horror novels, Bart used to read *Spiderman* and *X-Man* comic books.

Bart tends to "hang out" with friends who like to draw and make comic books. They show each other their work, just as writers and artists might show their works in progress to other artist or writer friends. The process Bart goes through when drawing with another person is the same as it is for Chris: "We go halfway through with one person doing the drawing and the other doing the writing. Then we'd switch so it would be from both of us."

It is obvious to us that Bart has a highly developed sense of critical literacy. He also knows what he likes and is pursuing it. Unfortunately, his high school, like many others, has a traditional idea about what students should and should not be reading in the classroom. It makes no difference that Bart—through his interest in books outside the traditional academic canon of literature, through his discussions about those books with his mother, through his desire to create his own stories, and through his need to share those stories with others—has developed his own ideas about reading and writing.

We do not mean to imply here that Bart should not be reading Shakespeare or that his English class is not furthering his critical development, but perhaps he should be reading Shakespeare when he decides he wants and is ready to read Shakespeare. In spite of the fact that Bart has done okay up to now in picking out his own literature, we doubt that many of his teachers have ever asked him to evaluate or discuss the relevance of King's work. In fact, we see value in combining Bart's interest in popular culture with the plays of Shakespeare. A synthesis combining Bart's established interests with the world of Shakespeare opens up some engaging possibilities for assignments. Along these lines, a teacher might have students rewrite a scene from Shakespeare as it might have been written by their favorite authors.

Despite what anybody may think of King or Koontz or even Marvel Comics, it is this literature that inspires not only Bart's critical literacy but also his own attempts at authorship. It is interesting that when we asked Bart what was most important in his comic books, the writing or the drawing, he answered, "The writing." Why? "You can see what's going on in the pictures, but with the writing you get the whole story line."

Bart has classes in science, English, math, photography, art, and ROTC. Is he allowed to do the kind of art he likes doing in his art class? "No, not really," he told us. "But sometimes when everybody's done, they'll let you do it." Can he write stories about the future for his science or English classes? No. English is for Shakespeare, and most of his science writing is devoted to laboratory assignments.

Besides the writing and drawing Bart does for his comic books, he also writes "back and forth" to his friends via a modem in his 486-DX2 computer. Bart's mom helped him get started with computers. He belongs to one of many on-line services that offers E-mail and a chance to communicate with people all over the country. Grace would undoubtedly be envious of Bart's computer.

Bart was not too sure how he would change school, although he did mention that he might shorten classes and make the breaks longer, "so people have more time to get to class."

Of all the teachers Bart has had since he has been in school, he remembers a favorite, his fourth-grade teacher, and a least favorite, his second-grade teacher. He said the favorite "let us have fun as long as we got our work done. Before the end of class, he'd ask if you got your work done, and if you did, he'd say okay. And if you didn't, he would make sure that you got it done the next day." What about the least favorite? "My second-grade teacher just told us what to do. She taught us how to write cursive, like how to write your name and all the letters." This teacher spent a lot of time with "grammar and spelling and handwriting," demanded that all assignments be handed in on time, and allowed no "fooling around in class." Conversely, his fourth-grade teacher did not emphasize the mechanical aspects of language. He spent more time doing collaborative activities with the students and allowed them to work at their own pace.

On the basis of Bart's observations, we have no way to gauge whether or not his fourth-grade teacher was more effective than his second-grade teacher. Obviously, not all entertaining teachers are necessarily competent and not all exacting teachers incompetent. However, allowing students choice in subject matter and then engaging them in collaborative settings is a more effective and natural path to literacy than compartmentalizing language skills for drill and practice. For each of our literate adults, the desire to become "literate" in some discipline grew from the need to be a member of some literate community. They made up their minds about what *they* wanted—a job, membership in an organization, or just to please a teacher; the discipline needed to achieve their goals followed naturally. We believe this can be carried over to the classroom. Choice in the classroom, as we have learned from our own teaching, leads to disciplined learning and helps foster intellectual curiosity.

Bart may not have many ideas about how to change school, but as a future literate citizen, his likes and dislikes with respect to reading, writing, and school need to be taken seriously (Bart C., interview with authors, Mar. 1995).

Laura: The Three Stooges Meet Voice

Laura H. is sixteen years old and a high school junior. She lives with her parents and two brothers. She is the middle child. This, Laura told us, is why she does not get as much attention as the oldest and the youngest child in the family. Although she seemed dissatisfied about her position in the family with respect to her brothers, Laura said her brothers were the main reason she took to sports at a very young age: "I was really good on my T-ball team. Every time I got up to bat, I'd hit a home run."

Laura was also reading and writing well before she started kindergarten: "My mom used to sit down with me with flash cards. They had colors on them, and we had math cards, too. I was ready to go to school at four years old. I was the only person in my class who could say the whole Pledge of Allegiance. I really wanted to go to school, just because I wanted to learn. I knew what I was talking about. I knew more than most kids in kindergarten."

But somewhere along the line, Laura believes, the other kids caught up with her. She remembers school as being "easy" at first, but "then it got harder and harder." We wondered why. "Because the material got harder to understand," she explained. "I think it was easier when I was doing stuff one-on-one with my mom. I had all her attention. Now there's twenty kids in the class, and you don't get all that attention that you might need. I like the smaller classes because you get more of the teacher's attention. There's not thirty kids asking questions of her all the time." If she were in charge, how small would Laura make the classes? "I would say about twelve or thirteen students. And I think we should have more different courses to choose from, too."

Interestingly enough, as we were writing this chapter, the Nevada legislature was in heated debate over proposals to reduce class size to sixteen in grades one to three, a move that would cost the state some $60 million per year. Research presented by education experts was divided on the relationship between class size and achievement. But as one legislator suggested: "There's no need to ask the researchers. Talk to the students. Ask the parents."

Laura was very outspoken in her criticism of school and students. She thinks, for example, that English as a Second Language (ESL) classes are a waste of time: "I see all these statistics, and these people still don't know how to speak English after all these classes. I saw it on TV." It offends Laura when students speak Spanish in her English class. "This is America," she said, "and you're supposed to speak English." We do not share Laura's views on these matters and cringed at her answer, but we realize that she represents commonly held views on second-language education.

Laura also believes, like Grace, that a lot of people at her high school are not motivated to learn: "On my first day of school, this place was packed. In my English class, we started with forty people, and now there's only nine or ten. There's just tons of people dropping out of school."

Laura told us that even her boyfriend is having a hard time trying to stay in school. According to Laura, his parents are divorced, and his mother does not give him any money. To support himself, he works nights at a convenience store. "I don't think he's going to graduate this year." she said. "He has to work so much just to support himself so he can go to school. He even has to buy his own food and clothes." Laura's boyfriend has just turned eighteen and is ready to move out of his mother's house.

Laura, however, looks forward to graduation. She has a 3.5 grade point average and plans to go to college. Furthermore, reading and writing are still important to Laura. As a Catholic, recently confirmed, she is now reading the Bible more often. She also enjoys reading Stephen King and romance novels. Laura has no problem reconciling her reading of romance novels and the Bible. In fact, as discussed earlier, this shows that students are capable of picking up conventional literature on their own.

Laura likes to write lots of letters to her friends and relatives. While we were interviewing her, Laura produced a letter from a friend that she had received just that day. She said she enjoys this type of correspondence for its communicative as well as its sentimental value. She writes to her great-aunt in Minnesota regularly.

How does Laura feel about the writing she does for school? "On the first day of class, most teachers have you write a story about who you are. Then you write different stories pretending that you're a different person. In my history classes, we write these term papers, and I wish I had a better vocabulary. No one gives vocabulary anymore. I don't learn any new words. It seems like everyone knows more than I do."

As with her comments about ESL, Laura's comments here echo the misconceptions most laypeople have about the correlation between teaching things like vocabulary and grammar and developing improved literacy. In fact, Laura was concerned that her vocabulary was not as large as her cousin's in California. She also wondered why her high school English teachers did not emphasize grammar more. "I think the English teachers need to go over more grammar," she said. "I haven't had grammar since my eighth-grade year, and that teacher really went through it. I didn't like her because she was really tough and hard, but after her class, I was able to read and write better."

Laura's dislike for her teacher may be telling, but that aside, the emphasis on the mechanical aspects of language, including studying and memorizing long lists of words out of context, does little to improve even basic literacy, and it enhances critical and dynamic literacy not at all.

Nevertheless, we were intrigued by her desire for more emphasis on the mechanical aspects of language, so we asked her more questions about how her writing was going in school now. We were not too surprised to find that her last English teacher had been quite critical of her work. Apparently, Laura had been told to write an "irony" paper. Laura's story was about the Three Stooges—Larry, Moe, and Curly—on a hunting trip. In the story, Larry and Curly go crazy trying to bag a big buck, but they never find one. Moe, however, does nothing the whole trip and without any effort at all ends up killing a buck that wanders into camp—an irony story.

Since her father and brothers are avid hunters, Laura based the Larry, Moe, and Curly characters and their exploits on what she had learned about hunting from the men in her family. Unfortunately, Laura's teacher gave her a "bad grade" on the story and told her that it had no "voice" and "not enough vivid details." There is also irony in the story that Laura told us about her story. Later, her older brother took the same paper to his college English class and received an A on it. As Laura tells the rest of the story:

So I went to my teacher and told her about my brother and asked why she gave me a bad grade. She told me I didn't have any voice in my paper. I said to her, "Well, what is voice?" And she said, "It's when you can hear a person speaking inside the paper." I don't know how to get that, and every paper I write she marks me down for having no voice. And that's what kind of turned me off on writing. I did my best to get a good grade, and she tells me that I'm no good because I don't have voice.

It is obvious to us that something is very wrong here. We could easily criticize the assignment itself. For instance, what is the purpose behind emphasizing irony as a topic for a paper? However, the ambiguous design of this assignment is not nearly as troublesome as the teacher's obviously vague understanding of the dynamic of voice as it emerges in a young writer's paper. In fact, Laura's desire to experiment with voice by using male rather than female characters is highly sophisticated and similar to the way professional writers use voice.

As we write this book, we adopt a variety of different voices. All professional writers do this. Novelists often talk about becoming the characters in their books. Laura was trying to do the same thing in her story.

Had she been writing about female characters in her paper, we asked, would she have used the same kind of voice? "Probably not," she said, "because I'm a female, and I know how that feels inside. I really don't know how a male feels or how they think about things." We asked if she had tried to show how they feel. "Yes, I tried," she answered. "I studied my brother and my uncle and my dad and could see how they act and how excited they get about hunting. So I kind of used them as my characters." In our opinion, Laura's story about the Three Stooges shows evidence of her maturity as a writer.

After Laura told us about her bad experiences with writing in this high school class, it became clear why she preferred grammar drills to writing stories. The structure that drill-and-practice language exercises provide for teacher and students may seem comfortable and beneficial, but they do little to advance writing development in children or adults. Researchers like George Hillocks, Jr., (1986) have stated "grammar study has little or no effect on writing" (p. 225). Further, he adds, "the same is true for emphasis on mechanics and correctness in writing" (p. 225). There are no benefits to emphasizing structure and mechanics over creative and critical skills.

So why is it still done in many schools? It is much easier to drill students on the mechanics of language. It is easier for teachers, since they can give standardized tests for this subject matter. And it is easier for students, since they do not have to struggle to create their own texts. All the student has to do is memorize information and give it back to the teacher on a test. However, it is much more difficult for the teacher to respond to actual written texts created by students. It is messier in terms of grading and assessment and requires much more work on the teacher's part. Obviously, for the student, making knowledge is also tougher than memorizing mechanical rules.

We asked Laura what was easier, grammar drills or making up stories. "Grammar drills," she said. "You have a book in front of you that tells you how to do it. It's easier for me to do the grammar. It's really hard for me to make up stories. But once I get started on a story, I can do pretty good."

Like Bart, like all of the people we have interviewed, Laura has a voice and a story to tell. Now what was it, again, that her teacher said about voice? "You can hear yourself behind the words. I don't know what she was talking about because when I write, it's me. That's how I write." For us, Laura's voice comes through loud and clear (Laura H., interview with authors, Mar. 1995).

Jason: When Learning Becomes a Job

Sixteen-year-old Jason S.'s mother has always been the driving influence behind her son's desire to do well in school. Even though Jason would rather have been doing something else, anything else, his mom always made him sit down and do his homework. "I didn't read good, but I read," he told us. "I was too impatient doing it, so I'd throw a fit. Then I would have to do it. It was boring. I'd have rather been outside doing something."

As a child, Jason took Ritalin to counter what his mother and doctor saw as a hyperactivity problem. "I had good grades," he said, "but I was just too immature." Jason told us that this immaturity caused him to be held back a grade. This, too, was at his mother's request. At sixteen, Jason is probably one of the oldest students in his freshman class. How does he feel about this? "It's okay. I don't care. At first I didn't like it, but now it doesn't matter."

Jason plays a lot of sports in high school, especially baseball. He does not care for reading and writing much, although he reads the sports page in the newspaper and *Sports Illustrated* once in a while. Jason's mom used to make him read books when he was younger, but he has little interest in reading them now. "Now," he said, "I just read magazines unless I have a book report due in school." When he was in the fourth grade, his mother took him to special classes for reading and writing. "At first," he said, "it [reading and writing] was really hard for me, but now it's really easy."

At first, Jason did not like school much either, but now he says, "It's fine." What, we wondered, has changed? "Well, I think I finally realized that it's important to get good grades. And it will really help me out later. And it doesn't cost any money or anything." It is important, Jason told us, so he can make money in the future: "Get an education and you can get a job and not have to worry about money."

No doubt Jason's desire to get an education and do well for himself comes from his mom. She owns her own home and works for the county in the treasury office. She is also taking classes and has hopes of becoming an accountant. Besides his mother, most of Jason's relatives have encouraged and continue to encourage him to do well in school. "All of my family—my mom, my grandmother, my aunts and uncles—they'll always help me no matter what they're doing if I need help. My grandmother will pay for me to go to college."

This type of support, as we said in Chapter Two, is essential to the development of basic, critical, and dynamic literacy in any young person. However, in Jason's case, we discovered what might be a negative consequence of his mother's desire to see her son succeed in the world. Jason likes school, but in the main, he sees it not as a place to learn interesting, new things about the world but as a kind of job he must show up for every day. In fact, without sports and his friends, this particular job would be, according to Jason, very unpleasant.

School, for so many kids, is merely something they have to get through in order to get what they want out of life. Jason has watched his mother, who never went to college, struggle most of her life, while his grandmother, aunt, and uncle, who all have college degrees, have done well for themselves. "Their lives," he told us, "are a lot easier than my mom's was."

We do not deny that a college degree is worth more in society than a high school diploma, but we wonder and worry about a child's desire to learn that is based mainly on material rewards. Is it possible to present knowledge as something to be desired for its own sake? Even more to the point, can schools learn how to make learning more intellectually engaging?

We think they can. In fact, Jason and the other kids we interviewed for this chapter gave us many examples of their teachers making learning fun. Most of them gave examples of what they thought good and bad teachers did. Jason was no exception. On the one hand, he hated (worse, he has almost forgotten) his third- and fourth-grade teachers because they made learning boring: "My fourth-grade teacher just did stuff out of the books. We did a lot of field trips in the fourth grade for like no reason." On the other hand, Jason loved his fifth- and sixth-grade teachers. Why? "My fifth- and sixth-grade teachers did a lot more different things that no one else was doing. My fifth-grade teacher taught ceramics. My sixth-grade teacher did a lot of Egyptian stuff."

Jason remembered visiting mines with his fifth- and sixth-grade classes, but the most memorable trip was to a geothermal plant in Nevada. This made quite an impression on him. Jason's sixth-grade teacher encouraged a lot of writing in her class, especially letter writing. As a resident of Carson City, Nevada, she arranged for her class in Reno to write to students at a school near her home. The trip to the geothermal plant not only allowed the children to see how this type of plant operates, but it gave them a chance to meet their pen pals. "When we went to the plant," Jason said, "we actually learned something. We didn't just go there and walk around, like those stupid museums and nature areas we went to over and over before the fifth and sixth grade. When we went to the plant, we met our pen pals, too. So we got to walk around and talk with these people we'd been writing to."

Can learning and schooling be pleasurable and fulfilling for its own sake? The answer is obvious to us, but Jason has been through so many "boring" and frustrating learning experiences that he no longer is sure that school can be fun: "I think they can only make it so interesting, since they [the teachers] have to *teach,* too. Some teaching you just have to do and you can't make it fun. Teachers can't make it more fun for all those people who don't want to do it. Some stuff is just not more interesting than it is. I don't think you can make math much more interesting."

Jason sees school as a "job" because, for the most part, his teachers, and perhaps even his mother, have presented schooling as something to be endured. Given what Jason and many of the other people we interviewed have had to endure in the name of education, we sympathize with them. We asked Jason if it would be better if schools could make learning more interesting, more exciting. Perhaps then educators would not have to rely so heavily on rewards and punishments for motivation. "Yeah," he said. "That was more like elementary school, when it was fun. Now it's more like this is your job. It [high school] is something you have to do if you want to get a job, so it's like a job."

We hope it is not too late to make learning pleasurable again. Jason, like the other kids we interviewed, told us that a lot of the students in his classes "just don't care whether they do well or not anymore." Even Jason admits that when he does poorly in school, "it's usually because I didn't think it was any fun." If schools and educators cannot figure out how to make learning more interesting and entertaining, they will lose a lot more than just students. "All men have an instinctive desire of knowledge," said Aristotle in the first book of his *Metaphysics.* (Smith, [1934] 1973, p. 4). Somehow, schools need to tap into this natural drive. Nurturing this innate desire to know is essential to the schooling of literate citizens. Our lives in this society, this world, depend on it (Jason S., interview with authors, Mar. 1994).

Jennifer: When School Becomes the Enemy

Our first high school interview with Bart took place in the school cafeteria. As we spoke with him, several students—seniors, we were told—were filling out applications to different colleges around the country. The seniors all appeared to be in noisy good spirits, excited about the prospect of moving on to another level of schooling, one that perhaps allowed more freedom, personal as well as academic.

In contrast to this convivial atmosphere, when we entered the same cafeteria for our interview with Jennifer P. a few days later, we found several students sitting in gloomy silence at some distance from each other. The teacher in charge told us with some uncertainty that we could do the interview, but we had to be quiet since it was detention time. The difference in the atmosphere of the same place between this visit and our previous one was startling.

We decided to find a more congenial place to talk with Jennifer. Finally, we settled on a conference room in the counselor's office. As we started the interview, a tall, handsome man came in and introduced himself. "I'm the vice principal," he said, and he gave us his name. When we gave him ours and told him about our book, he told us that he thought a good title might be *Schooling for an Illiterate Society*. It is, of course, this rather cynical view of literacy in society that we have been trying hard to counter. Implied in his comment is a somewhat elitist view of literacy that stifles rather than encourages it. Although we are fairly sure the vice principal made the comment as kind of an insider's joke, for our ears only, the fact is he made it in front of Jennifer.

Jennifer is a sixteen-year-old high school junior. She told us that she has held several jobs while in school—clothing store clerk, Baskin-Robbins ice cream clerk, and once, work with her aunt at a law office. She is looking for a job right now because she was recently in a car accident (in her car, but no one was hurt). Jennifer was quick to inform us that she was not drinking when it happened. "It was the other person's fault," she said.

Jennifer failed her freshman English class because of absences, so now she is taking it over again. She made no excuses for this: "In middle school, they gave us a lot of breaks. But in high school you can't fool around, and I had to learn that the hard way."

Now she is taking two English classes, freshman and junior. In spite of this, Jennifer includes her current English teachers, along with her home economics instructor, among her favorites. This may be because she likes to read and discuss books and movies, that is, "as long as they're not too boring or long." "If I have time," she said, "I read on my own, but usually not big books. Judy Blume used to be my favorite. She writes little novels. One of my favorites is *Tiger Eyes*. I like a book that once you start reading it, you can't put it down. They grab you."

Jennifer associates her earliest reading and writing experiences with her older sister. She even credits her sister, two years older, with teaching her how to read using phonics: "My sister explained how to sound out words and remember spelling them. She's a very intelligent person."

Although Jennifer had some good memories about her elementary school years, what we remember most about our interview is this comment: "When you're a kid, I think every teacher's your enemy." How many students view teachers as the enemy? We are convinced that most teachers and parents would be startled by the results of any poll taken to reveal the answer to that question. But perhaps they would not be, since a fair number of teachers (and students and parents) seem to subscribe to the notion that learning is by its very nature an unpleasant experience. Teaching under such circumstances is bound to turn teachers "old and grouchy" (as Jennifer remembers too many of her elementary school teachers) and cause students to think of school as a "job," and a very undesirable one at that.

There were, of course, good teachers in Jennifer's elementary school classes. The best ones, according to her, "didn't just stand up in front of the class with the same tone of voice and explain things, like 'This is this,' and 'That is that.'" There was a teacher who, Jennifer remembered, "actually got into it and sometimes had us get up in front of the class and act out an incident that happened." Significantly, Jennifer learned from teachers like this one to take advantage of the experiential approach to learning that nearly every literate citizen we interviewed for this book has espoused in one way or another:

> Usually when I learned something or picked something up, it's usually because I went out and did it. Field trips and stuff like that helped more, as opposed to reading about it. If I read about something and then went out and looked at it, I'd remember the looking at it more than reading it. Reading sometimes I don't comprehend. I can read a paragraph and look back and not even

remember what I read. It's easier actually to see it. And my favorite teacher did that. She physically made us see what was going on.

Jennifer is ambiguous in her feelings about high school. She complained mostly about teachers who she said "just want to pass you along and get you out of their classes." If she were in charge of hiring teachers, she would "want somebody to interview every single one of them and make sure they care about the students." Jennifer also thought some of her English teachers were too much like the worst teachers she had in elementary school, the ones who tended to force their views of the world on the students:

> I love my English teachers, but I get stressed out with them. Some-times if they're explaining a story, I don't think they focus on the right points of the story. But they don't care about what my opinion might be or what I get out of the story. The teacher might think that one thing is important, and I'll think something else is impor-tant. But they'll just go completely around what I think. So we all have to learn the teacher's lesson, but we might have learned some-thing else from the story on our own.

We responded, "So you believe what you got out of the story, and the teacher believes what he or she got out of it."

"Right," she said. "And I think it would be nice to combine all of that, share what everyone got out of the story." Jennifer's ideas about reader response and knowledge sharing are very close to modern theories about literacy and knowledge making. In fact, her notion of shared knowledge is as good a definition of how knowl-edge is socially constructed as any we have heard from a literate citizen. However, it does not sound like much of this type of learn-ing is going on in many of her classes.

In many ways, Jennifer was the most informed and outspoken young person we interviewed for this chapter, and perhaps that is why we saved her for the last. She certainly was the most fluent, since most of our questions elicited long and intelligent responses from her. The shortest answer we received was when we asked if she thought high school was preparing her for the future. "It's half and half. A lot of the time I don't think they're teaching us any-thing," she said (Jennifer P., interview with authors, Mar. 1995).

Are We Listening to the Kids?

It would be easy for school administrators, teachers, and parents to disregard Jennifer's last comment as simply that of yet another disgruntled kid in high school. We think that would be a mistake. Though it has been a long time since we were in high school, we still remember thinking some things very similar about our schooling. We wonder how many of you readers might say the same thing about what you learned in high school. Of course, we need to be cautious about interpreting testimonials or antitestimonials from our student interviewees as well as our own somewhat foggy memories. It must be noted, too, that students' concerns often do not discriminate between low- and high-level problems. They might express as much concern about having too little time between classes as they do about the substantive nature of writing topics.

Stephen Tchudi once sat in on a conference presentation where high schoolers talked about how to improve the schools. At first he was disappointed, finding the students' ideas unimaginative. Primarily, they wanted less homework and more entertaining teachers. But then Stephen realized that few kids have a vision of a genuine alternative (just as most laypeople), so the high schoolers' advice involved merely tinkering with the status quo. At first glance, the ideas of the students in this chapter might seem similar—more fun, less busywork, kinder teachers. But we want to emphasize that one must look beneath the surface and genuinely listen to young people.

Obviously, we think any school that is not listening to its students is not allowing them to participate in their own education. And we reject traditional ideas about how different kids are today than they were, say, thirty or forty years ago. We have even heard people say that the kids today expect more instant gratification, leading them to a sense that they do not have to work very hard to get what they want. We disagree that kids are lazier, less aware, or in any greater need of instant gratification than, say, our generation was when we were kids. As our interviews in this chapter suggest, the kids nowadays seem to know quite well what is going on in their world, probably because they are privy to much more information through computers and the abundance (some might say overabundance) of news programs on television. Before anybody jumps to the conclusion that this is part of the problem—that kids today place too much emphasis on computers and television—we have plenty of evidence to the contrary.

For example, one of the questions we put to every young person we interviewed was whether they saw a difference between television and other literacy activities. Here is ten-year-old Chris explaining the difference between TV and his favorite pastime, making comics: "TV is something you stare at. You don't do anything with it. In drawing, you use your *own* [our emphasis] mind." Chris said virtually the same thing about the difference between reading and television: "In reading, you use your mind and you think about it. TV you just stare at it, and it's so simple to know what's happening. In books, you have to think of a picture in your mind."

Jennifer told us that reading was "a lot more specific" than television. "You can paint your own picture in your head," she said. "Your imagination can go wild because you don't have any limits. Television limits you. You have only one view of any program you're watching. You see what you see, what others want you to see."

We received similar answers from every student we interviewed. Their answers convinced us that they were capable of distinguishing between different media as well as analyzing the variety of information being disseminated through them.

Perhaps the only real danger to the present generation of young people is not laziness but rather a kind of youthful apathy brought on by a sense of powerlessness in the face of the astounding amount of data available these days. This powerlessness is no doubt being exacerbated by teaching techniques that effectively deny students the opportunity to make their own knowledge. The only way we know of to relieve this sense of powerlessness is to empower them by allowing them to participate in their own education. Part of that empowerment involves looking at schooling for literacy as more than just reading and writing. It involves validating student experiences, and in effect, giving credence to what kids already know and understand about the world. It involves building a bridge between their need for fun and our recognition that the natural human desire for knowledge *is* "fun" of the highest and most important order.

Part Three

Schooling for a Literate Society

Chapter Eight

Dialogue and Synthesis

As intellectuals we need to learn to doubt things by weaning ourselves from naive belief: we need to learn the inner act of extricating ourselves from ideas, particularly our own. We need to learn how to cease experiencing an idea while still holding it, that is, to drain the experience from an idea and see it in its pure propositionality.
—PETER ELBOW, *EMBRACING CONTRARIES: EXPLORATIONS IN LEARNING AND TEACHING*

In Chapter One, we explained that the method we use in this book is Hegelian; that is, we examine opposing, conflicting, and apparently contradictory points of view about language and literacy and then push for broad synthesis—not hollow compromise—of the many and diverse responses garnered from our interviews. Continuing in a Hegelian vein, we present this chapter as a dialectic, a dialogue between the two of us. We developed much of the material for our dialogue by mail. Stephen Tchudi was teaching in London (which explains his frequent allusions to things British) while Paul Morris was in Reno. We found this chapter one of the most interesting and rewarding to write.

We do not and will not always see eye to eye on our interpretations. That is part of the challenge we have given ourselves. By chapter's end, we will have formulated a "model," or a picture or an outline, of literacy learning that will serve as a framework for our closing discussion of schooling. The model must not be Procrustean—narrow and constraining and arbitrary—and it must explain as much observed literacy behavior as possible. At the same time, it must not be so broad as to lack specificity.

Tchudi: I think we have posed ourselves a difficult problem here, in part because we do not see eye to eye on the significance of the interviews with the youngsters in the previous chapter. I had hoped that the connection between kid literacy and adult literacy would be immediately clear, but I am concerned by the number of times we talked about "fun" and about letting the kids "do what interests them." Now, let me say that I am not opposed to fun and have long been an advocate of student-centered learning, whereby instruction begins from students' current interests and needs and then moves beyond. But I am worried that the interviews seem to imply the stereotypical touchy-feely progressivism: just let the little children do what they want; ignore the basics like spelling and grammar; let them read Stephen King; do not bother to sweat the classics; and all will be well. I do not think that is a model we want to advocate. So how can we forge a connection between what these essentially school-disaffected students say is important and what we see as the requirements for literate adults to operate successfully in the world?

Morris: I see this connection in how our literate adults became excited about learning after they found a discipline that appealed to them personally. Their motivations for achieving literacy often were prompted by a desire to be part of some group: Ellen and Jeanie wanted to be teachers; Harold and Stanley wanted be part of AA; Eileen and Wes wanted to be writers; Stephen wanted to be a human communicator; Melodi wanted to be a scientist. The hard work needed to get what they wanted, in effect, became a labor of love. The kind of choice and fun in learning activities that we are advocating for the classroom follows naturally from this connection. And we have never said that the basics are not important; instead, we have reiterated what our interviews (and others' research) have shown—that language grows socially out of experience: the more people use it, the more competent they become. Further, I see no great divide between popular and conventional literature. Didn't Laura, a big Stephen King fan, begin reading the Bible on her own? I can envision King's obsession with evil and violence as a possible starting point for the discussion of literary themes in both the Bible and the plays of Shakespeare. It bothers me that the term touchy-feely, a stereotype of certain teaching techniques from the 1960s, has become an easy way to shame potentially progressive teachers back into line with more conventional teaching practices.

Tchudi: I see where you are coming from (to use a sixties phrase). To stick to our Hegelian construct, we need to explore the nature of experience for both young people and adults, and to see the links. We are talking about experience in several senses, I think. In one sense, we are discussing the experience of language itself, and our interviews provide strong evidence that language itself is learned primarily through experience—hearing or seeing it in use, figuring it out for oneself, trying it in new situations, gaining control. Steven Pinker's 1994 book, *The Language Instinct,* does a particularly good job of arguing for and explaining human powers of figuring out how language works. I am especially impressed by his argument that we learn much more about language experientially than we could possibly learn if we just sat down and studied it, bit by bit. Pinker shows how this implies a kind of grammatical (and I would add rhetorical) faculty of mind that lets us put discrete items into bigger and bigger patterns.

But we are also, and in some ways more fundamentally, convinced that people's experiences with the world— their lives—power that mechanism: people are driven to use language to make sense of, to record, to argue about their experiences. It seems to me that this view of *experiential learning* does a pretty good job of helping to explain what we have seen in our interviews—both for young people and adults. It also helps to explain the gap

we have seen between what schools teach and what society requires. Whether we are talking with the literacy
surprises, the folks who came to literacy late in life, or
with those who were high achievers in school, we see
that their commitments to or involvement with the
world have powered their voluntary uses of and their
growth in language.

I think of Janet B., for example, the hospital public relations person, who remains insecure about her public literacy but who shows by her use of language that she is
much more literate than she thinks she is. The memorable writing from her youth was voluntary—trip journals, diaries, love letters. The school writing did not do
much for her, especially that assigned by the professor
who always attacked her interpretations of poetry. Now,
as an adult, her writing is not voluntary in the same
sense, but it is motivated in similar ways, by the need to
get a job done. That is what I mean by experiential as a
model for literacy.

Morris: First, let me say that I agree with you that our interviews
support what you have referred to as the experiential
aspect of literacy and language development. Further,
there plainly seems to be a gap between what is taught in
school and what people learn through doing. It may also
be true, however, that some people are unable to connect what they were taught in school with what they are
doing now to make a living. I am thinking specifically of
Jane W., who claims her English literature degree did
not help her much in her port authority job. I would
argue that her interpreting of complex contracts is not
that much different from her interpreting of complex
literary texts. Perhaps the real gap between school learning and firsthand experience is that in the latter, people
get to learn for themselves what is important, while in
school oftentimes, students are not allowed to decide
what they believe is important.

Tchudi: There you go again talking about student decision making. How do you reply to my gadfly assertion that kids
may not know what it is they want or *need* to discover?

Morris: I would counter with Jeff W., the musician. Do you recall his comments about letting students get their hands on an instrument so they can learn how to make noise first, before anything else? What about Michael S., the artist, and Melodi R., the astronomer, who said something similar, as did many of the writers, artists, teachers, and other professionals we interviewed? I wonder if we, as teachers, should be taking this kind of experience—this firsthand experience—into account much more than we do now.

Tchudi: I think, in fact, that teachers have a tendency to underrate the value of kids' firsthand experiences. There is a tendency to ignore altogether what they learn on the outside and to bypass personal exploration of ideas and experiences in school. By contrast, one of my favorite science teachers advocates a kind of playful "messing about" in science. Rather than giving kids preset laboratory exercises, he gives them the equipment and lets them putter around with it. They find out for themselves: what can I do with a retort? Or with a balance beam? Experiments and ideas start to flow. What can we weigh on a balance beam? Why do scientists use a balance beam rather than a bathroom scale? I wonder if maybe there should be more "messing about" at earlier and earlier levels of schooling and in all disciplines.

Morris: There is a wonderful example of a teacher who uses this approach to science told by Ira Shor and Paulo Freire (1987). This physics professor sends his students into the community to find out what fishermen and farmers and other workers think about the stars and the universe. Then he asks the students to compare their cosmological visions with those of the people in the street. Freire calls this "the critical participation of the students in their education" (p. 107). I can really see the value of placing the students' ideas in context with those of others in the general society. For one thing, it makes their own ideas seem more real, since the students can begin to see how their knowledge fits in with everyone else's.

Tchudi: This is the next step beyond "messing about." The physics teacher gave his students freedom to explore, but he is also doing a nice job of connecting up people's intuitive interpretations with those of standard science. That is precisely what we need to do with literacy to avoid the charge of touchy-feelyism.

Morris: In responding to Freire's anecdote, Ira Shor supports the physics teacher's methods because the interviews with "working people" help "ground their [the students'] academic training in reality, rather than in conceptual abstractions invented on campus." Further, he says that it helps them to "become active researchers prior to listening to a lecture on reality" (p. 108).

This idea of the student as an "active researcher" appeals to me as a teacher of reading and writing because it is grounded in the student's experience with the real world rather than what some ivory tower professor thinks the student should know about being a literate citizen in the real world.

Tchudi: Admit it, Paul, it is much easier and far less messy to take a didactic approach to teaching literacy than it is to let the student participate in the *languaging* process on a more or less equal footing with the instructor. Yet, it is the collaborative approach that according to what we have discovered in our interviews, would be most effective for students in this society.

Morris: This reminds me, too, that the experiential approach to literacy is not at all in contradiction with current social theories about language and literacy development. Writing and reading develop out of our desire to be literate members of some group or community. Learning on the job *always* takes place in a social context. Educators have often talked about making schools more real (that is, educating students according to society's vision of what a literate citizen should know), but according to many of the people we interviewed, schools obviously are not doing enough. I also wonder how much educators are doing to facilitate old-fashioned intellectual curiosity.

Let me pose this question to you: can you see any parallel between Janet B.'s doubts about her powers of literacy and Jane W.'s inability to see a connection between what she learned in school and what she now does on the job? I think the answer to this question may help shed some light on that mysterious "it" we have talked about in previous chapters with respect to languageing.

Tchudi: Let me answer with a story. The very week your letter reached me in London, the chief school inspector here enraged educators by attacking what he called "woolly headed" and "progressive" approaches to education, which, he claimed, were bringing down "standards." From his perspective, the schools were playing too much to children's "needs" and paying too little attention to "didactic" instruction. He said British teachers were doing too much "group work," which I saw as an attack on the very sort of community learning you have described. The model of education he favors puts students in rows, teaches them what their elders think they should know, and tests them to find out what they do know.

I think *his* model is woolly headed and, in its way, terribly idealistic. What people on the street and our own interviewees tell us is that just because teachers believe that particular types of knowledge are valuable does not mean that students will learn them or be able to act on those types of knowledge.

The idea of checking out students' academic learning in the community, as the physics teacher did, is helpful, provided it is not viewed as intellectual slumming or trying to see how common or intuitive knowledge somehow differs from the real thing. The Hegelian approach demands more. We must be able to explain that such language uses are part and parcel of this thing—this "it"— that we are calling literacy. I am firmly convinced after our interviews that we are talking about a common process, or set of intellectual processes, for mastering language, and not just a bunch of different or mutually

exclusive languages—job English, literary English,
physics English, and so forth. It is not that learning happens in identical ways for diverse people, but it does
seem clear that on-the-job learning and other language
learning follow a core pattern. The failure of the
schools, I believe, is that they have abstracted the pattern
and have taught it didactically, trying to substitute rules
and procedures for firsthand experience.
In answer to your question then, I see multiple parallels
between Janet's and Jane's experiences. Janet, I think,
flouted schoolhouse tradition and taught herself to write
and read "on the street." Ivan Illich (1971, 1973) would
call this "deschooled" learning. Jane's private reading
was very much deschooled, but her English major nicely
coincided with her interests and enriched them. Both
Janet and Jane are thus literate in a full and rich sense,
and both have extraordinary skill in applying their literacy in new settings. As you are hinting, I think Jane's
major was probably of more use to her than she claims,
just as Janet's true literacy is much greater than she
acknowledges.
Let me float a possible definition-description of the "it"
of literacy. What do you think of this?:

DEFINITION: Literacy is the rhetorical ability to discover the rules
and principles of discourse and the power to use, extend, and
modify those rules to accommodate one's own experiences,
understandings, and needs.

Morris: Now, since you have connected the "it" of literacy to
rhetorical ability, I would like to bring up the example of
Harold from Chapter Two who, with little or no ability to
read or write, was able to copy Safeway advertisements in
order to sell the meat in his store. I would argue that
your definition of "it" comes very close to explaining
Harold's talent for getting around his problems with
reading and writing. Harold knew how to manipulate
the rules and principles of real-world discourse.

Moreover, the idea of rhetorical discovery is important, since how we use language plays such an important role in how we make knowledge. The gap between learning how to read and write—critically and dynamically—and learning about the universe is probably not all that great. If the critic-philosopher Kenneth Burke (1962) is right, and even human motives are rhetorical, then one could extrapolate and say that human knowledge is also rhetorical. Indeed, people like science historian Thomas Kuhn ([1962] 1970) and philosopher Michel Foucault (1988) have suggested just that about knowledge making in certain disciplines.

How, then, can we teach our students, most of whom know the basics of how to read and write, how to manipulate their worlds? Perhaps even more important, how can we teach them to understand when they themselves are being manipulated?

Tchudi: My answer is to teach them to adapt the rhetorical skills they already possess to situations and problems in their lives now. To make this even more effective, we probably have to find a way to synthesize this *on-the-street literacy* with what we teach in schools.

Morris: I cannot resist noting that the classical Greek Sophists were very much street-smart guys, arguing that rhetorical abilities are a way of shaping knowledge in human affairs. Their schools were very practical; indeed, one of the more famous Sophists, Isocrates, sought to create wise men who were adept at making decisions in practical matters, such as household responsibilities, as well as in the public sphere. How did Isocrates do this? Did he take his students into the *agora*—the Greek marketplace—and show them how business was conducted in the city-state? We do not know for sure, but the idea behind his practical schooling of citizens is worth considering even today.

Coming back to the present, on television recently, I saw one of those public service spots promoting literacy. The commentator, a well-known situation-comedy actor, told the audience he enjoyed reading stories to his next-door neighbor's daughter because he knew this was helping to prepare her for school. At first, I thought, "How nice!" since reading to any preschool child is very important. Later, it occurred to me that we probably need to stop preparing children for school and start preparing them for the real world. Many schools—elementary, secondary, and even college—are set up to prepare students for successive levels of schooling rather than for real-world jobs. I wonder if Isocrates's practical approach to schooling for a literate society would facilitate what you have defined as the "it" of literacy.

Tchudi: I just realized, Paul, that in this dialogue we have drifted into talking about literacy mostly as reading and writing. We need to hold true to our preaching and teaching in Chapter One and remind ourselves that literacy is a much more encompassing topic.

Here in England, I recently heard a talk by novelist-autobiographer–political activist Doris Lessing. She reminded her audience that writing is a relatively recent approach to storytelling. She observed that for aeons people told stories orally, and the storytellers were free to rework the tales a bit to suit their own needs. Thus, stories evolved over time, drifting from the "true" tale of the original. She went on to suggest that today the lines between fiction and nonfiction, between the biography and the novel, are really rather slight. Writing may freeze a story in time, but that does not mean it is a hermetically sealed truth. In response to an audience question, Lessing said that were she to rewrite her autobiography tomorrow, she would put in new stories, take other stories out, rewrite still others. The facts of her life as written down are a matter of perception, values, interpretation, and memory. Moreover, she pointed out that the writer—novelist or biographer—writes from a variety of personalities, or personae. The persona one chooses has a great deal of influence on what will be seen and reported as truth.

Morris: That is precisely what Isocrates and the Sophists realized. Plato unfairly represented them as playing fast and
loose with the truth. What they were doing, what Lessing
does, what you and I are doing at this very moment, and
what the people in our interviews clearly were doing is
forging a story, a truth, a statement that is valid, not only
for the present, but for the future. Oral truths can easily
be modified to reflect new understandings, new data,
new needs to reach new audiences. With writing, revision is less easy. As soon as this book is published, you
and I will probably wish we could go back and revise it
just one more time.

Tchudi: My previous, tentative definition of literacy (to which, I
notice, you did not fully respond) stressed the rule-
discovering part of rhetoric. Perhaps I need to reemphasize the part that mentions finding language "to
accommodate one's own experiences, understandings,
and needs." In this century, rhetoricians and linguists
have increasingly noted the linguistic nature of understanding. Literacy—the "it"— includes a very strong
component of being able to figure out one's world. At
one level, I think that is what the young people we interviewed are talking about. I do not think they read
Stephen King just for entertainment. King is attractive
to readers because he writes about things that scare
young people and adults—the unknown, things that go
bump in the psychological night.

I would argue that great literature is also about such
problems. King and Shakespeare (who also wrote about
the supernatural) both have entertained and both have
written about deep-seated human needs and fears (as
did the Greek dramatists, of course). They, like the
Sophists and Aristotle, have expressed concern with how
people sift through experiential data. They both have
recognized (as does Lessing) that truth is not absolute
and Platonic. The literate citizen, I would argue, also
knows this, and learns it as much on the street as
through schooling. Without the "it" of a rhetorical frame
for truth, the "it" of language use becomes hollow.

Without the "it" of verbal competence, the "it" of understanding one's world becomes imprisoned. (Have I
come back to Freire and empowerment through
literacy?)

Morris: The answer to your parenthetical question is obviously
yes, since Freire believes the literacy experiences (stories)
that any individual brings to the classroom (or job or
political activity) are part and parcel of the education of
that individual. I am more interested in what you (and
Lessing) have been saying about storytelling and oral
literacy. In our time, there is a resurgence in the oral tradition of storytelling. A friend told me that in California,
specifically in the Bay Area, people are gathering in
homes to listen to storytellers spin good yarns. Storytelling festivals are being held all over the country, all
over the world, drawing skilled storytellers and eager
storylisteners. That this lost art is returning at all is really
fascinating to me. I do not, by the way, see any of this as
regressive in terms of our development as a literate society. I find it very exciting and can easily imagine a classroom that emphasizes written and oral storytelling skills.

Tchudi: I could not agree more with you on the critical importance of storytelling, Paul. As you know, there is a good
deal of interest in the role of narrative in literature these
days. One of my worries is that academics in English
departments are now discoursing learnedly on "narratol-
ogy," a process that takes the good old story and turns it
into a specimen for academic study.

Morris: Gertrude Stein said, "A rose is a rose is a rose is a rose"
([1922] 1967, p. 187), and the same goes for communication. I am reminded here of you, Steve, and your having to revert back, literally, to pen and paper during our
correspondence for this dialogue chapter because your
laptop computer went on the fritz as soon as you arrived
in London. In fact, in our private correspondence, you
said you were taking "perverse pride in not letting electronic gizmomery" slow you down, since one can use a
pen and paper to write most anywhere.

I also agree with Lessing when she talks about the blurry distinctions between fiction and nonfiction. Facts, at least as we humans attempt to define them, are notoriously overrated, especially since knowledge making and language are so inextricably connected. Kenneth Burke says in *A Rhetoric of Motives* (1962) that "whenever you find a doctrine of 'nonpolitical' esthetics affirmed with fervor, look for its politics" (p. 552). I recently saw Charles Murray, coauthor of *The Bell Curve* (Herrnstein and Murray, 1994), on television, claiming that his book, which among other things classifies African Americans as being less intelligent than whites, is not political but based on scientific evidence. Our postmodern ideas about language suggest that we should question "ultimate" truths like this, especially when, as Burke warns, they affirm a nonpolitical stance.

Nevertheless, in spite of my earlier defense of the Sophists, I would like to defend Plato's search for absolute truths and his rejection of sophistic rhetoric for just a minute. One could see Plato's objection to the Sophists as a legitimate, though pessimistic, fear of humankind's seeming inability to make ethically informed decisions through language-rhetoric. Given the nature of political rhetoric being slung around during any election year in our own century, it is easy to understand Plato's lack of faith in the power of rhetoric as a force for the good in society. We do not know how fast and loose some of the Sophists of Plato's time actually were, but we do know how slippery sophistic language users in our own century can be. Plato wanted the Sophists to take ethical responsibility for their words. We talked about something similar with respect to teaching literacy in Chapter One.

You were right to point out that we were narrowing literacy to reading and writing and that I had avoided the experiential aspect of literacy by stressing the rule-discovering part of rhetoric. I suppose by restating Ira Shor's position regarding the student as researcher, I thought I was addressing the experiential component of literacy. But let me state my stance more clearly. If one were to expand on Shor's student-as-researcher concept and make everybody a student of literacy, then all language users would probably become language researchers, at least in the sense that they are constantly sifting through their experiences in order to come up with a workable and, I hope, ethical frame for practical truths. As you have already mentioned, Steve, our Hegelian method is attempting to do the same thing for literacy. I think it is important to get that word "ethical" into any definition we might come up with for the "it" of literacy. I also want to say something about Lessing's comments on how people write from a variety of personae and how those personae influence what a writer sees and reports as the truth. These different personae, by the way, become even more obvious in oral communication. For example, I am a writer, a teacher, a husband, a grandfather, a student, a war veteran, a golfer, and a lot of other things. Each of these roles requires different communication skills. I do not act like a teacher when I am at the auto shop talking to my mechanic; on the contrary, in that situation, it is usually me who becomes the student. It seems only natural that these personae, and a host of others, would also become part of my written communication. More important, as Lessing says, whatever personality I choose to adopt has a real effect not only on how I respond to the world but also on how I envision it. This gets me back to ethics, since my choice of persona affects how I convey my version of the truth to other people.

Tchudi: I was just reading Oscar Wilde on the topic of ethics. In an essay-dialogue, "The Critic as Artist" (Wilde, 1991), one of Wilde's characters (an undisguised spokesman for Wilde himself) argues, "The sphere of Art and the sphere of Ethics are absolutely distinct and separate. . . . Art is out of the reach of morals, for her eyes are fixed upon things immortal and everchanging." Wilde uses this point to argue against censorship and for the right of the artist to say or paint or write anything he or she pleases without being concerned about offending "Puritans."

We would both agree about restraining censors, I suspect, but we would sharply disagree with Wilde about ethics and art. An ethical system is inextricably a part of all composing—painting, sculpture, storytelling, essaying, and even chitchat or gossip. Human ethics are a part of our perceiving and our thinking and thus of our expressing. A story is a bit of ethics-in-action (thus, the "moral" of all stories, stated or implied). Wilde sounds surprisingly Platonic in his concern for "things immortal and everchanging," meaning beauty and truth and all that. I see your point about Plato's quest for permanent values and ideas but would argue that both Plato and Wilde sound absolutist about those elements of experience.

Morris: We need a middle ground between absolutism (my beauty and truth forever) and absolute relativism (anything you like is beauty and everything else is truth). That middle ground (not some hollow consensus) is what the Sophists seem to have been about. For better or worse, much of what passes for truth and beauty is a product of social agreement. Much of what we mean by literacy is, in fact, skill at shaping an ethical-moral-aesthetic system through language, language that is a product of human conventions, language that incorporates social consensus about the good, the moral, the ethical. We agree that teachers should not foist their ethical systems on their students (although they should not mask their ethics or pretend that teaching is ethically and politically neutral either). The best literacy training is that which helps students develop an ethical system, a system that will be both idiosyncratic and individual as well as social and conventional.

Tchudi: George Eliot once wrote that "the highest aim in education is analogous to the highest aim in mathematics, namely, to obtain not *results* but *powers,* not particular solutions, but the means by which endless solutions may be wrought" (Eliot, 1991, p.347). I believe the "it" of literacy is those "powers," which will vary for diverse people in diverse cultures and settings but will have a common set of characteristics we see in people called literate.

Let me push us in a new direction by posing a problem for you, a Platonic one in many respects. In *The Republic,* Plato gave his view of the ideal state (one that included no rhetoricians, as we know). I propose that in the balance of this chapter, we discuss what we have come to see as our ideal, our Platonic educational program for literacy and society, based on what we have learned from our research. Let me suggest that we avoid making this overly idealistic by putting a date on our republic, say, 2025. What is your idealized vision, Paul, of what schooling for a literate society should be and become over the next quarter century?

Morris: I like this question, although my first reaction is to ask for an extension, say, to about 2080. But I will try to stay within the twenty-five–year time constraint you have put on it.

First and foremost, I think we have to start changing the way we prepare new teachers. If we started now, then within a twenty-five–year period, we might begin to see some changes in our educational system. I am afraid too many colleges are turning out school technicians rather than schoolteachers. Technicians, to me, are instructors who are more concerned with technique than with knowledge making, more concerned with dispensing information than with allowing students to synthesize, more concerned with what they teach than with what students have to contribute, and more concerned with what they know than with what they can learn from students. The teacher as technician uses such things as basal readers (formulaic texts) and standardized exams and drills to test for memorized information. The real problem is, of course, that teaching technicians often have little or no theoretical foundation underlying their pedagogies. They are merely parroting the teaching techniques they have learned in school or following the guidelines in their basal readers.

While researching for this book, I spent several days observing a very well-meaning second-grade teacher using a mishmash of phonics and whole-language techniques to teach reading to her students. When I asked her what her theory was behind this practice, she told me that whole language never worked by itself; therefore, she used a little of both. (Actually, she used damn little whole language.) Although she knew who Jean Piaget was, she had never heard of most of the current researchers, who have gone to great pains to show that languageing (literacy) is socially constructed, that the urge to language develops naturally in young children, and that children already have a pretty good handle on languageing when they enter school. By using mostly phonics, this second-grade teacher is effectively saying to her young students: everything you learned about language up to now on your own is wrong. This is the way we learn language, by breaking sounds into parts and then being drilled on it.

Tchudi: Already I have to jump in and disagree. As one who spent twenty-plus years directly involved with teacher training, I quarrel with your implied assessment of what teacher-training colleges are failing to do. By and large, incoming teachers are getting a much better education than the public schools are prepared to accept. Moreover, because of public conservatism and media pressure, teachers find themselves pushed toward the mishmash you describe. If new teachers try to draw on the new research, they are likely to wind up on the street for failing to drill on phonics or spelling or vocabulary or for not wielding the infamous red pencil and marking every last error. I know from my association with teacher trainers all over the country that English education programs typically include a good amount of theory (often resisted by undergraduates, I admit).

Their students also get firsthand experience with such ideas and practices as process writing, literary response, oral language, and contemporary linguistics, including grammar.

A big problem, it seems to me, is in the model of English offered by university English departments. Whereas students' education classes offer them an introduction to modern English teaching, their literature classes too often stress history and criticism rather than engagement. Their writing is limited to academic forms that curtail fluency and breadth. Their linguistics classes are oriented to the requirements of future doctoral students in language science rather than to the needs of language users in the real world.

My own teacher-training courses have moved steadily in an experiential direction over the years, which means that to remediate the teaching of formalist colleagues (please forgive my arrogance here), I give education students lots of reading and writing experiences that model the kind of teaching we have been describing here, letting *that* direct the flow of conversation toward theory and classroom practice. But is that enough? From my observation, a single experience or even several with whole language is not enough to overcome years of training in a formalist model. So I would have to argue for a reform of English departments to parallel your call for changes in teacher training.

Such an English program would parallel the structures of my ideal school. Courses in English would be multidisciplinary and inquiry centered, would link real-world issues and problems to academic discovery and theory, and would use writing (and language generally) to tie things together.

Morris: Certainly any move away from the teacher-as-technician mentality will require a change, not only in the way college education is delivered but also in the way schools and kids think about education. A mutual friend of ours who teaches curriculum instruction heard recently that several of his student teachers are challenging the teacher-as-technician role in the schools where they are doing their internships. One student teacher in a high school film class asked the instructor why he insisted that his high school students memorize a list of technical terms. When the instructor told him that the information was necessary for the students to pass the final, the student teacher pointed out that having them watch films in a critical way would accomplish the same thing. Give me one or two hundred of these student teachers in every state, and my ideal school will very quickly become real.

If we can change the way teachers *approach* teaching, then we can begin to change the way they think about things like testing and grading. While we were interviewing, we discovered that many public school kids have an us-versus-them mentality when it comes to their relationships with teachers and administrators. Teachers are often the enemy, perhaps because they hold all the information (what the students need to get to college or just out of school). How well students memorize that information is usually controlled through a system of rewards and punishments called grades. Lately, as we know, a great many people have begun to question the value of rewards and punishments as motivation for human behavior. They suggest that extrinsic rewards like grades are even harmful, since they do not allow students to discover any intrinsic value in education or learning for the sake of learning. In fact, grades tend to encourage the sort of career-oriented goals we found in many of the kids we interviewed for this book.

In my ideal school, testing for particular information would eventually be phased out; instead, more writing would be introduced in all classes to assess how students have synthesized, assimilated, digested, converted the subject matter of the class into a body of knowledge that is valuable to them. As you know, Steve, good research has been done on the importance of writing in all subjects (Applebee and Langer, 1987), and much more needs to be done.

My ideal school would thus do away with grades. They
have outlived their usefulness. Adults are not graded for
the work they do in the real world; instead, they are
sometimes given performance evaluations. Further, they
are often allowed to respond to these written evaluations
orally or in a letter. When I worked for ABC television,
employees were allowed to respond in writing to any
management statement placed in their files. Written
evaluations, which allow both the teacher's and the student's observations, would replace grades in my ideal
school. There are already a few colleges that use this
method; I say we make it a nationwide trend by 2025.
To relieve some of the pressures on teachers to compromise, and to prepare (and garner public support) for
the changes I want to make in the school system, I would
initiate a media blitz using the Internet, television, newspapers, magazines, and radio to help change people's
ideas about literacy. Just the other day, I read another
article throwing around literacy statistics. This one
claimed that over half the inmates in prison are illiterate. The article implied that crime and the inability to
read and write are somehow connected. Although there
may be a correlation, the implication seemed to be that
teaching inmates to read would solve the crime problem, or that better reading programs in the schools
could somehow prevent hate and violence in our cities.
Such misconceptions, as we have already stated, give the
public a simplistic view not only of complicated social
problems but also of what real literacy is all about.
Those are a few of the ways I would try to change things,
Steve. I have some way-out-there ideas too, like changing
the way new schools are built. Most of the schools I have
seen look too much like prisons or hospitals. But we
might need more than twenty-five years to change the
way schools look. By the way, would you be willing to be
one of the front men for my media blitz?

Tchudi: I would definitely join you in the media blitz, but first, I
would argue for a reeducation program for journalists.
Good education does not so much need propaganda or

advertising strategies as it does writers and publicists who
deeply understand what learning is all about. In the past
thirty years (my teaching lifetime), the schools have
been greatly damaged by journalistic editorialized
reporting of crises, declines, and the like.

But aside from all our fussing about journalists, parents,
college English teachers, and teacher trainers, let us
briefly get back to the kids and the problem I raised at
the beginning of this chapter—the apparent gap between the kids and our adult interviewees. Two ideas
especially impressed me in our discussions with people
in the workaday world. First, they were incredibly inven-
tive in discovering rhetorical forms and strategies to
solve problems that they saw as important. Second, even
their business or real-world writing was linked to their
own needs to integrate their lives. In short, we did not
find any hack writers, people pounding out writing by
formula, indifferent to what it says or who it helps or
who it hurts.

This brings me back to the students I am worrying about
and back to the ideas of fun and choice. I would argue
that literacy teachers need to become more like mentors. A mentor is not a parent, not a professor, not a
teacher. Mentors, however, do give advice freely and do
push people in new directions. A good teacher-mentor
tries to enlarge the range of experiences that young people get through books, films, and discussion, but the
teacher-mentor also realizes that the range of experiences must originate with the students' needs and
desires to integrate their own lives. The good mentor
does not say that any old thing you read or write is swell
but instead will push and nudge: "Hey, read this; I think
you'll find it interesting," or, "Let's reach out for a new
audience for your writing. How about writing a letter to
the newspaper this time?"

Morris: Earlier we talked about people like Günter Grass and
Jerome Bruner, who praised certain teachers who, as
Bruner so aptly put it, were "human event[s]" and "not
transmission device[s]" (1986, p. 126). Most of the

people we interviewed remembered teachers who could be classified as mentors. My favorite English teacher in high school broadened my appreciation of literature simply by choosing me to read the character of Pip in Dickens's *Great Expectations*. I have no idea why he picked me rather than somebody else in the class. I was not a very good student, but perhaps he saw a chance to draw me into the world of literature. Whatever his reasons, I soon found myself relating my own life to Pip's in the novel, and then I was hooked. The evidence for a strong relationship between one's own experience and literacy is presented over and over again in our interviews with both literate adults and young people. Something catches the imagination of an individual, and a passion for learning takes hold. When teachers are responsible for igniting that passion, as Diane, our artist-teacher said, "They zoom you light-years ahead."

I would add this to the ideas you have already mentioned: the literate citizens we talked with seem to have a clear understanding of literacy as much more than just learning to read and write. In fact, they often had intelligent and insightful advice on how schooling should proceed. Margaret, the lawyer, suggested allowing students to make up their own stories about history to teach them synthesis and analysis. Jeff, the musician, gave an excellent example of how a teacher-mentor might inspire students by integrating technique and firsthand experience. What about Melodi, the astronomer? Like Freire's physicist, she tells her students to bring up topics like the big bang theory during Thanksgiving dinner to coax family members into revealing their own theories about the origins of the universe. I am especially impressed with Michael's advice in Chapter Five: "We have to remap the language, the educational structure, and everything else." Their advice covers a range of skills and motivating influences, from aesthetics to critical thinking to ethics, that we see as essential to schooling for a literate society.

Tchudi: Michael's comments ring both true and worrisome. This prompts me to ask these closing questions: (1) Do you think reform of college and school education can take place on a sufficiently large scale to bring about serious changes in literacy? (2) Can we remap language and education? (3) If it is not possible to envision such a total change (and I am anticipating that your answer will not be 100 percent positive), do you think we-you-they, citizens, can create enough pockets of change to push schooling on an evolutionary path toward higher and more satisfactory literacy?

Morris: I am optimistic enough to believe that changes can take place in the way literacy is taught. Why? Recently, I have been watching a marvelous TV program, *The Human Quest* (Bingham, 1994) on PBS, about how social we humans really are and why. Scientists are discovering that our tendency to be social may have as much to do with our biological makeup, that is, how our brains are actually wired, as it does with environment. While I was watching this series, it occurred to me that many of the government social programs that began in the sixties developed out of so-called woolly headed liberal ideas—such as that society as a whole might be responsible for how individuals behave within that society—that were founded on theories that are just now finding some basis in biological fact. The problem is that the more traditional ideas of rugged individualism and the self-made person are still with us.

Remember our earlier comments about the politics of whole language versus phonics? Phonics is based on a notion of language learning that separates the individual from the rest of society by discouraging the almost instinctive curiosity and creativity that comes through learning language in a more natural social context. I think this emphasis on the individual creates similar problems in our society. Politically, it is more expedient to encourage people to tend to their own gardens than it is to ask them to lend some fertilizer to their neighbors, but biologically, we like to share—need to share.

Bear with me now, and I will begin to lead you back to my point about literacy. Most of the ideas we have presented are based on the idea that language is socially constructed. Our view of literacy depends on this and on the notion that schooling in language should be first and foremost experiential; that is, learning must take place through the experiences of the language user. There is only one way I know to experience language and that is socially. Therefore, I believe, given the current scientific validation of modern social theory, reform will take place, and the present political winds will eventually shift to accommodate a more socially minded climate in this country and perhaps in the world.

Beyond all this, I see some fairly optimistic trends in education. Despite our earlier gloomy assessment of college English departments, more and more of them are offering graduate students programs that emphasize modern writing theory, rhetorical methods, and multidisciplinary and inquiry-based research. This, coupled with access for all writers in all disciplines to campus writing centers, is going to help change the way people look at writing as a tool for inquiry and knowledge making. In addition, we are seeing similar movements toward experiential learning in other fields—mathematics, sciences, history. We observed, too, that teacher-training programs are presenting more theory about language and how it is used by children and adults. Finally, ideas about schooling and literacy will evolve because they cannot do otherwise. In your third question, Steve, you mentioned the small pockets of change that might push schooling to a higher path. These small pockets already exist. What about the student teacher who I mentioned earlier, the one who challenged the formalist methods used by the film teacher? I think there are (and will be) a lot more people out there challenging traditional notions of education.

On a bleaker note, if our notions about literacy do not change, then we may be in big trouble. *The Human Quest* states that biologists and social scientists agree that we have evolved into the social beings that we are today. However, they also believe many of our ideas about how to solve social problems have yet to evolve beyond that of our hunter-gatherer ancestors. Their conclusion was that as evolving social beings, we must learn to be more creative in our attempts to solve the complex problems we face in modern society. To do that, I would argue, we need to change the way we teach languageing in schools. This, of course, will require that schools look at literacy (please excuse *our* arrogance here) in much the same way we have talked about it in this book.

Tchudi: Well, at this juncture, I think we have produced our promised portrait of literacy, and it is not Procrustean. I think we have demonstrated that the experiential model helps bridge various gaps, between fun and serious learning, between what drives the acquisition of literacy outside of the schools and what could drive it within the schoolhouse walls. It is important for us to recognize the historical roots of what we are describing. Some of those pockets of change have been around for a long time. Perhaps it is time for us to turn a page in this book and look at some proposals for the reform of literacy education.

Beyond the 3Rs: Responsibilities for Literacy

*Whom, then, do I call educated? First, those who manage
well the circumstances which they encounter day by day
and who possess a judgment which is accurate in meeting
occasions as they arise and rarely miss the expedient course
of action; next, those who are decent and honorable in
their intercourse with all men, bearing easily and good
naturedly what is unpleasant or offensive in others, and
being themselves as agreeable and reasonable to their
associates as it is humanly possible to be; furthermore,
those who hold their pleasures always under control and
are not unduly overcome by their misfortunes, bearing up
under them bravely and in a manner worthy of our
common nature; finally, and most important of all, those
who are not spoiled by their successes and who do not
desert their true selves, but hold their ground steadfastly as
wise and soberminded men, rejoicing no more in the good
things which have come to them through chance than in
those which through their own nature and intelligence are
theirs since birth.*
—ISOCRATES, *PANATHENAICUS*

Our morning newspapers are filled with school news, much of
it of reform movements that have failed or seem doomed to failure. An effort to teach "core values" in the schools is ridiculed
because a planning committee has been unable to narrow its list
of values to fewer than thirty-five (twenty-five more than the Ten

Commandments, the paper observes). Efforts to promote bilingual education are pronounced a failure by English Only, an organization contending that having an official language—English—is a way to bring us all together. The whole-language movement is said to have failed to teach a generation of California kids to read, and in Baltimore, an effort to privatize the schools (for profit) ends in rancor, with the school district leaders and the entrepreneurs each blaming the other for incompetence. National test scores in history are deemed a national embarrassment, even as a national survey indicates that Americans want education to deal with the 3Rs and not the liberal arts, even as efforts to reform the history curriculum by making it more relevant to global affairs are trashed in the papers as being un-American.

What are the reformers and the public to think? More important, what are they to do? In this chapter, we go beyond the 3Rs. As promised, we will examine a renaissance of Rs, as we discuss ways of extending and improving schooling for a literate society.

We start with the R of Reform. It seems that as long as there have been schools, there have been reformers—Plato reforming what he saw as the problems of sophistic education; Quintilian reformulating Roman education; St. Augustine reforming the educational role of the clergy; and many others—Francis Bacon, John Locke, Comenius, Horace Mann, Jane Addams, and John Dewey, to name just a few. In the three decades during which the two of us have been involved with the schools, we have seen numerous reform movements and measures—the new math and the new English, a National Defense Education Act, the elective movement in senior high school English, vocational literacy, whole language, back-to-basics, accountability and teacher testing, statewide proficiency testing, bilingual education and monolingual education, mainstreaming and tracking, behavioral reward curricula, school-to-work projects, exit examinations, cultural literacy, and national standards—again to name just a few.

Our positivist assumption is that all educational schemes, as well as all plans to reform or revolutionize the schools, have elements of visionary idealism to them. Moreover, it is incredibly difficult for a prophet or reformer to sift through alternative and competing schemes to predict which ones will work and which ones will not. Imagine, for example, if America's notion of free public education for all were to be proposed in today's political climate. We can hear the voices at public hearings:

"You can't possibly educate your entire citizenry and it's silly to try."

"It'll cost too damned much."

"Better not waste your money on the common folk; spend it on the people who are truly committed to learning."

"Let those who want it pay for it through user fees."

Yet, in America today we have a 350-year tradition of populist education, which, despite its drawbacks and failures, has been both astonishingly successful and remarkably stable, having provided a pretty good education for us common folk and having resisted efforts at reform. After all, the 3Rs of Puritan public education obviously continue to be a viable metaphor for the aims and content of public education.

We argue strongly against the notion that there is a single revolutionary solution to schooling for a literate society. As we have suggested with our discussions of Hegelianism, we believe that serious change comes about through synthesis, which requires finding a plurality of truths and shaping them into a coherent whole. At the same time, our Hegelianism rejects extreme relativism and argues that although one must embrace a multiplicity of ideas and alternatives, not all ideas are equal from the perspective of educational research and political practicality. Many of the recent reform movements have failed precisely because they have chosen a single idea, a single, limited truth, and pushed it without concern for a philosophical or pedagogical whole.

The back-to-basics movement, recognizing a partial truth—that there are some fundamental skills in any field, say, language or math—sadly ignored a broader truth—that fundamentals of learning are nowhere near as simple as one might suppose and that such skills seem to be acquired only as they function for a learner's genuine purposes. Therefore, these so-called basic skills have been reduced to a scheme for pushing drills and standardized tests.

The cultural literacy movement also recognized a partial truth—that cultures are centered around common knowledge and concepts. But under the leadership of E. D. Hirsch, it decontextualized its truth from human experience, thus creating curricula that would march children through mastery of a series of cultural factoids, a sort of basic skills approach to common culture.

The push for national standards for education—under way even as we write—finds its truth in the need for coherence in instruction and for maintaining high expectations for student achievement, but it obsessively turns those notions into arid and naive lists of what young people are supposed to know and be able to do at various school levels.

As parents and teachers know, such one-dimensional schemes seldom produce significant change in the schools. The new cure-all hits town through school in-service workshops in the fall and hits the road a week or a month or a year later. The educational museum has glass cases filled with these relics. Do you readers recall behavioral objectives? Teacher-proof curricula? The new maths? The new grammars? They are all on display as monuments to the failure of educational reform.

The 3Rs have, for us, come to serve as a metaphor for traditional education, a system that—to reemphasize—has enjoyed surprising success over the past 350 years in this country and has made millions literate and numerate. It has created citizens who, on the whole, have been sufficiently literate to elect reasonably responsible, occasionally imaginative leaders; to create a more or less successful economy; to win wars (seemingly less so recently); and to provide worldwide moral, ethical, economic, political, and social leadership (less so recently as well). As our parenthetical qualifiers suggest, times have changed. Manifest in the welter of educational reform efforts is a frustrated citizenry trying to assess what has gone wrong (or perhaps more aptly, trying to figure out why and how things have changed). People genuinely want to improve our systems—both the overall social-political-economic system and its intellectual heart, the school system.

Clearly, the 3Rs no longer will suffice, despite the efforts of some school reformers to insist that they will. As we reviewed the responses of our interviewees, we were struck by another thought—why only three Rs? Why not a Renaissance of Rs? So at lunch at the Breakaway Bar and Grill (our favorite place to talk about school reform), we pulled out our pencils and brainstormed for a list of Rs that in our opinion, would help explain the skills of literacy that we have seen in fully functioning, articulate adults and children.

We came up with thirty-nine (twenty-nine more than the Ten Commandments). So in addition to Reading and 'Riting, we propose that the schools teach:

Reflection	Relevance	Rationalism
Reliability	Responsibility	Ratiocination
Realization	Rhetoric	Resourcefulness
Resolution	Resonance	Revolution
Renovation	Reconstruction	Romance
Radicalism	Range	Razzmatazz
Reach	Reaction	Readiness
Recognition	Reciprocity	Reconnaissance
Redemption	Refinement	Renewal
Refreshment	Regeneration	Rejoicing
Relationships	Reformation	Remembrance
Repertory	Representation	Responsiveness
Revelation	Reverence	Rootedness

Probably most of these Rs are self-explanatory. We must annotate a few items though. For example, by Reverence and Revelation and Redemption, we do not mean that the schools should teach religion but that they should help young people be Reverent and Respectful to others and themselves and the universe; that kids should be open to truths and insights that are Revealed through study; that as the human products of schooling, they should be able to Redeem themselves as fully functioning literate citizens. We include Romance and Razzmatazz because of the need, as pointed out by the kids we talked to, for schools to be a fun place for them, a place for Rejoicing in themselves and in the mysteries and Revelations of the world around them. We see a need for Ratiocination and Reflection. We also think schools should be fertile ground for people like those we interviewed, people who are Revolutionary in their quiet ways, who are able to Reconstruct their own worlds, who can Recognize and Remember their Roots even while Reinventing society for their own purposes.

There are some Rs we left off the list, Ruthlessness for one (though some would say it is a skill worth knowing in our workaday world) and Revolvers (which, as our daily newspaper notes, has become the Fourth R in a number of schools). We invite the reader to add his or her own Rs, additional desirable traits for schooling.

One R on our list struck us as especially important, and we will focus on it for the remainder of the chapter. That R is *Responsibility.* About the time we were drafting this chapter, we attended a parents' night at an area secondary school. As we heard administrators and teachers talk, we were surprised to hear this R word come up time and time again:

"Students must simply realize that they are responsible for their own behavior."

"Students must learn to become responsible school citizens."

"Students must be responsible for putting covers on their books and arriving at class with freshly sharpened pencils."

As the evening progressed, we came to sense that in this school at least, responsibility was rather like a dose of medicine, something distasteful for students, but something that they would need to take if they were to be cured of the adolescent disease of irresponsibility. We understand, of course, and sympathize with the teachers and administrators who want their charges to exercise schoolhouse responsibility. It is no fun for an educator to spend time dealing with kids who are clowning around (or worse) in the halls, showing up in provocative (or worse) clothing, trashing schoolbooks (or worse), and coming to class unprepared and indifferent.

We argue, however, that like basic skills, accountability, and national standards, an imposed regimen of responsibility is no cure-all. In fact, we are convinced that responsibility deserves a place in reform plans, not as something to be imposed on the irresponsible but as something that fundamentally responsible people—kids, parents, teachers, administrators, businesspeople—can and will take on for themselves.

Based on our studies and synthesis, we want to discuss responsibilities for literacy, not as something obligatory, not as a one-dimensional or Procrustean plan, but as an invitation list, one that offers a number of ideas and suggestions that make sense for holistic, systematic reform of literacy education. We hope you will join us in embracing these responsibilities.

Literacy and Community

What does the community want from the schools? What does the community expect in a literate citizen? If one bases judgment on what appears in the newspapers and on TV, the answer is *basics*—academic basic skills and the alleged basics of responsibility—meaning *discipline*. The public clamors for demonstrations of mastery of skills, and legislators respond with more tests—proficiency tests, exit tests, tests of teacher mastery of basic skills.

We are convinced that the public actually wants a good deal more than the rather narrow kind of literacy of basics and tests. We are equally convinced that the community, frequently handcuffed by the press and by its own lack of vocabulary, fails to express its desire for critical and dynamic literacy to educators. Why should the public be expected to articulate the need for competence of the sort displayed in our interviews, or for that matter, to express its own considerable level of competence? Why should a community say that it wants critical and dynamic literacy integrated with phonics and spelling? Not recognizing their own literacies, good and responsible citizens express their school-reform demands in predictable ways:

"Spelling, yeah, that's the ticket. More spelling."

"Grammar. I never understood it. Hated it actually. Give my kids more grammar."

We do not think that community members, in general, need to become specialists or even to be particularly knowledgeable about the fine details of literacy, language, and language acquisition. But we do think the community needs to take responsibility, to *embrace* responsibility, for stating the best of what it wants for its young people. In conversations and workshops with parents in Nevada and elsewhere, we have discovered that freed from anxiety over basic skills and school discipline, parents express views of educational needs that are both expansive and "classic." We call them classic because much of what parents want is little different from the ideals expressed by Isocrates in the epigraph to this chapter. Parents want kids to learn to "manage well the circumstances which they encounter day by day" and to "possess a judgment which is accurate in meeting occasions as they arise." They hope for educated citizens "who are decent and honorable," for people "who do not desert their true selves, but hold their ground steadfastly as wise and soberminded men [and women]." Parents do not want their kids programmed with rote literacy skills suitable only for dead-end jobs or jobs that will become obsolete after the next economic or electronic revolution. They want kids who can master skills that will prepare them broadly for the twenty-first century—skills of critical thinking and cultural awareness, skills of discovery and on-the-job creativity. These are the skills that we have broadly represented as critical and dynamic literacy. Parents want their children given a shot at the range of skills, concepts, and processes represented by the thirty-nine Rs.

At the same time, we think that the public needs to evaluate critically the implications of broad and multiple aims of literacy for children. What if the schools were, overnight, able to produce a generation of dynamically literate children, children who, as school curriculum guides regularly invoke, are fully articulate, responsible citizens? Are we fully prepared to cope with and adjust to the products of schooling for a literate society? Are those of us awaiting our Social Security and Medicare benefits in the not-too-distant future willing to trust those systems to a bunch of sharp-eyed, literate-tongued youngsters who can think critically about the affairs of citizenship? What if they choose to balance the budget by cutting off our payments? Or what if they take the environment seriously and ban cars so that we have to take the electric bus? A major and nonsimplistic reform we propose is for the public to talk more about literacy and to get clear on what it wants, on just how much genuine dynamic literacy it is willing to accept. Despite some misgivings of our own, we think that the American tradition of populist schooling provides evidence of a strong commitment to that kind of literacy, even with its inconveniences and occasional participatory unruliness.

We also urge the public to develop skepticism of test scores as an accurate measure of literacy. As we talk with people, we find few who have fond memories of standardized tests and even fewer who think that those tests are adequate measures of what they know and can do. Yet the public by and large continues to act as if standardized tests are not only a measure of individual student performance but also of the overall performance of the schools. Think of the range of skills developed by our interviewees. Is there any reason to suppose those myriad skills can be accurately measured by a standardized bubble test or even by a timed writing sample? Further, is there any reason to suppose that any really good language arts program could be encompassed by a short-answer test? Could the reader's life be measured by a short-answer test?

We think the public, then, must accept responsibility for deepening the complexity of its discussions of literacy, resisting the temptation to find one-sentence answers to complicated questions. And in most communities, those opportunities do exist. Virtually any program of school change, any new curriculum, any new set of standards goes through a public-hearing process. In our experience, school leaders genuinely seek a variety of opinions on these matters, but too often, they find meetings either poorly attended or packed with vociferous objectors. We urge readers to take responsibility to redress those imbalances.

In the meantime, it is virtually axiomatic in our profession that literacy begins at home. This slogan is not an attempt to pass the buck to parents, but rather to recognize that the home-community environment for literacy is crucial. In exploring this, we want to distance ourselves from the widely accepted notion that there are good and bad home environments for literacy. Obviously, some backgrounds are more conducive to promoting the kind of literacy that is valued (and tested) in school. Putting it baldly, the kids who tend to wind up with the best test scores tend to come from the so-called literate backgrounds—where books and newspapers and challenging discussions are staple fare. However, the relationship is hardly causal; financial status and race are much better predictors of success in school than whether or not a family subscribes to a daily newspaper or reads award-winning books to the children at bedtime.

Every family is literate in the broadest and best sense of the word. Every family talks, worries, consumes print, consumes bread, consumes television. Whether the language is English or another, whether the dialect is middle-class standard or another, families and communities are clearly in control of languages that are developed to serve their own ends and purposes. Educators who understand the full implications of literacy research realize that schooling for a literate society requires not altering or dismissing those languages but enlarging the range of literacies, a common goal for all children, not just for those who have traditionally been perceived as sociolinguistically deprived.

Like many in our profession, we are deeply concerned about the so-called English Only movement, which would legislate English as our national language and move toward elimination of bilingualism both in education and in the political and economic marketplace. Recently, Paul Morris watched a culturally diverse panel of professional women discuss the English Only issue. As an aside, one of the women asked this very pertinent question about the movement: "Does anybody actually believe that bilingual education in our schools will in any way diminish the use of English as the preferred language of commerce and government in America, or for that matter, even the world?" It seems clear to us that English Only stems from the irrational, ethnocentric fears of some English-speaking Americans.

To repeat, it is the responsibility of the community to embrace multiple literacies, English and other languages, standard and nonstandard dialects, and above all, the amazing range of literacies demonstrated by people like the subjects in this book, in other words, by any group of citizens. The diversity of literacies in the United States is a cause for celebration, not concern.

But how the community can embrace this responsibility is highly problematic. The public needs guidance so it can understand what is best in schooling; it needs responsible leadership to be assumed by its political leaders, its business leaders, and its colleges and universities as well as its schools.

Responsibilities for Business and Industry

We laud the trend of the past two decades for business and industry to become concerned about the quality of public education. It is no coincidence in our minds that this interest expanded exponentially in the mid-1970s when industry became fully aware of the competition from overseas. We are dubious about the common belief that a decline in American education led to the decline in American industrial supremacy. Indeed, in curiously circular reasoning, many business critics of the 1970s blasted "progressive" education as leading to the downfall without recognizing that they—the adults, the fifty-somethings—were captaining the ship. If any education had failed, it seems to us to have been the traditional schooling of the 1930s and 1940s and 1950s, when many of the current captains of industry were educated. We are reminded of a particularly vicious argument made by George Meany about the young to the AFL-CIO in 1968: "To people who constantly say you have got to listen to these young people, that they have got something to say, I just do not buy that at all. They smoke more pot than we do and if the younger generation are the hundred thousand kids that lay around a field up in Woodstock, New York, I am not going to trust the destiny of the country to that group" (Rottenberg, 1994, p. 246). Our current president, most of his cabinet, many congressional representatives, many union leaders and corporate presidents were all of the generation about which Meany spoke.

We are also suspicious of the widespread notion that the ability to run a business successfully makes one an expert on how to run schools successfully, that the methods business uses to achieve profitability necessarily will lead to improved schooling. Moreover, we think some business and industry leaders have been guilty of confusing what they perceive as educational inefficiency in school management with processes of schooling that quite simply do not lend themselves to business streamlining or assembly line improvement. School is not business. Education is necessarily personal and not fully or even partially standardized.

Confusing schools with businesses is the sort of thinking that usually leads to dangerous faulty comparisons on the part of educators, like this one made by James A. Harris, former president of the National Education Association: "Twenty-three percent of the schoolchildren are failing to graduate, and another large segment graduate as functional illiterates. If 23 percent of anything else failed—23 percent of automobiles didn't run, 23 percent of buildings fell down, 23 percent of stuffed ham spoiled—we'd look to the producer" (Rottenberg, 1994, pp. 245–246).

Furthermore, we do not think it is the business of schooling to prepare students for jobs—at least not directly. We bristle at the suggestion that the schools ought to make writing a business memo or filling out a job application central components of the English/language arts program. This idea is, at best, a stopgap or quick-fix approach to a much, much broader problem.

Having expressed these concerns and possibly having alienated some leaders of the business community (who may brand us as typical academics, full of our theories and unwilling to test our ideas in the marketplace), we must add that we are fully sympathetic to the frustration of the business community over the lack of skills of entering workers at all levels. We understand the outrage of an employer faced with a high school graduate who cannot spell or read, or a college graduate who writes gobbledygook rather than crisp, efficient prose. We appreciate the frustration of the business community over the slow pace of change in the schools, over the fact that the schools talk reform, talk new programs, but nothing seems to happen, whereas in the business world, decisions are made and *things happen*. How then, can we merge—or Hegelize—these apparently conflicting concerns?

The resolution, it seems to us, may come about by reconsidering the concept of liberal or general education. Our research points to the pragmatic impossibility of preparing young people for all the explicit tasks that may be required of them in the real world—the writing of, say, a set of specifications for a heating system or a public relations brochure on trout stream management or a letter proposing marriage (if anybody actually writes such a quaint document anymore). We do think the schools and the business community might reach consensus on the responsibility of the schools to focus on the "it" of literacy, which we see as the essence of liberal education. We believe that the schools should embrace the responsibility of teaching basic, critical, and dynamic literacy (emphatically not in a hierarchical sequence). The schools should immerse students in the richest possible learning environment, moving toward specific technical skills through a wide-ranging liberal arts education, recognizing that the specifics of particular modes and genres can be learned—rather easily as we have seen in our interviews—on the job.

We believe that freed from the immediate concern of teaching the basics of job literacy (and freed, we hope, from the tyranny of standardized testing of the basics), the schools can potentially do a much more satisfactory job of integrating basic, critical, and dynamic literacy. It would be nice if literacy instructors could teach Shakespeare or Shel Silverstein without feeling that the business community regards such teaching as a frill, something to be achieved only after the spelling and vocabulary drills have been completed. It would be equally nice if literacy instructors could send their students into the community to interview business leaders, to study on site, without reducing such visits to occupational field trips. In sum, it would be nice if the business community and the teachers could agree that in a liberal arts education, both the practical and the aesthetic are critical; that good spelling and grammar matter as much in a poem as in a business memo; that articulateness covers a continuum that goes from the workaday to the ratiocinative; and that neither of these is the exclusive domain of business or school.

Having talked with members of the business community, we think the two sides may not be as far apart as they seem. One acquaintance talks to us about the changing pattern of business literacy: "We're doing more with groups and teams," she says, "and we'd like employees who know how to talk and negotiate and synthesize ideas" (rather Hegelian, we think). "The bottom line," she adds, "is not standard English—though that is important—but critical thinking, the management of ideas." As we think about our English classes at the university and what we see going on in progressive English classes in the schools, we find that the goals are virtually identical. Our acquaintance in business has looked beyond surface literacy, beyond correctness, to see the traits of general education and literacy that are really needed for success on the job. These traits, all three of us might add, are not the exclusive domain of the managers—they are just as vital for the full range of employees.

We urge business and industry leaders to look deeply at their workers' skills. We have looked deeply, not only at our interviewees but also at innumerable other literate people in our community (one of the top-rated spots in the country for small-business development)—the guy in the mall shop who has entrepreneured a package mailing service; the young couple next to him who have combined an espresso shop with a handicrafts and gifts mart; and the guy next to them who operates a sports bar and grill and who went out of his way to add our favorite nonalcoholic beer to the menu. The world of business is filled with such people, and if their only skill were spelling well or writing grammatically, they would fail. They succeed because they are literate in the fullest sense of the word.

We applaud partnerships between businesses and schools. We think it is superb that businesses see it as their responsibility to adopt a school and to donate funds and materials to supplement school budgets. We laud businesspeople who open their doors to kids, who show them how the ice cream business works, how the newspaper gets written and printed, how the stock broker communicates with Wall Street.

We do think, however, that the business community needs to be both more and less demanding of the schools—demanding that the schools turn out more generally literate people, while not demanding or even imagining that the schools can or should tackle teaching the endless forms of practical discourse.

Responsibilities for the Political Sphere

For almost three decades, we have seen a trend toward micromanagement of the schools by federal and state governments. Lacking confidence in the ability of local communities to manage their own affairs, government agencies have set up a welter of programs and requirements for the funding and execution of education. On the one hand, we must admit that many of these interventions have been positive. Without the federal government, for example, we would have no Head Start, limited Native American Education, little in the way of ESL and Bilingual Education.

On the other hand, we have also witnessed a national and disturbing trend toward long-distance management by political agencies, in particular through mandated legislative testing. In our state, which is fairly representative, students are tested annually for basic skills using a commercial test prepared outside the state of Nevada. These tests include a state assessment of reading, math, language, and writing at grades four and eight, and an eleventh-grade proficiency or exit examination of reading, math, and writing (with four chances for students to pass). On the surface, such legislative mandates appear to be in the interest of increasing literacy for students and accountability for teachers. In fact, in our considerable work with teachers, we find increasingly that some of the teachers we regard as the best—those who have read deeply in the professional literature and are working to implement progressive strategies—are seriously discouraged and disillusioned, in no small measure because of the pressure of tests, augmented by the spirit of public distrust that they generate. As we discussed earlier, we think these tests are a poor measure of what the community wants. The problem with the tests and the so-called standards is not that they are high but that they are low, dragging kids and teachers to narrowly conceived mastery of basic literacy rather than dynamic literacy.

Our recommendation to legislators will sound liberal and conservative and libertarian at the same time: supply more than adequate funding for the schools, then leave the professionals alone to figure out how to improve them. Horrifying as this might seem to some, it is based on our conviction that in the field of English, at least, the current crop of teachers is, contrary to popular belief, the best educated, best trained we have ever had in the schools. Although we are frequently appalled that within our own ranks many teachers stubbornly cling to practices that have been outmoded since the 1950s, a growing number are extremely knowledgeable about the kinds of methodologies supported by current research and by our own interviews. These include teaching writing as a process that involves writing for authentic audiences; integrating language skills across the curriculum; centering literacy on ideas and actions that are keyed to the world outside the classroom—a global village of mass communication, international politics and business, human needs and suffering, and achievement. All it takes to get teachers engaged in serious school change and reform is some time away from the job, an opportunity to explore new approaches firsthand and to implement those ideas in the schools.

However, testing and monitoring student achievement on low-level tests is extraordinarily expensive. Our state, with a modest population of 1.5 million people, budgets about a half million dollars per year for statewide testing. That does not count the cost of purchasing the tests themselves (paid by school districts), the cost of administering the tests (requiring teacher and staff time), and the cost of overseeing results (the larger districts in Nevada having full-time employees whose basic job it is to manage these unfunded testing mandates from the state legislature).

What should legislators do then? Obviously, we favor scrapping the tests and spending the money for on-the-job teacher retraining, but we doubt that will happen. But we can urge legislators to focus energies on recruitment and retention of the best and brightest folks for our teachers, to channel and rechannel funds away from the mandates based on a philosophy of skepticism and pseudoaccountability and toward the programs that invite and encourage teacher growth. Above all, we say to legislators: do not hamper and hinder your good teachers. Do not second-guess. Do not even imagine that implementing simplistic standards or authorizing student testing or teacher testing will make a substantial change in the schools. We urge legislators to consider the implications of the experiences of the interviewees in this book, whose literacy grew from face-to-face, person-to-person engagement with language users. There is no other way language skills can grow. Legislative action not directed to that end will prove to be futile, and we would like legislators to assume responsibility for knowing that.

Responsibilities for the Media

We will dwell on this area only briefly. We hope that this book—along with the kinds of books in the bibliography—will prove helpful to some media representatives in reconceptualizing their understanding of how literacy works. As faithful and in most respects admiring consumers of media, we respect the interest that media have shown through an array of reports on the schools. At the same time, from the infamous and presumptuous 1974 *Newsweek* exposé alleging to explain "Why Johnny Can't Write" to the recent headlines alleging that California's whole-language movement has "failed," journalists have not, on the whole, revealed themselves to be particularly knowledgeable about the nature of language and language learning. In our own state, for example, *Las Vegas Sun* columnist Debra Bass relied on accusations from an indignant but uninformed administrator and a former gym-coach-turned-English-teacher to launch an attack on a set of professional guidelines that had been developed by teachers from all over the state over a two-year period (1995, p. 3B). Although Bass made an effort to address the complexities, she failed to consult any knowledgeable language arts specialists and wrote a story that effectively brought a thoughtful and well-designed curriculum project to a dead halt.

One of the ironies and deep complexities in dealing with literacy issues is that often highly literate people are quite unaware of how they gained their skills. Although workaday journalists may assume they know how they got to be the way they are, we respectfully suggest that many of them could well afford the sort of introspection engaged in by our interviewees. Then, instead of offering simplistic solutions to the literacy crisis and displaying dramatic but unhelpful and misleading headlines, the media could offer helpful insights into what is happening with language and schooling, or at least, more journalistically accurate reporting.

We have high praise, by the way, for much of the media involvement in schooling, including school pages in newspapers, (some) educational programs on TV, and projects like the Newspapers-in-the-Schools program. As we look toward future evolutions of literacy, it is increasingly clear that mass electronic literacy will supplant traditional book literacy for many citizens. Without going into the complex issue of the quality of literacy being promoted by the media (about which we predictably have some doubts), we would like to see the media continue to embrace the responsibility of helping to educate its consumers, not through formalistic programs—no grammar of media literacy—but through partnerships with schools that get kids increasingly involved in using media resources to enhance their own literacy.

Schooling and the Literate Society

As we have pointed out, it is not our intent to offer a formula or a recipe for school change or school reform. Although we have our notions for bringing about major reform—our formula for ideal schools would essentially be interdisciplinary and community centered, with learners of all ages working together on projects of local as well as global concern—we will limit our discussion here to the direct implications of the interviews we have conducted. As desirable as massive school reform might be, we are convinced that the most important evolutions have always been and will continue to be based on what happens with individual teachers in individual schools. We offer some suggestions for change which, if implemented by enough teachers and administrators, would point in the direction of improved schooling for a literate society.

The Colleges

We think it is time that the colleges and universities stopped talking down to the K–12 schools, acting as if collegiate education is a model for what ought to go on below as if the major purpose of K–12 education is preparation for college. Although there are many exceptions, our accusations accurately describe a widespread attitude in academia. We not only think the colleges should stop talking down, we also think they should look more critically at their own programs, in particular, how well they are doing at teaching the thirty-nine Rs. While these generalizations may be sweeping, we believe them to be accurate. We think that collegiate education is anything but a good model of schooling, because of practices that have been common for generations: lecture predominates over discussion; courses center on content rather than on students; professors are more interested in their research than on teaching. On the whole, the K–12 curriculum is much more coherently organized than the college-level curriculum, which tends to consist of requirements rather than a set of integrated aims.

There are, of course, many encouraging trends in collegiate education. In the area of literacy, in particular, the writing-across-the-curriculum movement has linked writing courses to learning in other fields. Many writing programs have themselves undergone a transition from service courses that teach formula writing to process-based courses that focus on a range of student literacies.

At the same time, the colleges remain a poor model for teachers entering public education. How is a teacher to teach diverse literacies when the college where the teacher is trained offers a model of literacy that is essentially directed toward students preparing for graduate school? We are not saying that prospective English teachers need some sort of English curriculum that is different in kind from that given to other English majors. To the contrary, we believe that the best possible curriculum for teachers would also be a rich preparation for graduate school. Further, we believe that by and large, English departments are missing the boat by not dramatically expanding the range of literacy that they cover and by not radically changing the interrelationships and the interdisciplinary nature of their courses.

We need gatherings of school and college teachers—meeting on parity, with no distinctions between higher and lower school levels—to discuss the nature of literacy and learning. Of course, these meetings have great potential for turning into a kind of donnybrook, for university folk are so protective and provincial about their turf. Higher education has a lousy track record of trying to foist so-called basic literacy instruction onto the schools so that college professors can avoid teaching introductory courses. However, difficult as these discussions might be to manage, they could lead to the realization that a broad literacy curriculum is the best preparation for university work as well as for life in general. While some of these articulation discussions might take place on a national level, they certainly could and should take place in every region of the country, with school and college people getting together to review the particular educational, social, economic, and intellectual needs of their areas. In this way, we believe, there is a chance of breaking the stranglehold that college discipline-centered literacy has on the public school curriculum.

The K–12 Schools

Responsibilities for developing literacy are myriad, but again, please remember that we are calling for a voluntary embracing of responsibilities. Caught in a welter of conflicting demands—basic skills and spelling, ESL, English Only, literacy for the marketplace, literacy for values, values-free literacy, wide reading, censored reading—the schools have small chance of achieving the sort of massive, monolithic change that the school reformers dream of. But one can, we think, accept these responsibilities, one at a time per-haps, but also systematically, and in so doing can catalyze remark-able changes in the schools.

The District

At a recent conference of K–12 language arts educators, we were struck by the remarkable difference between what the presenters—most of them classroom teachers—were saying about their teach-ing and what the commercial textbook display in the foyer was offering. The most recent textbooks were lovely to look at, truly stunning books with bright, plasticized covers and four-color art-work inside, plus color-coded teachers' guides with lesson ideas highlighted by their emphasis on literature, language, or writing. The books all used recent pedagogical buzzwords, "integration," "whole language," "skills in context," "composing process." And in our judgment, they were awful—products of consensus, not syn-thesis, of the worst possible sort. Most offered alternative tables of contents so one could teach thematically or chronologically, two approaches to literature that are essentially contradictory. "Inte-gration" of skills was achieved in the weakest of ways, say, by show-ing grammatical principles in literary selections or by having students frame their responses in conventional literary terminol-ogy. The current cost of one of the glossiest was $48. Meanwhile, teachers at the conference were telling us, "We have no money to get trade books and paperbacks and magazines into our class-rooms. Once the district buys these textbooks, there is no money left for literary purchases." The curriculum, in short, is reduced to whatever commercial product the adoption committee has pur-chased. As if to reinforce our point, most major English/language arts textbooks are, quite simply, a hodgepodge, a carefully con-structed compromise intended to satisfy every possible consumer and, in the process, gutting the literacy curriculum of both con-tent and rationale.

The biggest single change that could take place in K–12 liter-acy education—and its effects would be instantaneous—would be this: do not adopt textbooks. Save the $48 per child and invest it elsewhere, mostly in paperback books for the classroom or new titles for the library. Actually, the English-teaching profession has known how not to use commercial texts for at least three decades. Fader and McNeil's *Hooked on Books* (1968), for example, showed how to structure classrooms around paperbacks, and the secondary English-elective movement of the 1970s had teachers constructing entire teaching units and courses without the rubber crutch of the adopted book. Unfortunately, these independent moves toward multiple literacy have been fairly well squashed by the back-to-basics movement and its successors.

Aside from the textbook issue, we think it is time for school districts to take a new attitude toward curriculum development. Curriculum needs to grow from teachers' perceptions of what young people do with language at various levels—a subject on which most teachers are extraordinarily knowledgeable—and from discussions about how the curriculum can provide the richest possible support for language growth and change. As we have seen from our interviews, the specific ways in which people come to use language in their lives are seldom predictable. Rather than a narrowly prescribed curriculum—textbook dominated—that presumes to know what all children should be reading and writing about simultaneously, the alternative is needed: flood the classroom with a rich supply of materials appropriate to students' needs and interests, that offers them the broadest possible range of writing, speaking, and thinking opportunities. Freed from obsession with test scores and textbook adoptions, many districts would be in a position to offer teachers strong support in developing just that sort of program. In such an environment, we think it likely that districts would be in a position to consider some serious alternatives to the status quo. Why not end the tyranny of the traditional disciplines in favor of interdisciplinary study? Why not move toward language as an integrated part of every classroom? Why not forge real links—not just guest appearances—with literate community members? Why not allow kids in the schools to be genuine participants in the community?

The School Building

It almost goes without saying that the individual school is the real point of contact between educators and the community. In the years we have been in the business, it has seemed to us that schools have become very much more skilled at communicating their aims to parents. The old-time parents' night has become more collegial and participatory. At the same time, school administrators have been under increasing pressure to respond to community concerns, so that for better or worse, the squeaky wheel still gets itself greased.

We would like to move beyond these concerns and to suggest that our concept, *schooling for a literate society,* could be useful to individual schools as a way of increasing curriculum coherence. We urge schools, as an in-service plan, to undertake the same sort of questioning we have done for this book; for example, inviting citizens into the school to discuss their concerns. Do not ask parents and the public: what do you want us to teach? Do ask: what is your own literacy like and how did you learn it? Your results may, of course, differ from ours. You may run into some people who diagrammed sentences and loved it and attribute their adult literacy to it. More likely, we think, you will learn, as we did, that people's literacy is diverse and that they pick up much of it on the job, provided they have the central skills of basic, dynamic, and critical literacy that allow them to operate fluidly and flexibly in a changing world.

From that, teachers can move to discussions of the natural literacy they see in their kids and what the schools can do about it. Opinions will differ, of course. However, we have found through many teacher workshops with this focus that surprising unanimity exists, *if* the focus is kept on what kids do with language. Hashing over piles of student writing, for example, teachers see that most kids have a better grasp of the basics than politicians and the public imagine. Talking about the books that young people most like to read, teachers begin to develop portraits of students' interests and achievements. Moreover, they begin to see a new kind of responsibility—not to prepare kids for the next grade level or for the mandated tests (although that may be important) but to enrich the literacy experience for kids in the here and now, at this grade level. This brings us to the classroom and the teacher.

The Individual Classroom Teacher

At one point toward the end of this project, we made a presentation about our research to a graduate class at the University of

Nevada. After we finished, one of the students, a bright, energetic second-year teacher at one of the area's best middle schools told us, "This is great. But you're preaching to the choir. The teachers I work with already know this."

We wish that were true in more schools. The following day, we talked with another teacher, who taught at a more conservative school and whose work has been regularly criticized by fellow faculty members and by the school administration for being too progressive. This teacher—whose progressiveness would be welcomed at the school of the first teacher—is alone, fighting not only for what she sees as a research-based approach to literacy but also for her own professional life.

Certainly, our research supports what a great many school and college teachers are doing in their classrooms. At the same time, progress is discouragingly slow in literacy education, in no small measure because of the negative influences we have cited in this chapter—the conservative effects of textbooks, mandated tests, overemphasis on basic literacy. A great many teachers find themselves demoralized these days, feeling as if every step forward is counteracted by shifting grounds, that they really could teach literacy if somebody gave them a chance. It is tempting for many teachers to acquiesce to the external pressures, and we find no fault with teachers who do.

At the same time, no teacher can afford to wait for the community, the businesses, the politicians, the colleges, the district, and the building principal and staff to come on-line in support of their (good) teaching. Many of us who are teachers work in our classrooms day by day to implement our own best visions of schooling for a literate society, even as we campaign for broader reforms that are necessary. There is a necessary doublethink, then, in the process of reform. Individual teachers need to know that they make a difference, even as they recognize that realistically, outside forces operate against or at least blur their efforts.

At the close of this book, then, we find ourselves affirming the role of the individual teacher in changing the shape of literacy in this country. We would like to believe that systematic, wholesale change is both possible and desirable, but the results of reform movements over the past decades persuade us that this is not the case, at least not without a radically restructured view of literacy and society. Perhaps that kind of change is closer than we think, but we are convinced that in the end, what will happen in individual classrooms will take place through the insights and literacies of individual teachers. As we have seen with our interviewees, often the literacy classroom is outside the schoolhouse and the literacy teacher is experience. We want to capitalize on that experiential structure so that literacy learning in the schoolhouse becomes inseparable from the broader realm of experience and language outside the schoolhouse, with each reciprocally leading to the ultimate aim—schooling for a literate society.

Postscript

In the film *Stanley and Iris* (1990), an illiterate worker (Robert DeNiro) learns how to read from a teacher (Jane Fonda) and in the process, falls in love with her. Although the film attempts to deal with the subject of illiteracy in a sympathetic way, it fails to present it realistically. Film critic Roger Ebert (1985–1991) comments: "I did not know whether to believe all of Stanley's problems in the movie, because I know that any smart person with a handicap soon figures out a way around it: putting the claim check in a special part of the billfold, for example, or looking for a skull and cross-bones on the poison, or grabbing all six little plastic bottles on the shelf in the company commissary and saying, 'We got everything here. What do you want?'" (p. 561).

In fact, Stanley *is* portrayed as smart in the film, but for the sake of the plot, he fails to use all the simple coping mechanisms mentioned by Ebert. Since he is unable to read, Stanley cannot find the claim check for his laundry in his billfold. He is fired from his job because, when his boss asks him to get the salt, he brings rat poison instead. Ebert only gave the movie 2.5 stars, claiming that it "makes illiteracy into the movie's gimmick instead of its subject" (p. 561). The real subject of the film, of course, is the romantic love affair between Stanley and Iris (or Robert and Jane). In typical Hollywood fashion, a serious subject, in this case illiteracy and literacy, is trivialized and sentimentalized so that the two big stars can be shown making love on screen.

It is this same sentimentalized view of illiteracy and literacy that we have challenged in this book. We believe the media and educators like Harold Bloom, E. D. Hirsch, and Jonathan Kozol are responsible for the sentimentalization of literacy. For Bloom, Hirsch, and Kozol, a certain kind of literacy is equated with everything from increased political awareness to better mental health.

Bloom and Hirsch are convinced that if students will just read the *right* books, the literacy of Americans will improve. Kozol implies that basic literacy is the cure for various social problems that threaten America, including unemployment, crime, and alcoholism. As did *Stanley and Iris,* Bloom, Hirsch, and Kozol have failed to define literacy as a complex problem with complex solutions, presenting it rather simplistically as a panacea for many of society's ills.

The same, by the way, can be said about people like John Taylor Gatto and Allan Bloom, who have essentially given up on the possibility of making people literate in their senses of the word. Here, the sentimentalization of literacy works in reverse, as they wallow in gloomy prophesies about illiteracy.

In John Le Carré's *Call for the Dead* ([1964] 1970), the first book in the series about his alter ego, spymaster George Smiley, the hero is introduced as a "sentimental man" who loves England, Oxford, baroque German literature, and his wife. But by the time Smiley appears in *Smiley's People* (1979), his years of service as a spy in "the Circus" have worn him down: "I am a thief of the spirit, he thought, despondently. Faithless, I am pursuing another man's convictions; I am trying to warm myself against other people's fires. He . . . recalled some scrap of poetry from the days he read it, *To turn as swimmers into the cleanness leaping/Glad from a world grown old and cold and weary*. Yes, he thought glumly. That's me" (p. 296, emphasis added).

"A cynic," a friend reminds us, "is merely a failed romantic." The two bleak lines of poetry by Rupert Brooke, especially, seem to capture the cynical sentiment of Gatto and Bloom. Gatto, the disgruntled, former New York schoolteacher who probably began his career as optimistically as Smiley, witnesses the worst the public school system has to offer, then declares it a failure. Late in his life, Allan Bloom, after years of teaching, said that cultured literacy had become an impossible dream.

This type of antisentimentalization is just as unproductive as the romantic views offered by Kozol, Hirsch, Harold Bloom, and the movie *Stanley and Iris.* For a more realistic view of the problem of illiteracy, one need look no further than Ebert's review. "What I did believe," Ebert writes, "was that Stanley felt cut off from ordinary life, just as a traveler in another land might feel strange to find that all of the street signs were in a language completely foreign to him" (p. 561). Here, Ebert has captured what it really must mean to be illiterate—not a criminal, mentally ill or stupid, but on the outside, cut off from the written word, and probably a little too ashamed or afraid to ask for help. It is not surprising to us that Ebert, a working writer, should have such a pragmatic sense of what it might be like to be illiterate. His insight is typical of what we learned about literacy from the literate people we interviewed.

This book is a synthesis of our own understanding of literacy as writing teachers and what we have learned from the literate people we interviewed. We believe the approach we have taken to studying literacy is best suited to the complex nature of the subject. From the beginning, we realized that learning how literacy actually worked in real people would require a particular type of research, one that went directly to the source. People are literate or not based on their abilities to communicate socially with the rest of humankind. We knew of no better way to find out how and why people become literate than to ask them.

We began our study—based on the research of a number of theorists—with the presumption that language develops socially and holistically. To this, we added our own theory—generated through years of teaching experience and language study—that literacy is essentially experiential, that people learn to use language critically and dynamically in society by participating in literate activities. Our interviews with literate people were what literacy researchers Russell Hunt and Douglas Vipond (1992) have called a "dramatization" of this theory. Hunt and Vipond, using the work of psychologist Kurt Danziger (1985, 1988), "question the assumption that the purpose of research is testing of theoretical claims." "Testing," they say, "is a worthy function of research, but it is far from the only one. . . . [R]esearch can also serve to 'dramatize' a theory in order that its implications can be explored. When a theory is dramatized, one can learn things one did not expect" (p. 70). Using Hunt and Vipond's dramatization method, we discovered that any meaningful view of literacy has to take into account the complex variety of language skills needed to operate in society; that the gap between learning-by-doing and schooling is bridgeable; and that happily, the printed word is far from obsolete.

As to our sample of literate citizens, we want to acknowledge that many of the people we interviewed live in the western states of America, and most are from Nevada. However, we are convinced that the range of literacy skills needed to function in a place like New York City or even Washington, D.C., is not that much different from those needed to operate in Reno or Las Vegas or Carson City. The fact is, thanks to twentieth-century technological advances in transportation and communication, many of the people we interviewed use their literacy skills to participate in aspects of art, business, and politics not just regionally but nationally and globally as well.

Finally, we hope we have convinced our readers that the sentimentalized version of literacy often presented is a false one. Most of the people we talked to see their work and their writing as a part of a larger picture for themselves. This tells us that our view of literacy, as something much more complicated than just being able to read and write, is an accurate one. If schools are serious about wanting to turn out literate citizens in this society, they are going to have to accept and meet that challenge.

Appendix: Three Literacy Projects

In the Preface, we pointed out that we are fundamentally optimistic—possibly even Pollyannaish—about the future of literacy education in the United States. We think the educational system has the know-how and the power to bring about a revolution in teaching reading and writing, and we do not think that it has to be a revolution of Copernican or Einsteinian proportions. We are believers in what we call *opportunistic reform*. There is no point in waiting around for the new millennium in the hope that sweeping changes will bring about what we want. Rather, we think it is the responsibility of every literate teacher, every literate citizen, to push for changes and reforms in his or her domain of influence.

With that in mind, we want to discuss our domain of influence and to describe three settings in which we have had opportunities to push for reform in modest ways. We will describe projects being conducted in school and college education in Nevada (one of them with international connections) under the auspices of our composition and rhetoric program at the University of Nevada. All three projects were ongoing during the time we were writing this book; therefore, the projects reflect our current thinking and show very clear connections between what we have discovered in our research for this book and what we are trying to achieve in our teaching.

The Nevada English/Language Arts Project

In Nevada, state guidelines regarding what subject matter should be covered at various grade levels are prepared and reviewed periodically. After public and legislative hearings, frameworks are approved by the state legislature and become law.

In 1992, when a cycle for revision of the Nevada English/Language Arts Framework was launched, the nation was excited about Goals 2000, a project developed by President Bush and sustained under President Clinton to establish national standards in the major subject fields. Teachers of math, science, history, and English/language arts developed descriptions of what "young people ought to know and be able to do" at various grade levels. The movement was enormously popular with legislators, the public, and the press because the national-standards effort gave the impression that something was being done to bring about major change in the schools.

We have been very skeptical of the concept of national standards in education, a notion based on a false analogy with science, in which standards are of a physical (if arbitrary) sort—the length of a foot or meter, Greenwich mean time, the standard weight of a centiliter of water at a standard temperature, and the like. As our interviews for this book so clearly demonstrate, the notion of strict standards in literacy—thou shalt spell "Mississippi" by grade four—is naive. Although one can see patterns in language growth over time, there is no lockstep pattern that all language users follow. The use of the standards model for literacy creates potential pseudostandardized curricula, with tests and measurements of an inaccurate—if standardized—list of surface language skills.

Nevertheless, in 1992, we found ourselves involved in a writing team from Nevada, seeking funds to develop the state framework in ways that would mesh with the national-standards effort. The federal Department of Education was seeking innovative programs to show how Goals 2000 might be implemented at a state level. Despite our reservations, we saw some potential for opportunistic reform in our own backyard, especially when we read the fine print and learned that the funding agency was seeking *innovative* approaches.

Many state standards or goals projects use a top-down model—defining levels of achievement in such areas as spelling, grammar, usage, reading, and the like; creating standards; then creating tests to match. We wanted to use a genuinely grassroots, bottom-up, student-centered approach. We began the project by looking to students themselves, in ways analogous to the approach we have taken in this book. We wanted to find out how young people use and learn to use language. Our initial questions, then, were not about what young people *should know* and *should do* but about what they *already know* and *already do* and what that implies for what they *can know* and *can do* next. Meetings with teachers all over the state centered on examining kids' work: what is it that youngsters K–12 do with language? What do they write about? What do they read? How do they demonstrate their knowledge of language? Where are they headed in their linguistic development?

We sought alternatives to the standards idea and explored the concept of *benchmark* (Jackson, 1982). In popular usage, the word benchmark implies a strict or rigid standard—literally, a mark or measurement on a bench. However, a dictionary search revealed that the term actually comes from the field of surveying, where mapmakers leave benchmarks—those brass markers you sometimes find anchored to rocks while on your country rambles—to identify geographical high points and landmarks. The aim of the Nevada framework is in the spirit of the surveyors' use of the term. We agreed that benchmarks describe the "topography" of student literacy more successfully than do standards, permitting educators to explore the lay of the land of literacy—the landmarks, the highs and lows, the variations of the terrain.

After an enormous amount of discussion and debate, all of it grounded in samples of student work, the framework writers—most of them K–12 teachers—developed a series of descriptors that sketch out patterns of growth, kindergarten through grade twelve. The writers saw literacy as extending like waves from a rock tossed in a pond. For the youngest children, the emphasis was on emergent or initial literacy skills in the first three grades—strengthening oral language, understanding the idea and techniques of encoding and decoding oral language into print. Then the circles expanded outward, from kids' exploring the basic uses of incipient literacy (grades three through six), to their establishing personal uses of literacy (grades six through eight), to their applying literacy in their communities (grades eight through ten), to their implementing *extended literacy,* which opens up the full adult world of language use (grades ten through twelve).

The first two years of the project centered on developing the benchmarks and shaping the draft of the framework. In the third year, just getting under way as this book is being published, participants from all over the state will focus on two tasks—implementing the framework and talking with the public. In a summer workshop, teachers will discuss how the framework ideas can be used in their schools, along with leadership approaches and strategies. Teachers will design innovative curriculum projects for their own schools, adapting benchmarks to the particular needs of their own students. The project has the potential to reach every English/language arts classroom in the state, although we are not naive enough to suppose that dream will be fully realized.

Then, in a series of forums, the framework will be taken to the public. Rather than simply seeking approval, the project plans to genuinely engage parents in discussions: what kind of literacy do you want for your kids? How do you suppose they will be using language? What do you see the literate citizen doing twenty or even fifty years from now? We anticipate that, given a chance to talk, parents will want for their kids what we have seen in the subjects for this book; that is, kids who know their way around in language, who can figure out new language settings and problems for themselves.

We suspect that parents do not so much want hollow standards and myriad standardized tests as they do reassurance that the schools are genuinely preparing their children for the real-world demands of literacy in years to come. To provide that assurance and to offer an alternative to standardized tests, the Nevada English/Language Arts Framework will invite teachers and schools to have students create *portfolios* or collections of their work—demonstrations of what they can do with language. As students complete various projects associated with the benchmarks, their work will be placed in individual folders. From time to time, teachers will ask their students to order their folders and to select what they see as their best work to be placed in the portfolio. Teachers may also specify that a portfolio needs to include evidence of a variety of kinds of writing and reading. A portfolio can contain other kinds of evidence of performance as well, for example, audio- or videotapes, artwork, photography, letters sent and received. In addition, the portfolios include student self-assessments, as young people describe what they think their work demonstrates.

In the final year of the program, we will take the framework document to leaders in teacher-training institutions around the state and invite them to adapt their programs to ensure that new teachers entering the system are well prepared in the kinds of goals and benchmarks that the Nevada framework offers.

We—Paul Morris, Stephen Tchudi, and the creators of the Nevada framework—believe that this kind of project gives a modest example of how to go about introducing reform in literacy into a large number of schools. Nobody expects this framework automatically to change and improve reading and writing instruction for every kid in the state; nor do we expect that there will be wholesale public and pedagogical approval for the somewhat unique approach we have taken. But the potential for substantial change is there.

The Nevada University Seminar Program

Freshman seminar programs at the college level are not a particularly new idea. For over thirty years, some colleges and universities have been giving entering students a special experience by putting them into classes taught by a full professor rather than a teaching fellow (Barefoot and Fidler, 1992; Upcraft and Gardner, 1989). When University of Nevada, Reno (UNR), decided to launch a small freshman seminar program in 1993, we saw this as an opportunity to put some ideas into practice. Drawn together by the English Department, a university-wide faculty committee began the process in the time-honored academic way by reviewing the literature that describes such programs and by interviewing the people who were conducting them. Although freshman seminar programs receive very high praise from both students and teachers, we were concerned about what we regard as the "star professor" phenomenon. Program after program boasted that it was putting its "best and brightest" faculty into the seminars, which was okay as far as that goes, but too often, the content of the course seemed to be centered in the star professor's research and academic celebrity, and too often, program descriptions talked about the opportunity "to brush elbows" with the professor or "to sit at the feet" of the great one.

We thought that a freshman seminar program—which we decided to call a university seminar—should have a different focus. Although we wanted good faculty to teach in the program, the focus was not to be on the professors themselves. Rather, we wanted these veteran teachers to introduce students successfully to the complex and sometimes frightening world of the university. The university seminars take a thematic rather than a content approach. Faculty members are invited to select a broad topic for exploration, a theme related to their particular disciplines, but they are not bound to it and students are not required to have specialized interest in it. Program offerings have included, for example, the following themes (home disciplines of faculty members are given in parentheses):

Garbage: Our War on Waste (agricultural economics)

What Do We Mean by Multiculturalism? (history)

Media Manipulation (university press director)

The Search for Self (student services administrators)

Multiculturalism and Hollywood (English)

The Automobile in American Life (physics, English)

Dance: Mythology and Ritual (health and physical recreation)

Crime in American Literature (criminal justice)

Medical Issues and Ethics (medicine and chemistry)

Life in the Universe (planetarium director)

Justice in the *Star Trek* Series (criminal justice)

To provide unity and consistency across these obviously different themes and topics, the seminars have common goals, divided into two categories, *personal knowledge* and *knowledge of the university*. The phrase "personal knowledge" is borrowed directly from Michael Polanyi's book of that title (1962), in which he argues that "knowledge" and "truth" are not something Platonic, or "out there," but rather are created by the individual in a complex interaction of experience, data gathering, assimilation, synthesis, and hypothesis testing. We want UNR students to gain that same sense of knowledge: true understanding is not something residing in textbooks or notebooks or to be delivered from the podium by professors, but it is something they create for themselves. We also want students to learn the practicalities of their own campus as a resource for personal knowledge, to learn to use the full range of library and other research tools and to develop a high degree of independence and confidence in seeking out university resources of the broadest possible kinds—museums, professors, fellow students, community resources.

Participating faculty members are, of course, free to develop seminars as they think appropriate for UNR students. Since participating faculty are drawn from all quarters of the university, no standardized design will be possible or desirable. However, a standard course pattern is suggested, one that roughly follows inquiry in all disciplines, from phrasing good or interesting research questions, through collecting data then forming reasonable conclusions or hypotheses, and ending with a debate on solutions and answers with a community of fellow inquirers. The seminars are offered for credit as Freshman English, so they are writing intensive, based on the philosophy (so often exhibited in our interviews for this book) that knowledge and purpose power literacy.

A highlight and end point for the seminars is a common meeting at the end of the semester. Students create poster displays of their individual investigations, show videos, and spread out their papers and notes in a country fair atmosphere of browsing and discussion, which is attended by both faculty and students. We supply the students with stacks of Post-it notes and ask them to write comments back to their fellow seminarians. For fun, but with serious educational intent, the instructors also give each student a two-inch gold sticker to affix to the project the student thinks does a particularly fine job of explicating an issue and presenting results. Students in the seminars also select one of two of their peers' papers to represent their seminar in the interdisciplinary journal I^2 (I Squared or Eye-Squared), published by the program for use by students in future seminars.

As we write, the seminars are in their third year of operation. Thirty-eight faculty and administrators have taught in the program, including the university president, three vice presidents, and the director of student services. The fourth year of the program has been filled with faculty volunteers, and there is a waiting list of people who want to teach in the fifth year. Although the program is small in comparison to regular freshman courses, the model is proving to be highly successful. When students have evaluated the course, 97 percent have said they would recommend a university seminar to other entering students.

This program runs on a very small budget. Academic departments voluntarily assign faculty members to teach the seminars; administrators teach on a voluntary overload. The program works because both faculty and administrators see the university seminar as valuable and are willing to contribute their time and energy to make it go. As we say each semester to the instructors: you were not required to teach one of these seminars, but we are mighty glad you chose to, and so are your students. These seminars offer another modest example of real-time opportunistic reform of literacy instruction.

The Mühlhausen International Writing Workshop

Just about every person involved with education dreams of running his or her own school. The thinking is: let me cut through all the administrative layers, the state tests, the pressures to conform and just set up my ideal curriculum. A few people we know have done so, setting up schools ranging from an independent school in the Sierra Nevada to the alternative of a home school. We know that, in reality, running one's own school is not easy. One fellow we know, who was running an independent school with a highly progressive curriculum, wound up looking for work elsewhere after two years, when it became impossible both to maintain a building and to collect sufficient fees to keep the place open and accessible. We have known home school teachers who had a tendency to drop out of sight, their lives dominated by the daily routines and responsibilities of teaching their own kids.

Still, opportunities outside the system present themselves from time to time, providing some an opportunity to teach in a setting removed from the problems inherent in institutionalized education. For those of us teaching at UNR, opportunity has come about through an international writing workshop in Germany. A staff consisting of English faculty and graduate students has twice traveled to Mühlhausen, in the former East Germany, to conduct a two-week writing workshop for students aged fifteen through twenty-five from Germany, the Czech Republic, Russia, Finland, Italy, Lithuania, and the United States. The Internationaler

Schreib-Werkstaat was created jointly by the Mühlhausen Initiative (a community-centered program concerned with developing international cultural and economic opportunities for this city of 50,000 people) and the Huron Shores Writing Project (a humanities and cultural exchange program based in Rogers City, Michigan). Participants and staff live in a youth hostel for two weeks, and the program is literally a dawn-to-postdusk experience.

As the Nevada teaching team developed a plan for the instructional program, we split events into three major strands, *writing*, *field trips*, and *community and culture*. (A fourth strand, *social*, includes such nonacademic events as a talent night, which has featured everything from jugglers to a German student who could instantly spell words backward—in English.)

The writing strand is centered on daily workshops, from nine to noon, with the participants working in small groups with UNR writing instructors. We begin the workshop with storytelling, having participants delve into past experiences and get to know one another by learning something of each other's pasts. After reassuring the participants that they have plenty to say, we move on to exploring diverse cultures through writing. People describe and teach one another childhood games, and they discuss how various games, hopscotch, for example, differ from one country to another. We have people pair off with someone of a different nationality and write a script showing a conflict between cultures; we then use script readings as an opportunity to explore how cultural differences come about and how they can be, if not resolved, at least understood.

As the workshop progresses, the focus of writing moves from immediate personal experience toward more abstract social, political, and cultural concerns and from writing about the here and now to writing about the future. We collect current newspapers in English and German, the two official languages of the workshop, and have the students make poster-collages of headlines, centering on what they see as crucial world issues. They have identified such problems as hunger, poverty, violence, terrorism, and the economy. They select an issue particularly important to them, consider its implications for their own lives and write and present "soapbox" orations describing what they think ought to happen to solve these problems. We tell them to think about a date thirty years beyond the writing workshop, and to write about their visions of the future. We have had them describe model cities reflecting utopian or dystopian perspectives on living in the coming century.

The writing phase of the program is supported by the extensive use of journals. We urge participants to carry their journals with them everywhere and to record notes on all of their experiences. It is not uncommon to see kids writing in their journals late into the night, sitting in the youth hostel commons room, even as the TV or the stereo blares around them.

The journals are also essential to recording responses to the field trip segment of the program. Our Mühlhausen hosts have arranged for us to visit a former concentration work camp in Dora/Nordhausen, a hellhole where 20,000 of 60,000 prisoners died working in subterranean tunnels on German weapons projects during World War II. Our visit coincided with a fiftieth-anniversary commemoration of the liberation of the camp, which was attended by survivors from France, Germany, Italy, and some of the liberating troops from the United States. At long tables underneath a tent, the workshop participants were able to interview the survivors and the veterans about their experiences. This led to a number of powerful journal writings.

We have also taken a bus trip to Berlin for a weekend, where we were all sobered by the remains of the Berlin Wall and by various memorials to World War II. Students have traveled to Weimar to visit the Goethe Museum and the state theater and to learn about and reflect on the pre-Hitler Weimar Republic.

Additional field trips closer to Mühlhausen create our community and culture strand. This city was relatively undamaged in the war: its twelfth-century walls still stand; its city hall archives contain documents dating back many centuries and include a note from Johann Sebastian Bach resigning his position as organist at one of Mühlhausen's churches over a pay dispute.

The Mühlhausen Initiative is concerned with workaday as well as cultural matters. It aims to help improve the state of the economy in postunification Germany, where unemployment is high. Field trips take our participants to the local vocational high school for a discussion of training and employment; to a potassium mine that has become unprofitable and been abandoned; to the village glassblower, who is struggling to make his products competitive now that state socialism no longer provides economic support. We have discussed the future of work with the students, who recognize that work patterns are changing globally; that in the future, fewer and fewer people will have secure, lifetime jobs; that young people, in particular, need to think carefully about the relationships between their lives and their life's work. At the youth hostel where they stay, participants have enjoyed an evening interviewing senior citizens from Mühlhausen, who have talked not only about the war but also about their own life's work—one a devoted botanist, one a world-class Ping-Pong player and coach, others members of senior citizen counseling groups or public officials.

The three workshop strands come together on the final day of the program. Each participant revises one piece of creative writing, and through cooperative efforts with staff and fellow students, prepares German and English translations. Participants from other countries also submit writing in their native languages—Italian, Russian, Czech, Lithuanian, and Finnish. They read their pieces aloud in the language of their choice while group members listen and applaud and then submit final copy for publication in *Breakwall*, an international anthology of young people's writing. This multilingual book has been recognized as a unique teaching tool and is now widely used in English classes all over Germany. It makes sense to teach language based on the writing of young people rather than from the traditional selections in textbooks.

By all accounts, from both participants and staff, the International Writing Workshop has been a smashing success. Although it can be argued that the workshop is far removed from the world of public education and that the participants and staff are a highly motivated, self-selected group, it is nonetheless true that the workshop provides a valuable laboratory for the kinds of ideas that have been suggested in this book. These concepts are nicely summarized by the workshop motto: *Cogitare, Scribere, Discere*—To Think, To Write, To Understand.

The Lesson of Opportunism

None of these three programs is without flaws or problems, of course. The Mühlhausen program, for example, is clearly too brief to create long-range growth in student writing, and one wonders if the dawn-to-dusk pace could be maintained or would even be effective over a longer period of time. The University Seminar Program, though rated highly by students, has not altogether succeeded in its aim of helping students truly feel a part of the university community. And it remains to be seen whether the Nevada framework will be anything more than just another state-issued document, ignored by teachers, failing to break the stranglehold of commercial texts as the real determiners of curriculum.

As we completed work on this book, we were impressed by the spirit and commitment of a local English teacher, someone knowledgeable about new directions in teaching and doing her best to implement them in her classroom. She described her frustrations—that staff members were overtly and covertly critical of what they saw as newfangled approaches; that the administration was not supportive; that parents did not always understand what she was doing and thus reported her to the administration; and that, above all, the kids in her classes were so conditioned by conventional teaching that they frequently failed to respond to invitations to explore new directions. By contrast, she described her teaching in a summer writing camp sponsored by the local writing project that permitted teaching in a different environment. With tears in her eyes, she told of the summer camper who wrote, "I like the way you read my work." The teacher added, "I wish I could get that going in my regular classes."

This led us to discuss pessimism and optimism. We asked her, "So how and why do you continue? Isn't this tilting at windmills? Do you see any real hope for significant change?"

"It will take time," she said simply. "And it seems worth doing. You have to work with the opportunities that come along."

We admire her answer. Although that answer does not in any way lessen the difficulties or pain of bringing about changes in literacy instruction in real time, it reinforces the not-too-Pollyannaish belief of ours that there is abundant hope and there are myriad opportunities to change the nature of schooling for a literate society.

References

Abbott, D. P. "Rhetoric and Writing in Renaissance Europe and England." In J. J. Murphy (ed.), *A Short History of Writing Instruction*. Davis, Calif.: Hermagoras Press, 1990.

Aiken, H. *The Age of Ideology*. Boston: Houghton Mifflin, 1956.

Alien Nation. G. Baker, director. Century City, Calif.: 20th Century-Fox, 1988. Film.

Applebee, A., and Langer, J. *How Writing Shapes Thinking*. Urbana, Ill.: National Council of Teachers of English, 1987.

Barefoot, B. O., and Fidler, P. P. (eds.). *1991 National Survey of Freshman Seminar Programming*. Columbia: National Resource Center for the Freshman Year Experience, University of South Carolina, 1992.

Bass, D. "Educators Worry About Proposed Standards." *Las Vegas Sun*, Oct. 2, 1995, p. 3B.

Bingham, R., and Campbell, J. *The Human Quest*. Los Angeles: KCET, in association with Science and Society Television, 1994. Television program.

Bissex, G. *Gnys at Work: A Child Learns to Write and Read*. Cambridge, Mass.: Harvard University Press, 1980.

Bloom, A. *The Closing of the American Mind: How Higher Education Has Failed Democracy and Impoverished the Souls of Today's Students*. New York: Simon & Schuster, 1987.

Bloom, H. *The Western Canon: The Books and Schools of the Ages*. Orlando, Fla.: Harcourt Brace, 1994.

Bloom, L. "Anxious Writers in Context: Graduate School and Beyond." In M. Rose (ed.), *When a Writer Can't Write: Studies in Writer's Block and Other Composing-Process Problems*. New York: Guilford Press, 1985.

Britton, J. "The Role of Fantasy" and "Response to Literature." In M. Meek, A. Wardlow, and A. Applebee (eds.), *The Cool Web: The Pattern of Children's Reading*. New York: Atheneum, 1978.

Bronowski, J. *Magic, Science, and Civilization*. New York: Columbia University Press, 1978.

Bruner, J. *Actual Minds, Possible Worlds*. Cambridge, Mass.: Harvard University Press, 1986.

Burke, K. *A Grammar of Motives.* Cleveland, Ohio: World Publishing/-Meridian Books, 1962.

Burke, K. *A Rhetoric of Motives.* Cleveland, Ohio: World Publishing/Meridian Books, 1962.

Covino, W. *The Art of Wondering.* Portsmouth, N.H.: Boynton/Cook, 1988.

Crawford, L. "The Digital Advocate." *PC World,* 1996, *14*(1), 193.

Crusius, T. *Discourse: A Critique and Synthesis of Major Theories.* New York: Modern Language Association, 1989.

Csikszentmihalyi, M. "Literacy and Intrinsic Motivation." In S. R. Graubard (ed.), *Literacy: An Overview by Fourteen Experts.* New York: Hill & Wang, 1991.

Damon, W. "Reconciling the Literacies of Generations." In S. R. Graubard (ed.), *Literacy: An Overview by Fourteen Experts.* New York: Hill & Wang, 1991.

Danziger, K. "The Methodological Imperative in Psychology." *Philosophy of the Social Sciences,* 1985, *15,* 1–13.

Danziger, K. "On Theory and Method in Psychology." In W. J. Baker and others (eds.), *Recent Trends in Theoretical Psychology.* New York: Springer-Verlag, 1988.

Diamond, J. "U.S. Planner Sees High-Tech Battleground of the Future." Associated Press article. *Reno Gazette-Journal,* Aug. 18, 1994, p. 2A.

Dinan, L. "Putting Language on Paper." In S. J. Tchudi (ed.), *Integrated Language Arts in the Elementary School.* Belmont, Calif.: Wadsworth, 1994.

Dixon, B. "Quotable." *Chronicle of Higher Education,* Apr. 21, 1994, p. B5.

Donaldson, M. *Children's Minds.* New York: Norton, 1978.

Drozdiak, W. "No Longer 'The Stranger.'" *San Francisco Chronicle,* "Sunday Punch," May 8, 1994, p. 5.

Ebert, R. *Roger Ebert's Video Companion.* Kansas City, Mo.: Andrews, McMeel, & Parker, 1985–1991.

Elbow, P. *Embracing Contraries: Explorations in Learning and Teaching.* New York: Oxford University Press, 1986.

Eliot, G. "Thomas Carlyle." In J. Gross (ed.), *The Oxford Book of Essays.* New York: Oxford University Press, 1991.

Eliot, T. S. *Collected Poems.* Orlando, Fla.: Harcourt Brace, 1936.

Fader, D., and McNeil, E. *Hooked on Books: Program and Proof.* New York: Berkley, 1968.

Faulkner, W. *Essays, Speeches, and Public Letters* (J. B. Meriwether, ed.). New York: Random House, 1996.

Flesch, R. *Why Johnny Can't Read and What You Can Do About It.* New York: HarperCollins, 1955.

Freire, P. *Education for Critical Consciousness.* New York: Continuum, 1992. (Originally published 1973.)

Foucault, M. *Politics, Philosophy, and Culture.* New York: Routledge, 1988.

Gatto, J. T. *Dumbing Us Down: The Hidden Curriculum of Compulsory Schooling.* Philadelphia, Pa.: New Society, 1993a.

Gatto, J. T. "We Need Less School, Not More." *Whole Earth Review,* Winter 1993b, pp. 54–69.

Graff, H. J. *The Literacy Myth: Literacy and Social Structure in the Nineteenth Century City.* Orlando, Fla.: Academic Press, 1979.

Grass, G. "After Auschwitz." In G. Grass, *Two States—One Nation?* Orlando, Fla.: Harcourt Brace, 1990.

Gusdorf, G. *Speaking* (La parole). Chicago: Northwestern University Press, 1965. (Originally published 1953.)

Halliday, M.A.K. *Language as Social Semiotic: The Social Interpretation of Language and Meaning.* Baltimore, Md.: University Park Press, 1978.

Harste, J. C., Woodward, V. A., and Burke, C. L. *Language Stories and Literacy Lessons.* Portsmouth, N.H.: Heinemann, 1984.

Herrnstein, R., and Murray, C. *The Bell Curve: Intelligence and Class Structure in American Life.* New York: Free Press, 1994.

Hillocks, G. *Research on Written Composition.* New York: National Conference on Research in English, 1986.

Hinchliffe, A. "In Search of Splendour." In L. Stratta (ed.), *Writing.* London: National Association of Teachers of English, 1968.

Hirsch, E. D. *Cultural Literacy: What Every American Needs to Know.* Boston: Houghton Mifflin, 1987.

Holbrook, D. *English for the Rejected.* Cambridge, England: Cambridge University Press, 1967.

Hunt, R. "A Horse Named Hans, a Boy Named Shawn: The Herr von Osten Theory of Response to Writing." In C. M. Anson (ed.), *Writing and Response: Theory, Practice, and Research.* Urbana, Ill.: National Council of Teachers of English, 1989.

Hunt, R., and Vipond, D. "First, Catch the Rabbit: Methodological Imperative and the Dramatization of Dialogic Reading." In R. Beach and others (eds.), *Multidisciplinary Perspectives on Literacy Research.* Urbana, Ill.: National Council of Teachers of English and National Conference on Research in English, 1992.

Hutton, E. "Say No to Trespassers." *Reno Gazette-Journal,* Aug. 13, 1994, p. 11A.

Illich, I. *Deschooling Society.* New York: HarperCollins, 1971.

Illich, I. *After Deschooling, What?* New York: HarperCollins, 1973.

Jackson, D. *Continuity in Secondary English.* New York: Methuen, 1982.

Joad, C.E.M. *Guide to Philosophy.* New York: Dover, 1957.

Kozol, J. *Illiterate America.* New York: Doubleday, 1985.

Kuhn, T. S. *The Structure of Scientific Revolutions.* Chicago: University of Chicago Press, 1970. (Originally published 1962.)

Langer, S. *Philosophy in a New Key*. Cambridge, Mass.: Harvard University Press, 1957. (Originally published 1942.)

Le Carré, J. *Call for the Dead*. New York: Pocket Books, [1964] 1970.

Le Carré, J. *Smiley's People*. New York: Bantam Books, 1979.

Lewis, A. *The Quotable Quotations Book*. New York: Crowell, 1980.

Llewellyn, G. *The Teenage Liberation Handbook (How to Quit School and Get a Real Life and Education)*. Eugene, Oreg.: Lowry House, 1991.

Llewellyn, G. *Real Lives: Eleven Teenagers Who Don't Go to School*. Eugene, Oreg.: Lowry House, 1993.

Lockridge, K. A. *Literacy in Colonial New England: An Enquiry into the Social Context of Literacy in the Early Modern West*. New York: Norton, 1974.

Mann, H. *Lectures and Annual Reports on Education*. Boston, Mass.: George C. Rand and Avery, 1867.

Mascari, J. "Learn to Speak English." *Reno Gazette-Journal*, Aug. 14, 1994, p. 5B.

McLuhan, M. *The Medium Is the Message*. New York: Random House, 1967.

Moffett, J. "Hidden Impediments." In S. Tchudi (ed.), *Language, Schooling, and Society*. Upper Montclair, N.J.: Boynton/Cook, 1985.

National Council of Teachers of English/International Reading Association. *Standards in the English Language Arts*. Urbana, Ill. and Newark, Del.: National Council of Teachers of English/International Reading Association, 1996.

Network. S. Lumet, director. Santa Monica, Calif.: MGM/United Artists, 1976. Film.

Newman, E. *Strictly Speaking: Will America Be the Death of English?* New York: Bobbs-Merrill, 1974.

Orwell, G. "Politics and the English Language." In G. Orwell, "Shooting an Elephant and Other Essays." Orlando, Fla.: Harcourt Brace, 1948.

Pinker, S. *The Language Instinct*. New York: Morrow, 1994.

Plato. *The Works of Plato* (I. Edman and B. Jowett, eds.). New York: Modern Library, 1928.

Polanyi, M. *Personal Knowledge*. Chicago: University of Chicago Press, 1962.

Pope, C. "Our Time Has Come: English for the Twenty-First Century." *English Journal*, 1993, *84*(3), 38–41.

Postman, N. *Amusing Ourselves to Death: Public Discourse in the Age of Show Business*. New York: Viking Penguin, 1985.

Reed-Jones, S. "'Faith in the Reality of Belonging': The Story of Alonzo A." Paper presented at the Conference on College Composition and Communication, Cincinnati, Ohio, Mar. 20, 1992.

Reno Gazette-Journal, untitled news item, June 15, 1995, p. 2A.

Rogers, J. "Language and Decalang." *English Journal*, 1977, *68*(2), 32–37.

Rose, M. *Lives on the Boundary*. New York: Viking Penguin, 1990.

Rottenberg, A. T. *The Structure of Argument.* Boston: St. Martin's Press, Bedford Books, 1994.

Sadker, M., and Sadker, D. "Confronting Sexism in the Classroom." In S. L. Gabriel and I. Smithson (eds.), *Gender in the Classroom: Power and Pedagogy.* Urbana: University of Illinois Press, 1990.

Sadker, M., and Sadker, D. "Failing at Fairness: How America's Schools Cheat Girls." *San Francisco Examiner Magazine,* Mar. 13, 1994, pp. 41–62.

Safire, W. *On Language.* New York: Times Books, 1980.

Sartre, J.-P. *Existentialism and Humanism.* London: Methuen, 1973. (Originally published in English 1948.)

Shaughnessy, M. P. *Errors and Expectations.* New York: Oxford University Press, 1977.

Shor, I, and Freire, P. *A Pedagogy for Liberation: Dialogues on Transforming Education.* New York: Bergin & Garvey, 1987.

Simons, H. *The Rhetorical Turn.* Chicago: University of Chicago Press, 1990.

Smith, F. *Joining the Literacy Club.* Portsmouth, N.H.: Heinemann, 1988.

Smith, T. V. (ed.). *Philosophers Speak for Themselves: From Aristotle to Plotinus.* Chicago: University of Chicago Press, 1973. (Originally published 1934.)

Stampel, J. D. "Birth Control Is the Answer." *Reno Gazette-Journal,* Aug. 9, 1994, p. 5A.

Stanley and Iris. M. Ritt, A. Sellers, and A. Winitsky, writers. Santa Monica, Calif.: MGM/United Artists, 1990. Film.

Steele, C. M. "Race and the Schooling of Black Americans." *Atlantic Monthly,* 1992, *269*(4), 68–78.

Stein, G. *Geography and Plays.* New York: Haskell House, 1967. (Originally published 1922.)

Stranglers. "No More Heroes." On *The Stranglers IV: No More Heroes* (lyrics and music by H. Cornwell, J. Burnel, and D. Greenfield). Los Angeles: A & M Records, 1977. Recording.

Tchudi, S. N. *Planning and Assessing the Curriculum in English Language Arts.* Alexandria, Va.: Association for Supervision and Curriculum Development, 1991.

Thomson, J. *Understanding Teenagers' Reading.* Norwood, South Australia: Australian Association for the Teaching of English, 1987.

Torrey, J. W. "Learning to Read Without a Teacher: A Case Study." In F. Smith (ed.), *Psycholinguistics and Reading.* Austin, Tex.: Holt, Rinehart and Winston, 1973.

Upcraft, M. L., and Gardner, J. N. "The Freshman Seminar." In M. L. Upcraft, J. N. Gardner, and Associates, *The Freshman Year Experience: Helping Students Survive and Succeed in College.* San Francisco: Jossey-Bass, 1989.

Vonnegut, K. *Slaughterhouse-Five; or, The Children's Crusade, a Duty-Dance with Death.* New York: Delacorte, 1969.

Vygotsky, L. *Thought and Language.* Cambridge, Mass.: MIT Press, 1986.

Whately, R. *Elements of Rhetoric.* Carbondale: Southern Illinois University Press, 1963. (Originally published 1846.)

Wilde, O. "The Critic as Artist." In J. Gross (ed.), *The Oxford Book of Essays.* New York: Oxford University Press, 1991.

Wilson, T. *The Arte of Rhetorique.* Delmar, N.Y.: Scholars' Facsimiles and Reprints, 1962. (Originally published 1553.)

Index